Reclaiming the Discarded

Life and Labor on Rio's Garbage Dump · KATHLEEN M. MILLAR

Duke University Press   Durham and London   2018

Interior designed by Courtney Leigh Baker
Typeset in Minion Pro and Trade Gothic by Westchester
Publishing Services

Library of Congress Cataloging-in-Publication Data
Names: Millar, Kathleen M., [date]–author.
Title: Reclaiming the discarded : life and labor on Rio's garbage
dump / Kathleen M. Millar.
Description: Durham : Duke University Press, 2018. | Includes
bibliographical references and index.
Identifiers: LCCN 2017033261 (print) | LCCN 2017043888 (ebook)
ISBN 9780822372073 (ebook)
ISBN 9780822370314 (hardcover : alk. paper)
ISBN 9780822370505 (pbk. : alk. paper)
Subjects: LCSH: Ragpickers—Brazil—Duque de Caxias (Rio
de Janeiro) | Dumpster diving—Brazil—Duque de Caxias (Rio
de Janeiro) | Ragpickers—Brazil—Duque de Caxias (Rio de
Janeiro)—Social conditions. | Refuse and refuse disposal—
Brazil—Duque de Caxias (Rio de Janeiro) | Recycling (Waste,
etc.)—Brazil—Duque de Caxias (Rio de Janeiro)
Classification: LCC HD8039.R462 (ebook) | LCC HD8039.R462
B6 2018 (print) | DDC 363.72/82098153—dc23
LC record available at https://lccn.loc.gov/2017033261

Cover art: Photo by the author

For Chris

Any recycled product is a collection of numerous pieces with multiple past lives and is the work of untold people whose labor often goes unseen. The same could be said for this book. First and foremost, I am indebted to the catadores of Jardim Gramacho who shared their lives and stories with me and who generously took me under their care as a "novice" on the dump. I especially thank Tião for having faith in my research from the very first day, and Glória for welcoming me into her home and for being my best teacher. This research also would not have been possible without my *truta*, the woman I call Eva, who taught me what it truly means to work in partnership. Numerous catadores whom I never came to know tossed me cardboard boxes or plastic bottles in my most exhausted moments. The gift of each box and bottle that fell at my feet became a reminder that so many catadores, not only those who appear in these pages, supported and contributed to this ethnography.

In Brazil, I also thank Comlurb for supporting my research and Valéria Pereira Bastos for sharing her expertise, gained through many years of dedicated social work in Jardim Gramacho. Special thanks to Luiz Antonio Machado da Silva for generously providing me with an institutional affiliation at the Instituto Universitário de Pesquisas do Rio de Janeiro (IUPERJ) and with guidance in my research, and Federico Neiburg for inviting me to participate in seminars organized by the Núcleo de Pesquisas em Cultura e Economia in the Anthropology Department at the Museu Nacional. I am also grateful for many years of support from Ruben Oliven and Claudia Fonseca in the Anthropology Department at the Universidade Federal do Rio Grande do Sul (UFRGS).

This project was shaped early on by the intellectual guidance of Brown University's Department of Anthropology. I thank Matt Gutmann for always asking the difficult questions, many of which I kept coming back to as I worked through the innumerable drafts of this book. Matt's continued generosity, support, and encouragement has helped me see this project to its very end. I thank Cathy Lutz for teaching me the craft of ethnographic writing and showing me how to approach ethnography as, itself, theory construction. Nick Townsend's kindness, patience, and profound intellectual curiosity broadened my thinking across time, regions of the world, subfields, disciplines, and theoretical paradigms. I thank Kay Warren for encouraging me to retheorize labor and for pushing me to consider why this matters in the Brazilian context. I am grateful to João Biehl for his generous and insightful comments on my dissertation, which helped me take this project to another level. I also thank my other mentors and teachers at Brown University, including Nitsan Chorev, Paja Faudree, Jim Green, Sherine Hamdy, Jessaca Leinaweaver, Dan Smith, and Rich Snyder. Special thanks go to Kathy Grimaldi, Matilde Andrade, Margie Sugrue, Susan Hirsch, and José Torrealba, who made the everyday logistics of university life run smoothly, all the while providing community and encouragement along the way.

My research in Brazil was made possible with generous funding from a Doctoral Dissertation Research Award from Fulbright-Hays and a Graduate Research Fellowship from the National Science Foundation. The Department of Anthropology, Graduate School, and the Center for Latin American and Caribbean Studies at Brown University provided support for several short-term research trips. Follow-up research was funded by grants from Duke University's Thompson Writing Program and Simon Fraser University. Preparation of the manuscript was supported by the University Publication Fund at Simon Fraser University.

I was fortunate to spend a year as a postdoctoral fellow in the Thompson Writing Program at Duke University. By teaching writing in the company of this remarkable community of scholars, I became a better writer. I especially thank Márcia Rego for guiding me in all dimensions of my work and Katya Wesolowski for her mentorship. I also thank my interdisciplinary writing group—Talia Argondezzi, Jim Berkey, Denise Comer, and Lindsey Smith—for evenings of laughter, conversation, and insight. At Simon Fraser University, I found a wonderful group of colleagues and friends who have supported this work. I owe a special thank you to Michael Hathaway who guided me through the publication process and gave me invaluable feedback on numerous drafts. My gratitude also goes to Liz Cooper, Alec Dawson, Parin Dossa, Sonja Luehrmann, Coleman Nye, Roxanne Panchasi, Stacy Pigg, Nick Scott, and Ann Travers for comments and conversations that helped me fine-tune my arguments.

For their insightful feedback on early versions of this work and portions of the manuscript, I thank Catherine Alexander, Aaron Ansell, Susan Ellison, Alexandre Fortes, John French, Rebecca Galemba, Daniella Gandolfo, Sohini Kar, Antonio Carlos de Souza Lima, Cristiani Vieira Machado, Duff Morton, Mariano Perelman, Andrea Muehlebach, Josh Reno, and Wendy Wolford. I owe the greatest debt of gratitude to Jennifer Ashley and Harris Solomon, who read this work in all its many iterations—from its inception in grant proposals to final revisions. Their wisdom and companionship enabled me to see the big picture, connect all the pieces, and keep going when I was stuck. I thank the audiences at Cornell University, Ohio University, Brown University's Pembroke Seminar, the Columbia University Brazil Seminar, St. Mary's College of Maryland, and the Universidade Federal do Rio Grande do Sul for their comments and questions that pushed my ideas in fruitful directions. Earlier versions and parts of chapter 2 appeared as "The Precarious Present: Wageless Labor and Disrupted Life in Rio de Janeiro, Brazil," *Cultural Anthropology* 29, no. 1: 32–53. I thank the editors, Anne Allison and Charles Piot, and the anonymous reviewers for their thoughtful suggestions as I developed that work.

I am immensely appreciative of Gisela Fosado, my editor at Duke University Press, for her enthusiastic support and guidance in this project. I also thank Maryam Arain for helping see the book through the final stages. I cannot express the depth of my gratitude to the two reviewers who read the manuscript with care and who gifted me with detailed, incisive, and constructive feedback. I thank Donna Goldstein, who was one of these anonymous reviewers until after the review process was complete, for pushing me in ways that helped me both situate and refine the book's ideas. I thank the second anonymous reviewer for showing me ways to "fully embrace" the implications of my arguments.

This book would never have materialized without the support of teachers, friends, and family over the years. I thank Greg Downey for introducing me to the wonders of anthropology as an undergraduate. Alessandro Angelini, Bhawani Buswala, Josh MacLeod, Casey Mesick Braun, Rebecca Fundis, Christine Reiser-Robbins, Yana Stainova, and Stacey Vanderhurst were wonderful companions through dissertation fieldwork and writing. Most of all, I am grateful for my family. I thank my sister, Maggie, for being my best friend and my biggest fan, and my brother, Matt, for his keen interest in all that I do. I thank my parents for instilling in me an openness to others, for encouraging me to write, and for sustaining me with their love and support.

Chris Gibson entered my life, a saving grace, just as I was beginning fieldwork and has been with me to the very end. His love, patience, wisdom, and insight made everything possible.

Introduction

The dump is a desert—dusty, shadeless, its dirt crust orange and cracked. Unless of course it rains, as it often does for days on end in the winter months in Rio de Janeiro. The rain turns the dirt into a thick sludge, revealing shreds of plastic bags buried just inches beneath the surface. Eighteen-wheeler trucks carrying hundreds of tons of garbage from across the metropolis sink into the muck, teetering dangerously to one side and then the other as they make their way to the unloading zone. But the rain seems a faint memory on this hot January morning. From the southeastern edge of the dump, we watch a hazy sunrise above Rio's tourist attraction Sugarloaf, fifteen miles away on the other side of Guanabara Bay. The murky water of the bay, well over a hundred feet below us, seems oddly inviting.

Seu Bernardo stops the truck, puts it in neutral, and leans over my lap to help pry open the rusted cab door.[1] He waits while I go to the back of the truck to grab my three burlap sacks. As I come back around to Seu Bernardo's side of the truck, he sticks his head out the window to tell me something about another load of plastics . . . back in the late afternoon . . . if I need a ride. . . . His speech is low and raspy, a consequence of having lost a lung to tuberculosis years ago, and I struggle to make out his words over the idling engine.

I watch as Seu Bernardo's truck pulls away, and then I hear a voice behind me, calling my name. I turn to find Eva and Fabinho waving me over to a cluster of burlap sacks overflowing with plastic bottles. Both Eva and Fabinho are *catadores*, or "pickers," who collect and sell recyclables on the dump for a living. Ever since trucks began emptying waste into the mangrove swamp at the edge of a peripheral neighborhood called Jardim Gramacho in the late 1970s, catadores have sorted through this garbage, retrieving scrap metal, plastic, and paper. In the early years, a few hundred catadores worked on the dump. Most came to Jardim Gramacho from other city dumps that had closed, "following the garbage," as they recounted. By 2005, the year I first came to Jardim Gramacho, the dump had become the largest in Latin America. Dozens of scrap yards dotted the neighborhood. Pigs, raised on reclaimed food scraps, roamed the streets. Used electronics shops, stands selling gloves and water, and shacks rented out for showers and changing rooms clustered at the base of the dump. Nearly all this activity was connected to the work of catadores. Their numbers now reached over two thousand.

As I approach Eva and Fabinho, I notice that Eva looks especially ragged. The hairnet and baseball cap she always wears are missing and a film of dust and sweat coat her forehead and arms. "I was buried last night," she tells me when I arrive. And then: "Do you have a cigarette?"

I drop my bundle of burlap sacks on the ground and rummage in my pouch for a pack of cigarettes and a lighter. I hand them both to Eva, who pulls out a mashed cigarette and then passes the pack to Fabinho. "What happened?" I ask.

It was a tractor, Eva tells me. She had been collecting all night. By early morning, she was tired and her legs dragged, and she ended up slipping in front of a tractor that bulldozed a mound of garbage on top of her. She was buried. She couldn't breathe. The weight of all that garbage. The tractor driver did not see her fall, but luckily another catador noticed and grabbed her arm. And what if no one had seen her? Eva's voice begins to quiver.

"Easy, *calma*," Fabinho says softly.

I suggest that Eva go home. But she wants to wait until Seu Bernardo returns with the truck so that she can take down her two sacks full of plastic. Fabinho offers to tie up Eva's two sacks, and I help him weave blue cord through frayed slits in the side of each sack, cinching the cord tightly over an assortment of empty drink bottles. The bottles crackle under the pressure.

"This is my last time on the dump," Eva suddenly announces. "When I leave, I'm not coming back."

"*Calma*," Fabinho says again, "you just had a scare."

"No. I'm serious," Eva insists. "I'm not coming back."

BUT EVA DID RETURN. That evening she called me to see if I wanted to go collect with her the following morning—early, before sunrise, to avoid the worst of the heat.

The next morning, as Eva and I made our way to the dump in near darkness, I kept thinking of the very first conversation I ever had with a catador in Jardim Gramacho, named Tião. At the time, I was just visiting. I did not even know that I would later return, over several years, to conduct ethnographic research on the dump. As Tião walked with me to the bus stop at the end of my visit, he commented:

"Catadores often say: I came here and I thought it was a horrible place and that I would never stay. But that was eight years ago or ten years ago, and here I am to this day."

"Why do they stay, then?" I asked.

"Oh, you'll see," he replied. "You might leave Jardim Gramacho, but you almost always come back."

WHY RETURN TO the dump? Why go back to working as a catador? In both scholarly presentations and casual conversations regarding my research in Jardim Gramacho, I have been asked many questions: whether the work is dangerous, how bad the garbage smells, who controls access to the dump, whether as many women collect as men, what the most surprising or valuable object was that a catador ever found. I have never been asked why catadores keep going back to the dump. Over time, I realized that this question is never asked because the answer is assumed. That is, the seemingly self-evident explanation for why catadores collect on the dump is that they do so out of necessity, as a means of survival. Eva, who insisted that she was finished collecting for good, must have returned to the dump because she had no other option. The story ends before it begins.

The tendency to frame work like that of catadores in terms of necessity stems in part from its classification as "informal." Ever since Keith Hart (1973) first proposed the concept of the informal economy in the 1970s to capture the income-generating activities of urban migrants in Ghana, wageless work in the informal economy has largely been understood as a recourse of urban poor who are left out or left behind by global capitalism. From this perspective, sifting through refuse on a city dump is one income-generating activity among a multitude performed by those who cannot find waged employment. Furthermore, unlike Karl Marx's (1990) concept of the industrial reserve army of workers who were meant to be brought back into employment once periods of stagnant growth had passed, the informal economy is increasingly seen not as a temporary fix but as a final destination for those no longer needed by global capital. The garbage dump thus appears as an end zone in a double sense: the burial grounds for unwanted things, the end of the line for urban poor.

This book takes a different perspective. It explores how work on the dump is not an end for Rio's poor but rather an experience of continual return. When I first began meeting catadores on the dump, I asked them where they lived, thinking they would tell me Chatuba, a bustling patchwork of scrapyards and makeshift bars at the base of the dump, or Maruim, a former swampland on the opposite side of the dump. To my surprise, many catadores told me that they lived on the far western side of Rio or in another municipality of the metropolitan area—a distance that required multiple buses to arrive home. Renting tiny shacks of reclaimed plywood in Jardim Gramacho, these catadores stayed near the dump for days or weeks at a time before returning home for periods that could also last days or weeks. Even in the case of catadores who lived in Jardim Gramacho, I found flows into and out of work on the dump to be common. Some departures, as in Eva's story, were abrupt. Others extended for so long that it could seem that a catador had disappeared. But almost always, as Tião had told me, catadores came back.

The comings and goings of catadores hardly fit the image of life subsumed by the work of subsistence. And yet persistent notions of informal labor as a product of scarcity or a last resort leave little room to ask why this work is *taken up* by those who pursue it, how it emerges from and fashions particular social and political relations, and how it expresses different visions of what life is for. As this book traces the departures and returns of catadores to the dump, it asks how wageless work coheres within the trajectory of a life as lived. These trajectories take their own paths. But as they do so, they weave together life and labor, value and waste, and the city and its margins in ways that this book seeks to understand.

When I began studying the work of catadores, I was struck by the numerous references to waste that suffused scholarship on work and unemployment. In 2004, just prior to my first arrival in Jardim Gramacho, sociologist Zygmunt Bauman published his book *Wasted Lives* in which he describes how modernization has made the unemployed "redundant," a population that is "disposed of *because of being disposable*" (12, emphasis in the original). Many subsequent works denouncing the pernicious effects of neoliberal capitalism echoed this discourse, referring to those whose labor is not needed by capital as being made into a "superfluous population," a "surplus humanity," or even the "human-as-waste."[2] Of course, the association of the wageless with waste is not entirely new. In the late nineteenth century, Marx described the lumpenproletariat—his term for the unemployable fraction of the working class, consisting of vagabonds, petty criminals, and beggars—as both the "refuse of all classes" (1963: 75) and as a mass "living on the crumbs of society" (1964: 50).[3] As in Marx's depiction here, I started noting a slippage in contemporary works between being discarded (by capital) and subsisting on the discarded, indexing catadores in a double sense. It seemed no accident that the cover of Bauman's *Wasted Lives* portrays an emaciated figure scouring a garbage dump or that trash-picking is commonly cited as the subsistence activity of so-called surplus populations. In studies of contemporary labor conditions, the figure of the scavenger has reemerged as iconic of wageless life. This led me to ask what prompted a language of waste to be revived. More importantly, what were the consequences—both for theory and for politics—of understanding the unemployed in these terms?

Such questions can only be answered by connecting the discourse of disposable life to increasing concerns over a crisis of work. Beginning in the 1980s, deindustrialization in North America and Europe led to pronouncements that these societies had reached the end of work (Rifkin 1995), the end of the working class (Gorz 1982), and were facing a jobless future (Aronowitz and DiFazio 1994). In the 2000s, unemployment skyrocketed in parts of Europe, particularly among youth, spurring marches and demonstrations that converged on a new worker identity of the "precariat." A composite of the words *precarious* and *proletariat*, the term *precariat* indexed the unstable work and life conditions of those in search of employment or those perennially moving from one temp job to the next.

The 2008 financial crisis in the United States and the rise in unemployment and inequality that followed seemed to further erode the expectation that lifelong, full-time employment was guaranteed, if not for all, then at least for the middle class. Precarity soon became a recurrent theme in studies of life in advanced capitalism, fueling the sense that the historical present is a time of crisis, at the center of which is work—or rather, its loss.

This discourse around a crisis of work has furthermore become global, though its content shifts significantly in the case of Brazil or other sites of the Global South where full-time waged employment was never the norm, especially for the urban poor. Here the narrative focuses not so much on the erosion of secure employment once associated with the Keynesian-Fordist era of capitalism, but rather on the explosion of urban slums and informality. Early work on the informal economy viewed the income-generating activities of urban poor as a transitional moment in a country's modernization process, or as a means for poor migrants from the countryside to eventually find a job or open a small business in the formal sector. The assumption was that the informal economy would eventually disappear as developing countries industrialized and gradually adopted policies and practices associated with modern capitalist economies.[4] But by the turn of the millennium, the trend seemed to be occurring in reverse. Urban populations in the Global South were growing rapidly, and many of the inhabitants in these new megacities lived and worked in unplanned settlements increasingly referred to, despite their differences, as "slums." In several high-profile publications by both scholars and policymakers, informality was declared not to be the past but the future of the urban world.[5] A 2008 UN Habitat report estimated that 85 percent of all new employment worldwide occurs outside formal relations of production (UN Habitat 2008: xiv). In response, pronouncements proliferated that we are witnessing the rise of a "new wretched of the earth" (Davis 2004b: 11) whose main livelihood is "informal survivalism" (Davis 2004a: 24). The expulsion from work and the forms of social exclusion that result has appeared in policy and academic accounts—at times, almost apocalyptically—as the final destiny for a billion human beings across the globe.

Though these crisis-of-work narratives gave rise to the metaphor of disposable life, its use has since proliferated beyond studies focusing primarily on work and unemployment. In anthropology, expressions involving waste or its many synonyms have appeared in ethnographic accounts of AIDS patients, indigenous communities, slum dwellers, refugees, the homeless, and marginalized youth. At times, the waste metaphor is part of a work's theoretical framework, as in Tova Höjdestrand's (2009: 20) conceptualization of the homeless in postsocialist Russia as "human refuse" and "excrement of the state," or as in João Biehl's (2005: 2) concept of a "zone of social abandonment" to describe an asylum in Brazil where those deemed unsound and unproductive are disposed of and left to die. In other cases, waste appears in isolated expressions that form part of a work's vivid, figurative language. Elizabeth Povinelli (2011: 129), for example, poetically describes indigenous Australians struggling in conditions of late liberalism as those "born at the far end of liberal capitalism's exhaust system." Anne Allison (2013: 16) similarly evokes this sense of exhaustion and exhaust in her powerful depiction of precarity as a kind of "straining"—both in the sense of pushing or stretching oneself to an extreme and in the sense of filtering out the undesirable. What results is a "social and human garbage pit." Each of these waste metaphors captures the extreme effects of today's global political economy, particularly its erosion of institutions and relations that once provided a degree of security and social belonging. However, when taken as a whole, these metaphors become a common refrain that reinforces the notion of human disposability. In other words, to repeatedly invoke images of waste, abandonment, excrement, exhaust, dumping, garbage, and disposal in contemporary ethnography "can lead us to imagine that there really are disposable people, not simply that they are disposable in the eyes of state and market" (Denning 2010: 80).

One reason that a vocabulary of waste has been taken up so readily is that it reinforces a persistent paradigm of seeing the poor, marginalized, and suffering in terms of scarcity. Specific concepts for understanding vulnerable human life have come and gone in anthropology and cognate disciplines, but they have all shared a tendency to define their object of study by what it lacks. In Latin America, for example, the concept of marginality arose in the 1960s at a time when huge numbers of rural poor were migrating to Latin America's growing cities. These migrants were perceived as marginal to mainstream society—as lacking the values and practices, including paid work, that would integrate them into the capitalist modernization process. Eventually debunked by scholars showing that the poor were bound into the political, economic, and social life of the city, marginality theory was quickly replaced by a focus on informality. The concept of the informal economy recognized and drew attention to the kinds of activities the poor performed to construct their own housing or generate their own income. However, these myriad activities were theorized in the negative, as lacking the order, state regulation, or employment relations associated with normative conceptions of capitalist wage labor. By the 1990s, a new term—*social exclusion*—began appearing in studies of urban poverty in Latin America. Adopted from public policy discourses in Europe on the unemployed, immigrants, and "delinquent" youth, the concept referred to those excluded not only from work but also from political processes and cultural worlds. Though it offered a multidimensional perspective on the ways that urban segregation, social identities, and economic conditions compound the lived experience of inequality, the concept of social exclusion revived the idea from marginality theory that the poor are cut off from society.[6] It was not much of a leap to go from notions of exclusion and expulsion to metaphors of disposable life that began proliferating in the early 2000s. If, for much of the twentieth century, the poor were understood in terms of what they lacked, by the new millennium they were perceived as the very embodiment of lack—made superfluous to the point of becoming human waste.

This book is a critique of scarcity as a persistent paradigm for understanding lives lived in precarious conditions. As unemployed workers who sift through garbage on a city dump, catadores seem to exemplify in extreme form today's notion of disposable life. Yet to see the work of catadores through metaphors of waste forecloses the most important questions. If catadores are superfluous to capital accumulation, then it becomes impossible to ask how the materials they collect are tied into a 200-billion-dollar global recycling industry.[7] Or to ask how their work shapes and is shaped by the political life of the city. Or even to ask what else, beyond mere subsistence, is produced by their labor—what values, social relations, subjectivities, lifeworlds. Though the crisis of work is an issue I address in this book, I do not adopt it as an analytic through which to examine the lives of catadores. Rather, I am interested in how life becomes livable through forms of labor commonly defined in terms of redundancy, abandonment, or exhaust—that is, in terms of waste. How do these forms of labor forge particular life projects? And what connection does this work have to pursuits of the good life, conceived by those who seem to live beyond its bounds?

I address these guiding questions in what follows by conceptualizing the act of collecting recyclables on a dump not as a survival strategy, not as informal labor, not even as a purely economic practice. Rather, I argue that the activities of catadores constitute what I call a form of living. This multivalent concept refers first to living in the sense of a means of income, sustenance, or livelihood, as in the idiom "to make a living." Work is thus a central dimension of a form of living, but it is not synonymous with the term. The word *living* in "form of living" is also intended to invoke its additional meaning as the pursuit of a specific mode of inhabiting the world. In other words, a form of living can be understood as, at once, both a livelihood and a way of life.

One of the values of approaching work as a form of living is that it departs from the attachment to waged employment. Wage labor has long been upheld as a source of social ties, dignity, and emancipatory projects in both liberal and critical leftist discourse (Weeks 2011). This is especially the case now that jobs, for many, are increasingly precarious or scarce—a situation that has prompted calls for "decent work" and "job creation," or what sociologist Franco Barchiesi (2011: 25) calls a "politics of labor melancholia." And yet what the celebration of labor and production ignores is wage labor's enduring history as a form of violence and technique of governance. Here I draw on Barchiesi's analysis of the "work–citizenship nexus," in which the linking of wage labor to state narratives of progress and programs of social security becomes a device for turning "unruly" subjects into a manageable, disciplined, industrious population (24). In the Brazilian context, the valorization of waged work as the foundation of the welfare state by President Getúlio Vargas in the early twentieth century, with lasting effects to the present day, has afforded social citizenship to certain (officially recognized, waged) workers while excluding those who do not conform to this model. The work–citizenship nexus is thus a useful reminder that capitalist wage labor is not only a socioeconomic relationship but also a state mechanism for forcibly reducing multiple subjectivities and modes of being in the world into just one—the predictable, governable subject of the worker (Barchiesi 2012b). My emphasis on forms of living aims to break open this reduction, allowing for a diversity of productive actions that do not fit easily into capitalist categories of labor and notions of work.

Wage labor as a reductive category is also echoed in the very language we use to speak about work. Beginning with the writings of Adam Smith (1976) and other political economists in the eighteenth century, the meaning of labor became narrowed from the sense of any productive action to specifically paid employment or work performed for someone else in exchange for a wage (Williams 1983). As capitalist production expanded, the meaning of "work" in common usage was similarly reduced to wage labor, making it possible, for example, for women caring for their households to be seen as "not working" (Collins 1990). Still today—despite several decades of critiques of the conflation of work with paid employment, largely from gender analyses of political economy—wage labor *as* labor remains hegemonic.[8] This is evidenced by the fact that the category of labor requires numerous qualifiers (such as informal, wageless, and unpaid) to accommodate the heterogeneity of productive actions that actually exist in the world. It is furthermore reflected in the idea that the loss of stable employment in neoliberal capitalism is a crisis of *work* that has made millions of workers across the world redundant and superfluous, as if those not employed in wage labor are not engaged in other productive efforts in their lives. In short, the tendency to view work like that performed by catadores in terms of what it lacks begins with the political economic category of labor.

By adopting forms of living as an alternative conceptual frame, I intend to leave open the question of what work is. Catadores were well aware that others often perceived collecting recyclables as akin to begging and therefore as not constituting "real" work, a notion they struggled to contest.[9] They also performed various kinds of activities on the dump in and amid the collecting of recyclables, such as constructing makeshift camps, cooking and sharing meals, playing soccer and other games, listening to the radio, lounging around, and chatting (*bater papo*), that defied work/life and labor/leisure dichotomies. Approaching these activities as composing a form of living draws attention to the ways different notions of work are fashioned, negotiated, contested, and performed in efforts to sustain and reproduce life. It furthermore allows us to consider how work as a category of action may be constituted by a wide range of practices beyond the purely economic.

My use of "form of living" also stems from my interest in the second meaning of "living" as a manner or style of life. This entails particular ways of constructing and inhabiting the world, values and beliefs about what constitutes a "good life," and the trajectories taken in pursuing life projects. One of the problems with seeing the work of catadores as a survival strategy or a last resort is that it reduces their existential concerns to the (merely) economic, pragmatic, or compensatory.[10] Through forms of living, I explore instead how the returns of catadores to the dump express distinct conceptions of human well-being and ideas of what life is for. The double meaning of form of living—as both livelihood and way of life—thus aims to overcome what arose within modern capitalism as a conceptual division between work and life. As historians and sociologists of capitalism have long shown, by splitting the day into the employer's time and one's own time, capitalist wage labor made it possible to think of work as separate from "life" and introduced related social categories of "leisure" and "free time" (Lefebvre 2008; Thomas 1964; Thompson 1967). This binary between work and life has tended to generate separate conversations in the social sciences between issues of political economy on the one hand and those of phenomenology and subjectivity on the other.[11] Yet labor is constituted not only through states and markets but also through the very meanings workers ascribe to their labor. And forms of living are also formative—shaping life rhythms, habits, and orientations to the world.

In arguing that livelihoods cannot be understood apart from modes of life, I am inspired by the work of the historian E. P. Thompson. In anthropology, Thompson is primarily known for his concept of "moral economy," though this term has often been appropriated by anthropologists indirectly through the work of political scientist James Scott and adapted in ways that diverge widely from its original and specific meaning as a model of economy based on customary and class-specific rights, obligations, and practices (Edelman 2012). To a lesser extent, anthropology has also drawn on Thompson's understanding of class not as a structural category but as a social relationship and historical process—a definition that appears only briefly in the six-page preface to his otherwise momentous tome, *The Making of the English Working Class* (see Goldstein 2003; Mitchell 2015; Walley 2013). While these appropriations of Thompson's thought have certainly been fruitful, I am interested here not in extracting any one specific term or definition from his work but in considering them in the context of what could be described as his overall anti-economistic approach to labor and political-economic change. For example, in the essay that introduces his concept of moral economy, Thompson (1971) begins by critiquing standard historical explanations of food riots in eighteenth-century England as "rebellions of the belly." That is, Thompson takes issue with the assumption that urban laboring poor rioted simply because they were unemployed, prices were high, grain was scarce, and they were hungry. Thompson notes that despite complex social analysis applied to other populations, somehow when it comes to laboring poor, the tendency is to interpret their actions through the reductive lens of economic need. But scarcity, Thompson argues, can never be the explanation for any human life. Instead, the question becomes: "Being hungry . . . what do people do?" (77). This leads Thompson into an exploration of deeply held notions of the good and the right among laboring people in eighteenth-century England, ultimately arguing that their rebellious actions were as much about moral outrage as they were about hunger.

The explanation of riots as "rebellions of the belly" parallels the assumption that collecting material on a garbage dump constitutes "informal survivalism." Not only does Thompson's anti-economistic stance help disrupt such conventional narratives of deprivation; it also reveals a profoundly humanistic sensibility in the way he constructed his histories of industrial capitalism, always showing how political economy is interwoven with what he called "the arts of living" (1967: 95). For Thompson, this meant that labor is not just a means of subsistence, source of surplus value, or structural condition; it is also fundamentally an *experience* that shapes inner life processes and modes of inhabiting the world. One of his most famous examples was that of the factory bell that rang at fixed times and partitioned the workday—a new experience for workers introduced to wage labor that radically shifted their inner sense of time as well as their rhythms of everyday life.

While retaining Thompson's emphasis on the phenomenology of labor, this book focuses on the experience of work not in wage labor but beyond it. Ethnographically, this has required paying attention to the somatic qualities of collecting on the dump, as in the *feel* different objects have through the lining of a plastic bag. It has meant staying attuned to catadores' own commentaries on their experience, such as their common claim that collecting on the dump radically transforms the self in ways that make it impossible to readapt to the conditions of wage labor. And above all, it has involved tracing how work is not only a livelihood but also a key site of struggle in everyday efforts to construct the good—not in the sense of the normative and prescriptive but in the sense of what is valued, desired, and aimed for in the living out of life—in this case, within the precarious conditions of Rio's periphery. In short, the returns of catadores to the dump manifest how work is fundamentally entangled with moral and existential questions of what it means to live well.

Finally, by exploring forms of living, I aim to draw attention to form itself. Work that unfolds in relations other than those of wage labor continues to be described as informal, though what exactly it means for work to be informal remains an unresolved and heavily debated issue.[12] This is partly due to the expansiveness of the category, encompassing such a wide range of activities as street vending, home brewing, car-watching, busking, begging, shoe shining, domestic work, moto-taxis, piracy, pawnbroking, gambling, hustling, sex work, and drug dealing. What these myriad income-generating activities share is their divergence in some way from state-regulated, officially recognized, institutionally organized forms of work in capitalist societies. In other words, these diverse types of work are defined primarily by what they are *not*. In the case of catadores, their work does *not* occur in relations of wage labor. Their earnings are *not* recorded or taxed. Their presence at a waste disposal site, their activities there, and the conditions of the dump itself do *not* comply with several of Brazil's environmental laws. Their work is informal because it does not con*form*.

This does not mean that the work of catadores lacks form. If anything, collecting on the dump is all about creating form out of spaces and materials that are otherwise amorphous. I realized this for the first time on a day, early on in my fieldwork, when I arrived on the dump alone. That morning, having overslept, I had missed the stream of flatbed trucks that carry catadores to the dump's summit at dawn and had decided to hop a ride with a scrap dealer I knew during his midmorning trip to pick up a new load of plastics.

After the scrap dealer let me off, I stood at the edge of the staging area with my bundle of burlap sacks perched awkwardly against my shoulder and scanned the scene for someone I recognized. There was no one. Three garbage trucks had just pulled in, prompting most catadores to race off to the unloading zone a few dozen yards in front of me. I knew that all I needed to do was to spread out my three sacks on the ground, grab the oversized plastic bag I used to gather cardboard, and head out to the pile of freshly unloaded waste. But I had no idea where I should drop my sacks. There didn't seem to be an obvious spot unless I opted to leave my sacks quite far from all the action. I hesitated for several minutes, feeling increasingly self-conscious, and then I noticed a fairly open space in the dense patch-work of burlap sacks before me.

Relieved, I dropped my bundle and began arranging the sacks one by one. Just as I spread out the third, I was startled by someone shouting obscenities at me. I looked up to see a young guy immediately in front of me, carrying what was clearly a heavy barrel of loose paper, books, and magazines. I quickly jumped to the side and he passed, swearing and yelling that I was in the pathway. What pathway?

But then I saw it. A gap between burlap sacks, barely a couple of feet wide, led all the way to the unloading zone. I was standing in the middle of this trail. During all the times I had trekked back and forth between unloading trucks and my partially filled sacks, I had never realized that I was following a passageway that was marked off and respected by catadores. Though previously unable to see any order to the sacks, their arrangement was now glaringly obvious. It was like looking at one of those "Magic Eye" posters whose hidden image had suddenly come into view.

This was not the only time I had had this kind of experience while learning to collect on the dump. The constant movement of trucks and tractors in open space—arriving, departing, backing up, stopping, turning, dumping, and bulldozing—felt chaotic before I gained a sense of their rhythms. And then there were the ubiquitous black garbage bags whose contents I struggled to discern. The trick, I was told, was to feel for different shapes through the bags and, once found, to distinguish types of plastics by the way their form gives or resists when squeezed. I began to see the flatbed trucks carrying neat rows of rectangular bales of plastic, all sorted by color, as a product of form creation. This plastic was once lumped together with a seemingly indiscriminate mass of stuff that poured from the backs of unloading garbage trucks. To collect on the dump, then, primarily involved recognizing and re-creating order—identifying, gathering, sorting, and bundling. The Portuguese verb *catar*, the root of catador, does not exactly translate as the English verb *to collect*. Rather, it means to sift, select, and separate. It is to search for by way of discriminating.

Given that creating form is central to the activities of catadores, it hardly makes sense to describe their work as informal. But when Keith Hart (1973) proposed the concept of the informal economy, he was not thinking of form in its multiple instantiations—as order, as shaped materiality, as distinction. Rather, he was drawing on a specific meaning of form found in Max Weber's (2003) concept of rationalization in economic life (Gandolfo

2013). For Weber, "the formal" referred to formal rationality, action based on abstract laws that enable systematic, means–end calculation. Hart saw the degree of rationalization of work—the extent to which an enterprise was bureaucratic, institutionalized, and amenable to enumeration—as the key variable separating the formal economy from the informal economy. The income-generating activities of the urban migrants Hart came to know in Ghana in the 1960s convinced him that these new city inhabitants were not so much unemployed as alternatively employed in enterprises with different logics and modes of operation than those of modern capitalism. Yet to call these activities informal inadvertently implied that only one form exists in the world—form based on rational, economistic behavior.

This book dispenses with the conceptual language of the formal and informal economies. In its place, I examine the specific form that work takes, which is why I consider the activities of catadores to constitute a *form* of living. Here, form is not just a synonym for "type" or "kind," but a means to call attention to the ways that different materials, relations, and practices in economic life *take shape*. That is, my aim is to theorize the positive qualities of the economic forms I encountered in Jardim Gramacho, positive in the sense of what something is rather than what it is not. I argue that much of what we associate with informality—the variability, transience, fluctuation, spontaneity, and imitation that characterize many of the practices deemed informal—is instead plasticity or the quality of changing form. However, plasticity is an attribute not only of the activities of catadores, but also of entities that would conventionally be categorized as "formal," such as the waste management company that owned the dump. Indeed, tracing the various actors involved in Jardim Gramacho's recycling industry shows how the plasticity of economic life often emerges out of the interplay between different forms of living, and is therefore fundamentally relational. Plasticity as an analytic thus breaks open the dualistic division of the world into the formal and informal, revealing an array of economic forms with the potential to both shape and be shaped. Ultimately, this inquiry into what form *is* constitutes a critique of formlessness—the notion that some things in the world, whether matter like garbage or an act like collecting recyclables on a dump—lack order in themselves.

By setting aside the concept of the informal economy, this book furthermore contributes to a growing effort to rethink the very idea of economy—arguably the last remaining concept in modern science to be deconstructed by critical theory (Mitchell 2002: 3).[13] Ever since Malinowski (1984) described the Kula Ring in the Trobriand Islands as a system of exchange based on principles of gift-giving, reciprocity, and social prestige, anthropology has provided innumerable examples of societies whose practices of production and exchange diverge from the utilitarian and calculative orientation of modern market economies. However, by emphasizing alternative kinds of economies (gift economies, peasant economies, moral economies, among others), these studies reinforced the notion of the economy—that the economy as a distinct material domain of human life is something that exists everywhere, even if it looks different in different places (de L'Estoile 2014; see also Mitchell 2002). The concept of the informal economy continues in this vein. The "informal" functions merely as a qualifier, one that furthermore emphasizes lack, thereby leaving the unmarked category of *the* economy intact. As J. K. Gibson-Graham (2006) has argued, the problem is not only that the economy has become naturalized by the failure to deconstruct this concept, but that this has attributed to the (capitalist) economy an internal coherence and totalizing force. In contrast to the category of the economy, the concept of forms of living emphasizes process and practice—how certain material relations take shape through everyday actions. Rather than implicitly invoking a norm, it draws attention to a multiplicity of forms, and it captures both material and existential dimensions of life, refusing to uphold the material as somehow more fundamental or "real." In short, forms of living as a theoretical frame allows us to ask what is entailed in producing and reproducing life without reifying the economy as a universal, eternal, and essential domain of social worlds.

JARDIM GRAMACHO AND THE WORK OF THE FAVELA

Less than five miles as the crow flies from the international airport and less than twenty miles from Rio's downtown, Jardim Gramacho is not far from the center of the city. However, depending on traffic, it can take anywhere from forty minutes to two hours to make one's way from Rio's bus hub at Central Station to the last stop in Jardim Gramacho, located in the neighboring municipality of Duque de Caxias. Along this journey, the urban landscape changes. Rio's beaches, high-rises, and hillside favelas give way to congested highways and car, furniture, textile, and cigarette factories. A multitude of buses clog the side lanes, as they pause momentarily to let passengers on and off. Pedestrians and street vendors cluster at the base of footbridges that span the highway, Avenida Brasil, every kilometer or so. At times, it is possible to catch a glimpse down one of the narrow streets that lead off the main highway and into dense neighborhoods of half-built houses, some piled three stories high. Merging onto the highway Washington Luiz from Avenida Brasil—thus crossing from Rio de Janeiro to Duque de Caxias—cheap motels and roadside restaurants are interspersed with industrial warehouses.

Bordering Rio's northeastern edge, Duque de Caxias is one of eight municipalities in the metropolitan area that together make up the Baixada Fluminense, a low-lying region of rivers, swamplands, and floodplains.[14] In the eighteenth and nineteenth centuries, the Baixada's rivers irrigated plantations of sugarcane, rice, corn, and beans and served as transportation routes between the gold-mining region further inland and the ports of Rio de Janeiro (Ferreira 1957).[15] Beginning in the mid-nineteenth century, however, intensive logging destroyed much of the original forest of the Baixada, leading to increased flooding, pools of stagnant water, and the proliferation of miasmas and malarial mosquitoes. Health and living conditions deteriorated to such a degree that many residents simply abandoned the area. The population of what is today Duque de Caxias plummeted from over 10,000 inhabitants in 1872 to 800 by 1910 (Beloch 1986: 22).[16] Still today, many residents of Jardim Gramacho, especially those who have built shacks on land below sea level, struggle to keep their homes from flooding during rainstorms. Mosquitoes are so prevalent that one subsection of the neighborhood bears the name Maruim, after a type of mosquito that thickens the air at dusk.

The relationship between the Baixada and the city of Rio de Janeiro has long been fraught. As Rio pursued modernization projects in the latter half of the twentieth century, the Baixada became the choice location for heavy industries, including the largest refinery of Brazil's petrochemical company, Petrobras. While many government officials and residents of the Baixada welcomed industrial projects in the hope that they would bring much-needed infrastructure to the region, the Baixada has also borne the wider social and environmental costs of these development projects. Nothing illustrates this relationship more powerfully than the Jardim Gramacho dump. In September 1978, garbage trucks began arriving in Jardim Gramacho to unload, at the time, three thousand tons of Rio's daily waste into the mangrove swamp at the edge of the neighborhood. Despite federal guidelines prohibiting solid waste dumping in waterways and federal

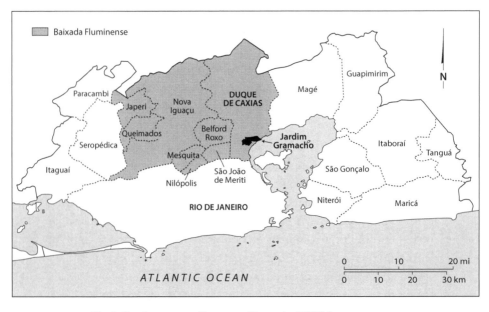

MAP I.1. Rio de Janeiro metropolitan area. Drawn by Bill Nelson.

legislation that established mangrove swamps as protected areas, the City of Rio de Janeiro selected one million square meters of mangrove swamp in the neighboring municipality of Duque de Caxias as the new destination for the metropolis's refuse. The establishment of a garbage dump in Jardim Gramacho was considered a development project, sponsored and coordinated by FUNDREM, the Foundation for the Development of the Metropolitan Region, which was created by the governor of the state of Rio de Janeiro in 1975 in an effort to recognize the urbanization of Rio's periphery and incorporate neighboring cities into urban planning projects. The site of the new dump belonged to a nineteenth-century plantation that had been appropriated by INCRA, Brazil's National Institute of Colonization and Agrarian Reform. INCRA donated this land to the state of Rio de Janeiro, and FUNDREM coordinated an agreement among the city of Rio and neighboring municipalities to use the area as a garbage dump servicing nearly the entire metropolitan area.[17] Since 1978, roughly seventy million tons of garbage have been dumped in Jardim Gramacho. Ninety percent of this waste has come from the city of Rio de Janeiro.

Though nearly every banana peel, soiled napkin, or plastic wrapping thrown out in Rio de Janeiro eventually ended up in Duque de Caxias, few *cariocas* (residents of Rio) ever venture into this part of the city. The Baixada has also received relatively little attention, either in the media or in scholarly work, in contrast to Rio's hillside favelas, some of which have featured in internationally acclaimed films, hosted "slum tourism" programs, and more recently become targets of urban development projects and "pacification" campaigns in connection to the 2014 World Cup and 2016 Olympic Games.[18] This does not mean, however, that the Baixada is marginal to the life of the city. The region's role in the social and political life of the city became clear in several incidents, large and small, during my fieldwork. For example, during a spat between the mayor of Caxias and the mayor of Rio over maintenance of the access road to the dump, the mayor of Caxias shut down the road by bulldozing a trench across it. No trucks could pass, and Rio's garbage was left uncollected on the streets for several days. Outraged, one resident of Rio wrote the following in a letter to the editor in Rio's main newspaper, *O Globo*: "The mayor of Duque de Caxias does not want Rio de Janeiro's garbage deposited within his city. Now, imagine if the mayor of Rio prevented Rio's municipal hospitals from receiving residents of Duque de Caxias?"[19] The observation that Caxias is home to the city's dump, whereas Rio is home to the city's best hospitals, received no comment.[20]

There are other, more subtle ways in which places like Jardim Gramacho fail to be recognized within the social geography of the city. One of these concerns the ways Jardim Gramacho diverges from hegemonic notions of the "favela" through which poverty, inequality, and informality are understood in Brazil. Usually translated as "shantytown," the favela has historically signified an informal settlement constructed by the poor on illegally occupied land that lacks access to public services. In Rio, many of these settlements were built on the rugged hills that rise above the city's middle- and upper-class neighborhoods. The favela is therefore often defined in opposition to the *bairro* (an officially recognized "neighborhood" of the city) or in opposition to the *asfalto*, or "pavement," the part of the city with well-maintained urban infrastructure and public services. Though favela urbanization programs in the past two decades have brought pavement, sewage systems, and other basic services to favelas and many are now officially recognized by the city as bairros, the favela–bairro or favela–asfalto distinction continues to operate in the public imaginary (Cavalcanti 2014). Since the late 1980s when drug-trafficking organizations began operating in these hillside communities, the favela also became synonymous in the public imaginary with drug dealing and armed violence, both between rival gangs and between drug dealers and police.

According to these ways that Rio's communities have been defined, Jardim Gramacho is *both* a bairro and a favela. Officially, the city of Duque de Caxias classifies the community as a "sub-bairro" of a larger area called Gramacho. The part of Jardim Gramacho that is closest to the bordering Washington Luiz highway, where various industrial warehouses are located, has long been paved and has received basic services for several decades. Many of the brick-and-mortar homes in this area are well constructed and in good condition. In contrast, the part of Jardim Gramacho that is closer to the dump, which residents often refer to generally as "the inside," is lined with shacks built from scrap materials or with partially built, autoconstructed brick-and-mortar homes. Some of this area was paved in the early 2000s, but sections of it continue to expand along dirt paths that flood in rainstorms. This area has also served as the location for Jardim Gramacho's *boca de fumo*—the name given to a site where drugs are sold, literally meaning the "mouth of smoke." While shifting its specific location periodically to avoid detection, during my fieldwork the boca always operated within one of the sections closest to the dump (or when hiding out during a police invasion, on the dump itself). Yet while Jardim Gramacho has elements of both a bairro and a favela, this is not to say that there are two separate, clearly demarcated areas of the community. Residents frequent the same schools, day care centers, bars, and grocery stores. Scrapyards, which cluster in the more favela-like areas, are also interspersed among other warehouses on the main road. Some residents rented homes on more established streets of the neighborhood and at a later point built their own shacks in areas of Jardim Gramacho that began expanding into land that was formerly mangrove swamp. And despite its official designation as a sub-bairro, Jardim Gramacho is part of the wider constellation of favelas in Rio whose relations to each other are shaped by the relations among drug-trafficking organizations. For example, it would be dangerous for a resident of Jardim Gramacho, which was controlled by the drug-trafficking organization Comando Vermelho (Red Command), to attend a *baile funk* party in a favela where a rival gang operates. The difficulty in defining Jardim Gramacho as a bairro or a favela demonstrates that this distinction is more of a symbolic construction than an objective representation of urban space.[21] This leads to the question of what ideological work the category of the favela performs—to ask not only what the favela–bairro distinction reveals about poverty and inequality in Rio de Janeiro, but also what it masks.

One answer to this question of what the favela–bairro distinction masks is work. The favela has long been associated with the absence of work. In the early twentieth century, depictions of favelas as sites of vagrancy or *malandragem* were common in public debates on poverty. In her intellectual history of the favela, Brodwyn Fischer (2014) quotes a 1908 essay describing the people of a favela as "making merry in indigence rather than working, managing to construct a camp of indolence in the midst of a great city . . ." (18). By the late twentieth century, the association of the favela with the figure of the *malandro*, the vagrant or hustler who disdains waged work, shifted to the association of the favela with the *bandido*, the criminal involved in drug trafficking. Both of these figures have been perceived in Brazil's public imaginary as the antithesis of the "honest" worker. This is not to say that such portraits of favelas have gone uncontested. Many policymakers and social scientists have expended great effort on showing that favela residents are indeed workers. One of the best-known examples of this work is Janice Perlman's (1976) study *The Myth of Marginality*, which argued that favela residents contribute significantly to the political, economic, social, and cultural life of the city, including through their provision of labor. But even these critiques of marginality have tended to emphasize work that favela residents perform *outside* the favela, as domestic workers, repairmen, construction workers, janitors, doormen, and security guards in Rio's middle- and upper-class neighborhoods. That is, even if favela residents are perceived as workers, the favela itself is rarely seen as a space of production.

Much like the category of the informal economy, the favela has persistently been defined in terms of lack—a lack of order, services, security, and, most importantly for the case of Jardim Gramacho, a lack of work.[22] As a result, scholars of urban poverty have tended to represent the favela as a "symptom of contemporary crisis" and to focus on the more spectacular or dramatic aspects of favela life such as drug trafficking and urban violence (Fischer 2014). Certainly the voluminous literature on violence in Rio's favelas has provided much-needed insights into social relations among drug traffickers, residents, police, and the wider city.[23] But this predominant focus on armed violence has left other dimensions of life in urban poverty in the dark, fueling widespread notions that the drug trade, policing, and violence are the only, or at least the most significant, attributes of favelas. The work that catadores perform in Jardim Gramacho's bustling market in recyclables complicates this singular portrait of Rio's favelas. Far from an absence, work is a central dimension to this community's history, development, and relationship to the broader city.

Jardim Gramacho not only defies dominant understandings of favelas as spaces of nonwork but, more importantly, reveals the centrality of work to the life projects of urban poor across Rio de Janeiro. Few catadores grew up in Jardim Gramacho, and even after coming to the dump, most continued to maintain a home, families, or friendships in other parts of the city. The time that catadores spent away from Jardim Gramacho led them to the far western side of the city, to favelas that rise above the wealthy South Zone, to other favelas that line Avenida Brasil in the north, to the Ilha Governador where Rio's international airport is located, to other municipalities of the Baixada Fluminense, and to other neighborhoods in Duque de Caxias. As home to the city's largest garbage dump, Jardim Gramacho is unique. Yet it is also a place where people gathered from the city's farthest reaches. This meant that when catadores returned to the dump, they brought with them histories, networks, and forms of living that crisscrossed Rio's urban expanse.

THE WORK OF ETHNOGRAPHY: INQUIRIES AND METHODS

I first came to Jardim Gramacho the way almost everyone does—by word of mouth. A street catador named Paulo told me about the place on a quiet morning in January 2005 when I met him while wandering through downtown Rio de Janeiro. I saw him from across a wide avenue, hunched over, methodically pulling a cart laden with flattened cardboard boxes. A flag pinned to the back of his cart caught my eye. Bright green with a simple black drawing of a cart at its center, I recognized it as the flag of Brazil's National Movement of Catadores of Recyclable Materials (MNCR). At the time, I was interested in the political mobilization that had recently sprung up around this type of work. I crossed the street.

"If you are interested in the movement here," Paulo told me, "you should also meet the catadores from Gramacho, Jardim Gramacho."

A few days later, I found a taxi driver who lived near Jardim Gramacho and knew where to go. When we eventually arrived in Jardim Gramacho, we pulled off the highway onto a dusty road, following a lumbering eighteen-wheeler truck with an orange trailer and the word *Prefeitura,* "The City [of

Rio de Janeiro]," painted in thick black letters on the side of the cab. The truck rocked clumsily on spots of broken pavement, making brutal sounds of stressed metal and engine as it pounded through the street. We drove by warehouses, corner bars, a grocer, a chicken shop, a bakery, and several evangelical churches. Children wearing public school uniforms chased each other. In front of a bar, several young guys gathered around a jukebox that played a music video accompanying the blaring *funk* song. A couple of pigs roamed at the edge of the sidewalk. Coming from the opposite direction, a flatbed truck passed us, stacked with bundles of crushed plastic bottles. Another truck followed, this one carrying a dozen or more burlap sacks filled with what looked like sheets of paper. Perched atop these sacks sat several men and women, all wearing tattered orange or yellow vests. Some of these riders seemed half asleep, while others shouted boisterously to acquaintances below. I began to notice many people on the sides of the street wearing these same vests and carrying bundles of burlap sacks or large plastic containers on top of their heads. The dust had now thickened into a haze, making the scenes to my left and right seem like photographs developed with a brush effect.

Transfixed by all this activity, I did not immediately notice the mountain rising up in front of us, nor the sign at the end of the road that read "The Metropolitan Landfill of Gramacho."

We stopped at the entrance. A guard approached the taxi and then directed us to a small, single-story white building that housed the dump's administrative offices. I spent the next several hours chatting first with the manager of the dump and then with Tião, who, at the time, was the twenty-five-year-old leader of a newly formed Association of Catadores. I learned in those initial conversations that trucks bring eight thousand tons of garbage to Jardim Gramacho every day. That the garbage dump rests on a former mangrove swamp, where locals once caught crabs. That dozens of scrapyards fill the neighborhood of Jardim Gramacho where materials are sorted, bundled, and then sent out again into the world. And that for the last thirty years, hundreds and eventually thousands of catadores have made their lives reclaiming plastics, paper, cardboard, metals, rubber, and a multitude of other objects that still hold some use-value.

I would return to Jardim Gramacho several times between 2005 and 2012, though the majority of this book is based on fieldwork I conducted in 2008 and 2009. During this time, I lived partly with a catadora, Glória (Tião's sister), and her daughter, whom I met during my first visit to Jardim

Gramacho. Later, when I found my own place, I lived in a small house located behind a bar on Monte Castelo, Jardim Gramacho's main street. This location had its advantages. It was a quick walk to the entrance to the dump and on the road where nearly every garbage and scrapyard truck passed. I also benefited from proximity to the bar, owned by my neighbor Deca, which served as a gathering spot not only for catadores but also for numerous truck drivers en route to recycling plants. Living on Monte Castelo, however, had its disadvantages. The constant traffic of eighteen-wheelers clunking along the pothole-filled road kept me awake at night and kicked up a thick, black dust that gathered on the house floors. It was necessary to sweep and mop the floors each day to keep the layers of dust to a minimum. At times I felt that much of my effort was expended on an unceasing battle against the rats, ants, poisonous centipedes (*lacraia*), cockroaches, and dirt that threated to overtake the house with any lapse in cleaning—the residue of a juice glass overlooked on the table, a couple of days without mopping floors, or a week without pouring bleach in the cracks of the wall where centipedes gathered and multiplied.

I spent much of my time in Jardim Gramacho collecting alongside catadores on the dump. I first collected cardboard because I found it to be one of the easiest materials to identify (though not to carry, as I quickly learned, given that it tends to be soaking wet and therefore heavy). When the price of cardboard dropped precipitously in October 2008, a consequence of the U.S. housing market collapse and ensuing economic crisis, I switched to collecting PET (polyethylene terephthalate), the type of plastic found in water and soda bottles, and other hard plastics. There were days, especially at the beginning of my fieldwork, when all my energy focused on the physical act of collecting—identifying material, filling my sack, and carrying it back to the staging area, all the while paying attention to the pathways of trucks and tractors. But over time, many of my conversations with catadores occurred in the midst of collecting and pulled me into other kinds of activities on the dump, such as meals and soccer games. Furthermore, learning to collect as a *novata*, or "novice," as catadores called newcomers, inspired my interest in the phenomenology of work. That is, my own (terribly inadequate) training in the labor of catadores drew my attention to the ways experiences of work do work on the self—reshaping bodily sensations, daily rhythms, and ways of being in the world.

In addition to collecting on the dump, I spent time at a cooperative run by the Association of Catadores in Jardim Gramacho (ACAMJG).[24] My first visit to Jardim Gramacho in 2005 happened to coincide with the initial process of forming ACAMJG (pronounced *ah-cán-jee*), and I was therefore able to follow the development of this association from its beginning as an informal group of catadores who held weekly meetings at an outdoor neighborhood bar, to its creation of a separate, registered, self-sufficient recycling cooperative. This cooperative, which catadores referred to as the *Polo*, was inaugurated in May 2007 and consisted of an open-air shed and a small building with an office, kitchen, and bathrooms. Though catadores often circulated in and out of the cooperative, at any one time there were roughly fifty active members. These catadores collected material individually on top of the dump, brought it to the Polo to sort, and then sold everyone's material jointly, either to recycling plants or to larger scrap dealers—bypassing intermediary scrap dealers in Jardim Gramacho. Each catador received payment in accordance with the amount of material in weight that they contributed to the total sale.

ACAMJG's Polo became my own base for collecting. I often rode up to the dump on ACAMJG's truck, brought my sacks to the Polo at the end of the day, and sorted my material there if needed. I also helped out with day-to-day operations at the Polo, assisting with the week's accounting, sweeping and cleaning the patio, helping weigh material, running errands, and attending meetings. My involvement with ACAMJG enabled me to address questions regarding the potential for political mobilization and collective action. But I was also careful not to allow ACAMJG to dominate my focus. Most studies of catadores in Brazil (and elsewhere) focus on those who are members of recycling cooperatives, despite the fact that these catadores represent a small fraction of the laboring poor who collect on city streets or atop dumps.[25] This disproportionate attention on cooperatives might stem from what Orin Starn has described as a tendency for scholars to study social movements that meet their "own vision of the right kind of activism" (1999: 25).[26] By working with catadores who were involved with ACAMJG and with many who were not, I was able to explore a fuller range of collective projects among catadores and to question what counts as a politics of labor.

Though both the dump and the Polo were my two most important research sites, I also spent a great deal of time visiting catadores in their homes (sometimes in other parts of the city), chatting with neighbors, interviewing scrap dealers, visiting recycling plants, recording oral histories of the neighborhood, conducting archival research on the development of the dump and the surrounding region, collecting cans on the streets of downtown Rio during carnival, and attending and hosting all kinds of social events—birthday parties, funerals, barbecues, dances, and gatherings at the Sunday fair. Accompanying catadores in their lives beyond the dump allowed me to trace the threads that weave together life and labor. It was also in moments and sites away from the work of the dump that I began to understand the stakes of catadores' returns.

OVERVIEW

Each of the chapters that follow provides a different piece of the puzzle of why catadores return to work on the dump. Most anthropological work on the experience of return, most notably in studies of migrants and refugees, examines the return to place. Though catadores certainly return to a place (the dump), I am more interested in their return to a condition—that is, to a particular form of living. Nonetheless, I draw from studies of return migration the emphasis on return as an ambivalent process with political, social, economic, and cultural consequences (Oxfeld and Long 2004). My adoption of return as an analytic thus differs significantly from the idea of a cycle frequently invoked in popular representations of poor families as trapped in "cycles of poverty." A cycle is a set of events that recurs again and again, leading back to the same starting point. In contrast, one can return to a place or condition and find that it has changed or that one's experience of it has shifted, as is often the case for refugees or migrants returning to a homeland after many years. Furthermore, a cycle suggests a fixed series or structure in which one can become "stuck," whereas returns are not necessarily either forced or liberatory. A return can be a relapse, but it can also be a response or an act of restoring something to the world, as in the act of picking up discarded objects and placing them back into relations of exchange.

As the book gradually unravels the puzzle of why catadores return to the dump, it simultaneously builds my conceptual approach to work as a *form of living*, a term I use to capture the relations between livelihoods and ways of life. Each instance of return illuminates how labor and existential conditions intersect in ways that defy standard interpretations of wageless work as either a strategy of survival or (more rarely) an act of resistance. It is a central argument of this book that work is tightly interwoven with values and beliefs about what constitutes a good life and with human struggles to realize these visions even within brutal social constraints.

Chapter 1 introduces the question of return by first examining narratives of arrival. Reflecting on the stories catadores told of their very first days on the dump, I consider what it means to arrive on the dump in a phenomenological sense and what this reveals about the ways catadores experience and perceive their place of work. These entry narratives, which span three decades (from 1978 to 2008), point to important historical shifts in the political economy of Brazil, while challenging standard depictions of Brazil's social and economic policy in the first decade of the twenty-first century. But most importantly, these narratives address the stakes of arrival—what catadores knowingly take on each time they hop a truck to the top of the dump. In these tales of both first arrivals to the dump and their arrivals on a day-to-day basis, catadores complicate the common notion that garbage is an experience of the abject. Instead, their stories speak to the ontology of the dump as a burial ground and the labor entailed in what I conceptualize as its vital liminality, the experience of being at the border of life and death. What it means to arrive, then, opens up the book's inquiry into labor not only as an economic relation but also as an ontological experience.

Chapter 2 begins to unpack the question of return by exploring moments in which catadores leave the dump for other jobs and then later go back. Specifically, it examines how everyday emergencies that disrupt the present in Rio's periphery often clash with the rigid conditions of regular, wage-labor employment. Such emergencies arise from multiple insecurities in the lives of Rio's poor, including urban violence, makeshift housing, deficient health care, poor infrastructure, and relations of debt. I argue that the comings and goings of catadores emerge from a tension between the desire for "real" work and the desire for what I describe as relational autonomy, made possible by the conditions of wageless work. On the dump, catadores are able to collect at any hour of the day or night and can determine how frequently and intensely they work. Moreover, catadores perceive their experience of the fluidity of work on the dump as changing them in ways that make them no longer able to "adapt," as they say, to the structures of waged employment. Collecting on the dump thus fashions a distinct form of living that implicates everyday rhythms and embodied habits. The chapter concludes by suggesting that the act of leaving a job for wageless work constitutes a politics of detachment that enables life to be lived in fragile times.

Chapter 3 explores the returns of catadores to the dump—not over weeks, months, or years, as in chapter 2—but rather within the microtemporality of the day-to-day. Attending to moments in which the earnings of catadores seem to "vanish," this chapter examines how income, expenditures, credit, and debt influence when and how often catadores go back to work on the dump. Faced with a continual barrage of financial needs and requests, the ability of catadores to earn cash payment each day they work on the dump takes on added significance and paradoxically transforms spending into a form of saving. The experience of being broke among catadores furthermore emerges from a moral critique of work as an end in itself, rather than a means to sustain life. Emphasizing the interlocking dynamics of economic and moral value, I argue that catadores' decisions on a daily basis to work on the dump (or not) constitute a diverse set of arguments about what it means to live well.

The conditions of return explored thus far in the book might suggest that catadores move in and out of the dump without restraint. Chapter 4 provides an essential, if complicating, piece of the puzzle by shifting focus from the question of what draws catadores to the dump to a question of what impedes their returns. For years, city waste-management personnel implemented a series of (continuously unsuccessful) policies and practices intended to shape the dump into a "proper work environment." One of these policies involved the requirement that catadores wear identifying work vests as a means of access to the dump and that they sell their material only to the scrap dealer who provided the vest. Yet despite the fact that every catador I encountered on the dump wore a vest (including myself), catadores continually insisted that the vests controlled neither access to the dump nor their sales to scrapyards. I unpack this apparent contradiction by tracing the social life of work vests as they circulate between the semipublic waste management company, unregistered scrap dealers, and catadores. This story illuminates how actors usually associated with different sectors or types of economy—the formal, informal, and illicit—are deeply integrated in everyday practice. Rather than ask what is formal or informal, I shift the question to how form is made. I am interested in the interplay between different forms of living that are fluid, mutable, and malleable—that is, plastic, to borrow a term from the most ubiquitous material that catadores collect. This chapter thus contributes most directly to the book's aim to rethink economy. It is also about how struggles over the contours of what constitutes "work" are struggles over different forms of inhabiting the world.

Chapter 5 provides the final piece of the puzzle by examining the most contentious kind of return to the dump—one that occurs as a result of catadores withdrawing from ACAMJG's self-organized worker cooperative. This chapter traces the history of ACAMJG from its early years of mobilization, to its establishment of the recycling cooperative, to its increasing expansion and institutionalization. It seeks to understand why many catadores who were, at one point, centrally involved in ACAMJG eventually left the cooperative to go back to collecting on their own. Rather than frame these returns as "failures" in political consciousness and collective organizing, I consider how the withdrawal from ACAMJG enables catadores to pursue more anarchic forms of cooperative practice. These include work partnerships, a self-organized camp called "the union," and strikes in which catadores refused to sell their material to scrap dealers at different moments in the dump's history. I suggest that work outside conditions of wage labor is often seen as an unorganized, competitive, and apolitical space because the kinds of ephemeral, noninstitutionalized forms of collective action that do occur among wageless workers diverge from standard conceptions of what counts as politics. Yet, I argue, the very act of turning back to the dump can be understood as a political project. That is, to return to the dump is to break with normative forms of capitalist labor, opening up possibilities of other ways of fashioning work and life.

The book concludes with a description of my own return to Jardim Gramacho in July 2012, a month after the garbage dump closed. Taking catadores' insistence that "the garbage never ends" as a point of departure, I follow how catadores remake forms of living in the wake of this closure. Though at the time employment was said to be booming in Brazil and job-training programs were being offered to catadores to address the consequences of the dump's closure, few catadores pursued these possibilities. In addition, activities at ACAMJG's recycling cooperative—a possible work alternative to collection on the dump—nearly came to a standstill. Most catadores emphasized instead that they were "waiting" (*aguardando*), in the sense of holding out for something. Their waiting reinforces many of the themes of the book—particularly how wageless work is not simply a last resort for urban poor, but rather articulates with visions of what constitutes a good life. Ultimately, I consider what it means to lose work outside conditions of wage-labor employment by exploring the significance of the dump as a site to which catadores can no longer return.

WRITING ON GARBAGE

When I told cariocas in the center of the city where I was conducting research, those who knew about the place told me that Jardim Gramacho is a "hell."[27] Indeed, the most common reaction to the image of human beings sifting through garbage is one of disgust and horror. Such revulsion resonates with the way anthropologists and other social scientists have long conceptualized garbage as the abject product of order creation.[28] This approach draws heavily on Mary Douglas's famous insight that dirt is "matter out of place" (1996: 36). For Douglas, dirt is what gets eliminated in the human effort to create meaningful order out of what is an inherently chaotic world. Dirt offends and disgusts us precisely because its presence threatens the integrity of the order we have produced.

This structural and symbolic perspective on waste might explain why the Jardim Gramacho dump was located in the outskirts of Rio or why visitors to the dump pinched their noses or rolled up the car windows when approaching the entrance. It says nothing, however, about what happens to garbage once it is dumped, what garbage produces over time, or how those who interact with (and not just produce) garbage experience it. In other words, it fails to account for the social life and generativity of waste itself.[29] Furthermore, the perception that garbage is disorder, nonbeing, or formlessness prevents any engagement with its specific qualities. As any novice quickly learns on the dump, not all garbage smells, feels, sounds, moves, rots, shrinks, or weighs the same. Knowing these differences, which is essential to the labor of catadores, means recognizing that garbage is matter and that all matter has form, even if it is not the form we might desire.

The refusal to engage with the materiality of garbage leads to a tendency to either sensationalize or aestheticize waste in its representation. Throughout my fieldwork in Jardim Gramacho, I witnessed numerous journalists and other visitors arrive on the dump and immediately pull out cameras to photograph it—often without asking catadores for their permission. In addition, several professional artists and filmmakers have developed photographic projects of Jardim Gramacho, including Marcos Prado's (2004) film *Estamira*; Vik Muniz's (2008) series *Pictures of Garbage*; and Lucy Walker, Karen Harley, and João Jardim's (2010) Oscar-nominated documentary, *Waste Land,* which follows Muniz's project. For some of these image-makers, the picture of garbage is aimed at rendering brutal degradation, as in the case of a news crew that showed up in Jardim Gramacho to use it as backdrop for a live report on poverty in Brazil. For others, like the photographer Vik Muniz, the image of garbage is meant to turn waste into art—though the reason garbage is so compelling in such work is precisely that it is thought to be antithetical to beauty. Despite their differences, these images depict garbage as an indiscriminate mass, the particular contents and characteristics of which do not matter, either because garbage is taken to be the *totality* of all that society rejects or because the goal is to transcend this refuse by giving it aesthetic value. These two tendencies crystallized in a scene from the documentary *Waste Land* in which Vik Muniz's assistant photographer asks a catador, named Tião, to collect items from the dump that will be used in the pictures he is creating. After Tião responds by showing him the *specific* materials that catadores collect, the photographer decides that he wants mostly *carina*—a flexible plastic found in a wide range of goods, from flip-flops to tubing. Carina is best, the photographer explains, because it "gives the impression of *tudo*"—garbage as anything and everything.

But garbage is not *every* thing. To depict it as such is to erase the singularity of its contents. It is telling that in both English and Portuguese the word *garbage* (*lixo*) did not originally refer to refuse of any kind but rather to a specific thing that was commonly discarded: the viscera of butchered animals in fifteenth-century Middle English and the ashes of an oven or hearth in the Latin root of the Portuguese. Indeed, the very labor of catadores was premised on the fact that garbage consists of particular objects that are predictably present and identifiable. It mattered to catadores, for example, that certain known trucks or types of bags contained discarded medical supplies (usually to be avoided), stacks of used office paper (to be collected and sold), or nearly, but not yet, expired cartons of yogurt (to be enjoyed).

Furthermore, garbage is not *every* thing because it is its own thing—its materiality distinct from other materialities. Garbage is gaseous, belching methane and carbon dioxide that must be trapped and released lest the methane spontaneously erupt into fires. Garbage leaks, creating streams of black, noxious leachate that drain through its layers and, if not contained, seep into surrounding groundwater. Some of its contents, in varying stages of de-composition, attract all kinds of critters including vultures, flies, and mag-gots as well as plenty of microbes invisible to the naked eye that catadores blamed for the occasional abscess or rash. All this belching, leaking, at-tracting, and infecting are part of the generativity of waste, as are the value, sociality, and forms of living produced through recognizing and reclaim-ing its contents. To embrace the materiality of garbage—what catadores did every time that they reached a hand into a ripped bag—is to confront waste as both toxic and life-giving. It means refusing to appropriate, glo-rify, or transcend its abject qualities and instead to engage with the vitality of waste that is concealed when we view garbage from the perspective of order, when we view garbage as merely the discarded.[30]

How to do this in writing, how to put the materiality of waste into words, is not an easy question. In writing this book, I have struggled with the images of garbage and of the work of catadores that I sketch on the page. In an effort to capture waste not as a symbolic category but as a lived experience, I have chosen to adopt the language and expressions that cata-dores use themselves in depicting their place of work. Most often, catadores referred to the objects they collected not as garbage but as "material," a semantic shift that signals the differentiation of what is usually assumed to be an indiscriminate mass. If garbage, I was told, is that which is worth-less, then paper, plastics, metals, and other recyclables that still hold value cannot be garbage. For this reason, I retain the Portuguese term *catador* rather than rely on terms commonly used in English including scavenger, garbage picker, or trash picker—all designations that imply that the objects catadores collect are waste. However, despite passing under a sign read-ing "Metropolitan Landfill" every day that they worked, catadores referred to their place of work not as a landfill but as the dump (*lixão*), or simply the slope (*rampa*), the specific area within the dump's one million square meters where waste was unloaded at a particular time. In doing so, they refrained from participating in the sanitizing work that the word *landfill* does to hide the toxicity, contamination, infection, and inequality that cat-adores endured in their everyday labor.

I also seek to foreground catadores' own representations of the dump in the stories they tell each other, narratives that I present in the chapter that follows. These stories reveal that the materiality of waste can disrupt corporeal integrity, subjectivity, and everyday experience, but that this disruptive power also breaks open possibilities for transformation. In this chapter and throughout the book, I approach garbage not as "the degree zero of value" (Frow 2003: 25) but as the material basis through which catadores rearticulate notions of value and the good life. As Gastón Gordillo (2014) suggests in his analysis of rubble produced by capitalist and imperialist projects, waste is often perceived as nothingness, negativity, or the void. The modern conceptualization of waste is thus similar to that of the informal economy. Both are characterized by the *absence* of particular qualities or values. Both are defined by lack. The forms of living catadores create through actions and materiality that are only seen by what they are *not* challenge us to rethink both work and waste. The smashed blue water bottle, the outdated high heels, the dented Coke can, the school notebook with half its pages still blank inside, the cardboard box soaked with the juice of rotting tomatoes, and even the ubiquitous black bag are not garbage in the sense of a homogeneous, worthless mass. In the pages that follow, I aim to show how the act of reclaiming these particular objects and many more is also an act of remaking the world. In doing so, this book illuminates how waste lies at the heart of both relations of inequality and transformative social projects.

1 · Arriving beyond Abjection

ORIGINS

"Jardim Gramacho was a paradise."

My neighbor, Deca, told me this on an unusually quiet afternoon at his open-air bar. I was the only one seated on one of the plastic stools that lined the counter, though a couple of guys were busy choosing a song at the juke-box in the corner of the bar. Deca seemed to be in the rare mood to talk, and so I had asked him what he remembered of the neighborhood before the garbage dump existed. I knew that his family, having migrated from the northeastern state of Paraíba in the 1960s, was one of the first to arrive in Jardim Gramacho.

"This road," Deca recalled, indicating the main street in front of us, "was just a dirt path. I think my house might have been the seventy-eighth in the whole neighborhood. We were surrounded by fruit trees and natural springs."

I thought of the old stone hitching post at the edge of Jardim Gramacho where the nineteenth-century Emperor Dom Pedro II would stop on his way from Rio de Janeiro to his summer residence in Petrópolis so that his horses could drink from the spring. Today, the dust-covered hitching post is the only sign that a natural spring once flowed nearby.

FIGURE 1.1. Stranded fishing boats. *Photo by the author.*

There were also tidal pools, Deca told me, where neighborhood children would go swimming and where crabs could be caught among the mangroves. Residents supplemented their income by catching these crabs and other fish that entered from Guanabara Bay to lay their eggs. It was possible to fill a whole bag with mussels (*sururu*), mullets (*parati*), or blennies (*maria-da-toca*)—too much for any one family to eat. Lacking refrigeration, they would lay the excess fish on the tin roofs of their homes to dry in the sun.

Not that life was easy at the time. Like most early residents, Deca spoke of everyday struggles resulting from a lack of electricity, sanitation, paved roads, and bus service. There was also no pedestrian bridge over the highway, Washington Luiz, that borders Jardim Gramacho. Leaving the neighborhood required crossing eight lanes of traffic moving at speeds of sixty to seventy miles per hour. I recalled Glória telling me, soon after we first met, that her older brother had been hit and killed crossing the highway when he was nineteen years old. When I mentioned this to Deca, he shook his head.

"Before the garbage began arriving, they told us that Monte Castelo would be paved. We were told about the dump, but none of us knew to what extent the garbage would affect our lives." His words hung in the air, as if laden with sadness or perhaps *saudades*, the bittersweet remembering of something loved and lost.

"Did you know my wife?" Deca asked me. "Did you know her before she died?"

I recalled the day that I found a house to rent in Jardim Gramacho, not an easy feat in a place where most families built their own homes. Mariana, who sold clothing door-to-door in Jardim Gramacho and knew more about neighborhood news than did the most committed gossiper, had offered to take me to a couple of residents who she thought had a vacant house in their family's yard that they might be willing to rent out. We arrived at Deca's bar. Deca was not there, but Tom, another longtime resident of Jardim Gramacho, was working the bar and showed me a house behind the bar owned by Deca's brother, who had moved in with his grown children. As I finished making arrangements with Tom to rent the house, Mariana inquired about Deca's wife, and Tom replied that she had recently passed away. "She was such a good person, kind to everyone," Mariana kept repeating, her voice trembling, as we walked away.

I told Deca what Mariana had said.

"My wife had breast cancer," Deca replied. "We fought it. We did the mastectomy and the reconstructive surgery. After five years, the cancer came back. When it comes back, there is nothing to be done, *não tem jeito*."

"I'm so sorry," I replied.

Deca picked up a rag to wipe the counter and then stopped, shaking his head. "There are so many diseases in Jardim Gramacho. Cancers. Tuberculosis. Skin diseases. Other horrible diseases. I think it's the garbage. It's the dust that we breathe in Jardim Gramacho, a dust like no other dust, a dust that comes off the garbage trucks on their way to the dump. The leachate drips from the trucks onto our streets. All this toxicity. It causes these diseases."

I wanted to ask Deca why he had stayed in Jardim Gramacho, but I knew enough to realize this question had no simple answer. Most of the clientele who frequented Deca's bar were tied in some way to the dump. Truck drivers often stopped for a plate of Deca's rotisserie chicken on their way to and from recycling plants in the south of Brazil. A team of engineers working on a new piping system for the dump's methane gas had drinks each night at Deca's bar before heading to the local motel where they were staying. And many catadores unwound at his bar after a day of collecting—sharing rounds of drinks, playing dominoes, and listening to music that blared from the bar's jukebox.

Instead, I asked about the early days of the bar. How did it start? Deca's voice became more animated, as he described how he sold *quentinhas* (to-go lunches kept warm in an aluminum container) to the employees of Queiroz Galvão, the company contracted to remediate the dump in the 1990s. It was possible to sell sixty quentinhas at lunchtime and another forty throughout the day. At a certain point, Queiroz Galvão began giving employees tickets that they could use to go out and buy lunch at one of several locations. The bar was established to provide these sit-down lunches. Eventually the rotisserie was acquired. In a single week, 120 chickens were sold.

Deca paused, seemingly lost in a memory and then smiled: "Those were good times, you know, very good times."

FOR A LONG TIME, I understood the history of Jardim Gramacho as a straightforward story of environmental degradation. The arrival of garbage in Jardim Gramacho polluted the surrounding bay, clogged springs, smothered mangroves, and dripped on its streets and into its groundwater leachate—a black, acidic, nauseating liquid that seeps through decomposing waste, carrying concentrated amounts of copper, lead, nickel, and mercury, among other contaminants. The neighborhood that derived its name *Jardim*, meaning "gardens," from its history as a densely vegetated plantation dating back to the eighteenth century, had now become a toxic site.[1] Deca's own story of loss certainly echoed this narrative. It recounts the loss of beauty, the loss of resources in fruit trees, crabs, and fish, and most painfully, the loss of life. For Deca, there was never any doubt that it was the garbage that caused his wife's cancer and ultimately her untimely death.

Yet Deca's story also speaks to what I began to see as the entangled relations of life, labor, and the dump. The everyday labor of running his bar—a business that first emerged to serve sanitation workers—depended on and intersected with materials, activities, and individuals tied to the dump. I saw this web of work and waste in Deca's simple act of wiping the bar counter of dust kicked up by passing garbage trucks. It was also apparent from observing his customers, most of whom either worked on the dump or worked in transporting waste and recyclables to and from the dump. As a result, his work routines shifted with those of the dump: peak hours at the bar coincided with the times of day scrapyard trucks made their trips back from the dump, carting sacks of recyclables along with tired catadores in search of meals, drinks, and rest. Deca's story captured these ambivalent connections to the dump. He certainly knew now to what extent the garbage would affect his life, leading in his eyes to the death of a loved one. At the same time, the dump both initiated and contributed to his form of living. As Deca's narrative shifted from fruit trees and springs, to dust and disease, to hot lunches and "good times," it became clear that there was no easy relation to the garbage. There was no such thing as a singular experience of the dump.[2]

The ambivalence that Deca expressed in his reflections on the arrival of garbage in Jardim Gramacho was echoed in catadores' own stories of arrival—their accounts of how they first came to the dump. To arrive is often understood as a conclusive act, in the sense of reaching a destination or attaining some end. But in the stories of catadores, I came to understand arrival more as a fraught condition, an unsettled and ambiguous moment when everything has yet to be resolved. These stories of arrival therefore became particularly useful windows onto the complex ways catadores experience the dump and the labor they perform in reclaiming the discarded. In listening to their narratives, I also began to realize that to understand the returns of catadores to the dump, it is necessary to understand how they first arrived.

FOLLOWING THE GARBAGE

Catadores came to Jardim Gramacho for a host of reasons, but as I pieced together their accounts, I began to trace how the pathways that initially led them to the dump told a larger story of historical shifts in the political economy of Brazil. In tracing these connections, I follow Donna Goldstein's (2003: 45) insistence that any "ethnographic snapshot" of Rio de Janeiro must be situated within "Brazil's particular historical, political, and economic framework." In her richly textured ethnography of domestic work and class relations in Rio de Janeiro, Goldstein shows how the everyday life of favela residents is both a product of and an oppositional response to

Brazil's historical and spatial structures of elite privilege, dominant racial ideologies, and differentiated forms of state governance. This commitment to political-economic critique is part of a long tradition in Brazilianist ethnography and Latin American anthropology more broadly that sought to bring questions of power and inequality to the study of cultural practices, local histories, and social worlds.[3] More recently, anthropology has shown that weaving together ethnography and political economy does not just entail placing ethnographic subjects within their larger historical contexts. Rather, as João Biehl (2005) argues in his person-centered ethnography *Vita*, singular lives can uniquely illuminate the workings of structural forces and challenge accepted interpretations of the world. In the case of catadores, their continued arrivals to the dump in the early 2000s tell a story that calls into question hegemonic narratives of Brazil's economic growth (and subsequent decline) at the beginning of the twenty-first century.

The first arrivals of catadores to the dump date back to the late 1970s when the dump first opened. Most catadores from this older generation were migrants who had come to Rio de Janeiro in the 1960s and 1970s, part of a massive exodus from Brazil's rural areas, particularly from the drought-ridden northeast. Beginning in the 1950s, the rise of the modern sugar industry in the rural northeast uprooted the traditional plantation economy, evicting many peasants who had had customary arrangements of land tenure (Scheper-Hughes 1992). Migrants were also drawn to cities like Rio de Janeiro and São Paulo by the prospect of finding jobs in new industries that were booming at the time as the result of state-led development efforts. However, increased employment opportunities were insufficient to absorb the labor force pouring into Brazil's major cities. Inequality also continued to rise, a sign that the fruits of Brazil's "economic miracle" continued to be held by a small, elite segment of its population.

It was at this time that Carolina Maria de Jesús, a black, single mother of three who had migrated from rural Minas Gerais to a favela in São Paulo, published her diary, *Quarto de Despejo* (1960), literally "Room of Garbage," which had been discovered by a local journalist.[4] Surpassing sales of the Brazilian novelist Jorge Amado and eventually translated into thirteen languages, the diary described de Jesús's everyday struggles to support her children by collecting paper, bottles, cans, and food from junkyards and garbage cans. In addition to de Jesus's diary, scholarly literature on rural–urban migration and shantytown life in Latin America portrayed scavenging as an element of this new urbanization. For example, in her study of a

Mexican shantytown in the 1970s, Larissa Lomnitz (1975) argued that the poor survived by gathering what the industrial system discarded—used clothing, leftover materials from construction sites, even odd jobs—calling them urban "hunters and gatherers" (96). Though the Jardim Gramacho dump did not open until the late 1970s, the first catadores who arrived there had been collecting recyclables for years. When one dump had closed, they had simply moved to another—"following the garbage," as they recounted.

By the 1980s, Brazil's state-led industrialization led to an acute debt crisis, soaring inflation, and stagnant to negative economic growth. Unemployment began rising at a rate of 5.6 percent, while the real value of the minimum wage dropped by 1.8 percent (Pochmann 2010: 641). Brazil's economic restructuring in the 1990s did little to ameliorate the situation of Rio's poor. Deindustrialization, privatization, outsourcing, and reductions in the public sector meant that employment possibilities that did exist tended to be temporary and precarious. During these two decades, those who were new to the dump often came in the wake of a supporting family member's job loss. Glória's father, for example, lost his job as a shipyard worker in the late 1980s. Faced with little means to feed eight children, her mother went to the dump in search of food, returning the first day with a sack full of rice, beans, and vegetables. She soon began collecting recyclables regularly, along with Glória's father and at times with Glória and some of her siblings.

This was also a time when street children began arriving on the dump, prompted by heightened concern over their presence on city streets in the late 1980s and 1990s. Though the number of street children in Brazil at this time was relatively small (797 in Rio de Janeiro in 1993), they became the target of police "death squads" seeking to clear the streets of those perceived to be perpetrators of crime.[5] One of the most widely denounced incidents occurred in Rio de Janeiro in 1993 when several off-duty police officers shot and killed seven children who were sleeping on the steps of the Candelária Church located in the center of the city. Street children did not fare much better in state institutions for minors. Facilities run by the National Foundation for the Welfare of Minors (Fundação Nacional do Bem-Estar do Menor or FUNABEM) became notorious for their crowded rooms, squalid living conditions, and abuse by overseers.

Several catadores whom I met as adults on the dump told me that they had first arrived in Jardim Gramacho as children seeking to escape life on the streets or in state institutions. For instance, a catador nicknamed "Funabem," for having spent time in the state institution, ran away from an abusive mother when he was eight years old. He lived on the streets for two years, sleeping on sidewalks under newspapers and begging for food, clothes, and other necessities. When he was ten years old, he was apprehended and placed in a FUNABEM institution that was located in Rio's neighboring municipality of Niterói. After two years in the institution, Funabem managed to escape along with several other children, and having heard about the dump, made his way to Jardim Gramacho. Though the pathways that led Funabem and Glória to Jardim Gramacho differed, they both formed part of a cohort of catadores who started collecting in their early adolescence. The friendships that formed among these young catadores became, years later, the basis of the political organizing that generated ACAMJG. By the time I came to Jardim Gramacho, there were no longer children collecting as young as Glória and Funabem had been when they first arrived. In the late 1990s, the waste management company, Comlurb, began enforcing rules prohibiting minors (those under eighteen years of age) from entering the dump as part of a larger social and environmental effort to remediate the dump. However, older adolescents who were still minors were often able to pass as adults and slip by the guards who monitored entry and exit at the dump.

Paradoxically, it was in the first decade of the 2000s—when Brazil was lauded in the dominant political and academic discourse for having explosive economic growth *alongside* pro-poor policies—that the numbers of catadores on the dump skyrocketed. In 1996, Comlurb recorded 960 catadores in Jardim Gramacho. By 2008, there were over two thousand.[6] It was during this period that Luiz Inácio Lula da Silva, a former metalworker and union organizer, won the presidential election and launched what became called a "neodevelopmentalist" program. Lula maintained the neoliberal macroeconomic policies of his predecessor, Fernando Henrique Cardoso, such as privatizations, the payment of foreign debt, free capital mobility, and support for export-oriented agribusinesses (Rocha 2007). However, Lula combined this macroeconomic approach with the expansion of a set of social assistance programs. The most important of these was Bolsa Família, which involved direct cash transfers to families with incomes below the poverty line. Lula's administration also extended consumer credit to the poor, expanded social security coverage, and increased the minimum wage by 67 percent between 2003 and 2010 (Morais and Saad-Filho 2011: 35). With an approval rating of over 70 percent in the final months of his two-term presidency, Lula received praise in Brazil and internationally for achievements in economic growth, declining inequality, and poverty reduction.

On the surface, the numbers were impressive. Brazil sustained an average economic growth rate of nearly 5 percent between 2004 and 2008.[7] During this period, the unemployment rate in six of Brazil's largest metropolitan areas fell from 11.5 percent to 7.9 percent. Though still among the highest in the world, Brazil's Gini coefficient (a measurement of inequality with 100 signifying that one person owns all the wealth and 0 indicating complete equality of wealth) also declined—from 0.592 in 1998 to 0.537 in 2009 (Lustig et al. 2013). Finally, poverty decreased from 35 percent of households in 2001 to 21 percent in 2009, while 32 million Brazilians entered what became called "the new middle class" ("Classe C").[8] Such indices led *The Economist* magazine to publish a 2009 issue featuring an image of the statue of Christ the Redeemer launching from Rio de Janeiro's Corcovado Mountain like a rocket. The headline read, "Brazil Takes Off: A 14-Page Special Report on Latin America's Big Success Story."[9] Such optimistic reports emphasized not only Brazil's economic success but also its emergence on the international stage, symbolized in its selection to host the 2014 World Cup and 2016 Olympic Games.

However, such economic indicators can obscure more than they reveal. Most of Brazil's economic growth resulted from an expansion of exports (mostly natural resources and other primary goods) during a boom in commodity prices generated by increased demand from China (Rocha 2007). This export-led growth weakened the domestic market and failed to generate new jobs in industry that would be accessible to urban poor. The cash transfer program Bolsa Família mitigated situations of extreme poverty and hunger, particularly in rural areas, but this kind of social assistance did not create improved employment opportunities for workers, build infrastructure, address land reform, or alter social policy patterns that historically have benefited the privileged in Brazil.[10] Among these social policies were pensions, which date back to the early twentieth century when the Brazilian state privileged certain kinds of workers over others by granting social protections on the basis of regular, wage-labor employment (Hunter and Sugiyama 2009). At the turn of the twenty-first century, Brazil's top income earners continued to receive 65 percent of pension funds, while the bottom took home only 2.4 percent (Paes de Barros and Foguel 2000).[11] While certainly helping to improve the living conditions of the poorest Brazilians, Bolsa Família did little to ameliorate this history of inequality, which would require fundamentally restructuring social protections that primarily benefit Brazil's middle and upper classes. Targeting those in situations of extreme poverty (making less than R$60 per month on a per capita basis, or roughly less than a dollar a day), Bolsa Família's goal was never to achieve a more equitable distribution of income but rather "to provide a floor, however low, below which living standards do not fall" (Hunter and Sugiyama 2009: 48). Furthermore, as Gregory Duff Morton (2015) has shown in his insightful ethnographic analysis of Bolsa Família beneficiaries in rural Bahia, the program has had depoliticizing effects that stem from the fact that it is not a right but a privilege that can be stripped at any time. Such observations have led several analysts to argue that programs like Bolsa Família are little more than a bandage stemming the detrimental effects of neoliberal policies in Brazil. In other words, such programs fail to address deeper structural change. As a 2006 United Nations report argued, "shifting public finances away from investment that can have long-lasting effects on the causes of poverty to social spending that might temporarily cure the symptoms of poverty can be counterproductive in the long run" (UNCTAD 2006: v; cited by Rocha 2007: 143). By 2015, the Brazilian economy was in recession and any gains achieved by the much-celebrated "new middle class" were being lost, contributing to a growing political crisis.

Furthermore, reports on the unemployment rate in Brazil tend to be reductive of a much more complex labor context. Though the first decade of the 2000s brought the greatest expansion of added jobs in forty years, nearly all of this new employment (95 percent) was extremely low-paid work, earning workers less than 1.5 times the monthly minimum wage (Pochmann 2012: 19). To put this in perspective, in 2012 a worker needed to earn four times the minimum wage to achieve an estimated *salário mínimo necessário* or living wage (Luce 2013: 176). The official unemployment rate also does not capture workers in the so-called informal economy, which in 2008 made up well over half of the Brazilian labor force (Leone 2010; Marques and Mendes 2008). Those who do meet the definition of unemployed and are counted in unemployment statistics actually tend to have on average a higher education level than the employed, suggesting that the official unemployed population consists of workers with more resources who are able to hold out for desired jobs.[12] Finally, improvements in Brazil's labor market as a whole since 2003 do not reflect significant differences that still exist between social divisions of race and gender. The largest portion of workers defined as "informal" in Brazil continues to be made up of nonwhites (*negros*, *pardos*, and *indígenas*) and especially women of color (Leone 2010). This trend was well recognized by catadores, nearly all of whom self-identified as negro or pardo and who, though rarely discussing racial differences in the day-to-day life of Jardim Gramacho, often explicitly commented on race in situations related to employment.[13] For instance, Glória's niece, who was applying for a job as a store attendant, asked half-jokingly if she could take my photo to use on her application form since I was "very white" (*bem branquinha*). Moreover, nonwhite Brazilians perform the most precarious, poorly remunerated forms of work even *outside* regulated relations of production—for example, cleaning as an unregistered domestic worker in contrast to operating a microenterprise. Such inequalities were reflected in the economy of waste recycling in Jardim Gramacho, in which nearly all of the catadores were black or brown but many of the scrap dealers were white, referred to by nicknames such as "The Russian" or "The Portuguese."

The stories of the hundreds of catadores who came to the dump in the first decade of the new millennium complicate what were then celebratory portraits of Brazil's social and economic policies. Their arrivals to a place of work that involved collecting the discards of what others consumed—a relation of inequality—became testament to the limits of a political-economic approach that failed to address the continued concentration of wealth and political privilege in Brazil. Many of these newcomers came to Jardim Gramacho in the wake of increased policing of street vendors and other self-employed workers, which I describe in more detail in the chapter that follows. Knowing why catadores first came to Jardim Gramacho, however, reveals little about what it meant for them to arrive on the dump and captures even less about the experience of being a novice catador. This struck me at the end of an especially long and tiring—if otherwise typical—day on the dump. It was on a day that catadores still insist on calling my "first" that I began to see journeys to the dump less as arrivals to a place and more as arrivals to a particular condition.

A FIRST DAY

During my walks to the dump, I often tried to picture the fruit trees, springs, and tidal pools that Deca described. It was hard to imagine the bright colors of *maria-da-toca* along the mud-caked curbs of Monte Castelo.

FIGURE 1.2. Pathway. *Photo by the author.*

Sometimes I took a longer route that passed along the banks of a polluted canal, lined with shacks that flooded in heavy rainstorms. The water of the canal was stagnant, almost black, and smelled of raw sewage. But if one crossed the canal and headed west toward the Polo instead of east to the dump, shacks gave way to dense vegetation. It was along this remote, partially overgrown pathway that led to the backside of the Polo that I thought I could catch a glimpse of what Jardim Gramacho had once been.

On an early Monday morning in October, as I made my way to the Polo, it was too dark to see much of anything. It had rained the night before, filling the air with the smell of damp foliage and leaving deep puddles that I struggled to avoid along the muddied path. Though I walked slowly, I still arrived before Eva. We had made plans the previous day to meet at the Polo at 5:00 AM to pick up burlap sacks that we were storing there before heading up to the dump to collect together. I waited for Eva for a half hour, eating the bread I had brought for breakfast and swatting the mosquitoes that swarmed at dawn.

"The bus was late and traffic already horrible," Eva exclaimed when she arrived, throwing up her arms in exasperation. She quickly changed into her work clothes—switching out her blouse, skirt, and flip-flops for a stained long-sleeve shirt, tight shorts worn over leggings, two thick mismatched socks, ankle-high brown boots, a green hairnet, and a baseball cap. Most of these items had been found on the dump.

"Ready," Eva announced. I looked up from my task of rolling our burlap sacks and stuffing them into two plastic barrels.

"Where's your work vest [*colete*]?" I asked.

Eva explained that she had lent it to her teenage son, Maicon, so that he was able to collect over the weekend. Being underage, Maicon was not officially able to acquire one of the limited number of bright orange or green work vests from ACAMJG or from a scrap dealer. These vests were a requirement for entering the dump during the day (hence, Maicon often worked at night), and were part of efforts by Rio's waste management company, Comlurb, to control the number of catadores. However, like Eva and Maicon, catadores commonly shared or duplicated vests.

"Don't worry," Eva told me. "I told Maicon to meet us at the entrance [to the dump]." With one hand grasping the top of the barrel and the other lifting from the bottom, Eva placed one of the barrels horizontally atop her head. I followed suit, though I fought to keep my balance, and we set off again through the puddles.

Sure enough, just as we were approaching the dump's entrance, Maicon ran up to us. He was agitated, talking hurriedly. Eva asked him to calm down. What happened?

Maicon recounted that he found the person who had stolen his burlap sacks (full of the material he had collected over several days), along with his barrel, last week. He confronted the guy, demanding that he return his sacks as well as the barrel. When the guy resisted, Maicon punched him.

"I gave him two black eyes," he told us.

Maicon explained that the *bandidos* (literally, "bandits") were then called in to resolve the dispute, referring to the neighborhood drug dealers.[14] Though Jardim Gramacho lies beyond the hillside favelas at the center of Rio's drug trade, it is tied to the Comando Vermelho, one of Rio's dominant drug-dealing gangs, and operates its own *boca de fumo* (point where drugs are sold) that supplies marijuana, powder cocaine, and crack to a local clientele. Bandidos rarely intervened in the day-to-day operations of the dump, but they were known to intercede if a conflict escalated.[15] Scared that he could be beaten up or worse, Maicon left the dump—empty-handed.

Eva urged Maicon to go home. It was best to wait these things out. I thought Maicon was going to resist his mother's prodding, but he handed her the work vest, gave me a quick *tchau*, and disappeared through the winding, narrow paths of the favela.

I was astonished that Maicon's sacks had been stolen. I knew that catadores frequently left sacks of material in one area of the dump while collecting in another, or sometimes left partially filled sacks overnight. I mentioned this to Eva.

"It's not common for sacks to be stolen. But sometimes it happens. Then people go to the *boca*. If the bandidos are in a good mood, they will go to the scrapyards to look for them and get them back for you. The problem with Maicon—" Eva stopped short, shaking her head. "The problem with Maicon was that he waited too long. His sacks were stolen last week and he's only doing something about it now."

Eva picked up the barrel she had dropped while talking with Maicon and continued onward. Though she did not say it, I knew that Maicon's fight probably made the situation even more complicated. Maicon had had a few other run-ins with bandidos in recent weeks. But I didn't push the conversation any further, sensing that Eva did not want to talk about it.

We crossed to the other side of the street to catch a ride on one of the flatbed trucks used by scrap dealers to pick up material at the top of the dump. A truck soon approached and I could feel the tension in Eva's arm as she helped me hop onto the slowly moving vehicle. We both perched on the railing of the truck along with a half dozen other catadores. A few moments passed in silence and then Eva turned to me. "Do you have a cigarette?" she asked. I handed over the pack.

We collected plastic bottles and containers all day with little rest. Eva needed to pay a credit card bill by the end of the week, which added pressure to keep working no matter how tired we felt. Around nine o'clock, it started to rain. I put on my yellow poncho that another catadora, Tatiana, had found in the garbage and given me a couple of weeks before. The more it rained, the more our boots sank into the mud. It became difficult to trek back and forth between the unloading zone, where garbage trucks poured out their contents and catadores filled barrels or large bags with recyclables, and the staging area where catadores emptied these barrels or bags into large burlap sacks. In the late morning, Eva suggested we pause to eat lunch. I pulled out a leftover container from my backpack, which I had stashed inside one of our burlap sacks. We split the rice, beans, and a few pieces of fried chicken, but I ate little, as the pouring rain quickly turned the lunch to mush.

"Why aren't you eating right?" Eva asked, as she reached over to pluck a chicken wing from my container. "Look, you can't get dispirited. Not yet. Let's have some fun."

Before I knew it, Eva was shouting out to a catador I did not recognize. "Hey, you! Come over here!"

"Me?" he responded, seeming confused. Apparently, Eva did not know this catador either.

Eva asked him if he would do us a *big* favor and go over to that hill (pointing to a hillside we could see from the top of the dump far in the distance) to a bodega there and fetch us a *guaraná*, a type of Brazilian soda. She picked up an old two-liter guaraná bottle that I had refilled with water.

"I'd like a *real* guaraná," she told him, starting to laugh. He chuckled in response but continued on his way to the unloading zone. Eva kept repeating her joke each time a young guy passed near us. One catador finally agreed, joking back to Eva: He would get us a guaraná but would have to go all the way to the farthest hillside, because he'd just heard that the bodega on the nearer hillside was closed. What bad luck! It would take a long, long time to get our guaraná, but he'd even buy it for us. This made all three of us laugh. Later, each time Eva and I ran into this catador in the unloading zone, he would shout: "The guaraná is coming! It's almost here!" On a day of rain and mud, I was grateful for this momentary relief.

After lunch, my legs dragged and my lower back hurt. I had recently switched from cardboard to plastics and was still getting used to the different muscles and skills that collecting plastic required. Cardboard tended to pour from the back of garbage trucks in waves, making it possible to grab a bunch at once. In contrast, plastic bottles arrived in garbage bags amid other tossed-out things. It was necessary to bend over, rip open bags, and sift through their contents. This furthermore required quick movements to avoid being hit by a truck or by one of the bulldozers that followed in the wake of unloading trucks to disperse the mounds of waste that they left behind. Bend over. Sort. Collect. Carry. Move out of the way of an oncoming vehicle. How to do all of this at once? I expended so much energy in just staying alert.

Toward the end of the afternoon, I lifted a full bag of plastics and metal cans onto my head to take back to our burlap sacks. As I took a first step, striving to balance in the uneven mud, I failed to see what must have been some construction debris—an iron rod sticking out from a chunk of stone on the ground. I tripped on the stone and fell forward onto the rod. The weight of my bag collapsed on top of me.

Though I struggled to stand up again, I eventually made it back to our burlap sacks. I noticed that my leg was scratched and beginning to swell. I was shaking a little. I needed to sit down. Eva was busy smashing down the plastics in one of our sacks to make room for more—standing inside the sack, holding onto slits cut in its sides, and jumping up and down. When I told her what had happened, she suggested I rest, drink some water—pointing to the old guaraná bottle that had been the source of her jokes. Too tired to protest, I agreed. Eva climbed out of the sack, grabbed her barrel, and went back out to the unloading trucks, while I sat inside an empty cabinet that she had pulled out of the garbage earlier in the afternoon and that we had been using as a shelter from the rain. When she returned with another load, I rallied and went back out with her to collect. It would be our last collection of the day. By that point, Eva and I had filled all three sacks.

We were planning on taking down our material on ACAMJG's truck on its first trip of the evening. But the truck was full and so we agreed to wait until the second trip. We waited a long time. Eva suggested that we just leave our sacks overnight, that it wouldn't be a problem. She'd simply ask a friend to keep an eye on them. I could not endure the thought of having to walk the half mile to the base of the dump and then another mile to the Polo. At least if we loaded our material on the truck, we could catch a ride back. A couple of catadores told us that they saw ACAMJG's truck picking up material at the other unloading zone, called the *rampão*, literally "the big slope," and that it would likely return soon. The rampão was "big" because it was where large semitrailers, brimming with garbage picked up from one of several waste transfer stations in the city, disposed of their contents. The unloading zone where we had been collecting—the "little slope" or *rampinha*—was the designated area for compactor trucks that came directly from neighborhoods closest to Jardim Gramacho. Both of these zones moved every few days to a different part of the dump so that the waste would be dispersed. Some catadores became accustomed to collecting only at either the rampinha or rampão, while others, like Eva, alternated between the two spots depending on the day.

It was almost dark before ACAMJG's truck arrived. I fell again, sliding through sludge, as I tried to drag one of our sacks over to the truck. Two other catadores, Miguel and Geraldo, helped us raise the sacks onto the bed of the truck. Three of us lifted from below as Geraldo, standing on the truck, pulled up from above. After we climbed onto the truck, Eva took my hand and squeezed it encouragingly. "We made it," I said in reply.

Suddenly, the truck lurched and then stopped. It had blown a tire. No, two tires. "I don't believe it," Eva cried, jumping to her feet. I couldn't believe it either, but this commonly happened when it rained; the rain exposed all kinds of sharp objects beneath the surface and a truck, loaded with hundreds of kilos of material, tended to sink into the mud. It would take several hours to find not one but two spare tires. There was nothing to be done but to get out and walk.

On a deserted stretch of the path to the Polo, a man stumbled out from the woods in front of us. Eva put out her right hand to stop me. She suggested that we keep our distance, since we could not make out who this person was in the darkness. And so we slowed our pace and the walk stretched on, seemingly without end. It was difficult to see the deep puddles in the dim light of the moon, and many times my boot sank into a pool of water and filled with pebbles and debris. The tension from the day built— Maicon's fight, my fall (and what if it had happened in front of a bulldozer?), the blown tires, this nervous, painful walk. My leg throbbed. I no longer had the strength to keep going. I couldn't do it. I stopped, sat down in the mud, and cried.

THE NEXT MORNING I woke late. Eva and I had decided to spend the day at the Polo, sorting the plastics we had collected. There was no rush, and I was even more grateful for not having to go up to the dump. We finished in the late afternoon and Glória, one of the founding members of ACAMJG who was in charge of day-to-day operations at the Polo, suggested that I go home early. I was living at Glória's house at the time, and she offered to leave early too and walk back with me. When we arrived, she sent her fourteen-year-old daughter, Lohany, to a corner stand to buy a beer, handing her an empty brown beer bottle for the necessary bottle deposit. Though weekends often involved outings to the local fair or family barbecues with plenty of beer, it was rare for Glória to break open a bottle on a Tuesday night. Lohany returned within minutes, and Glória set down her cigarette on the edge of the kitchen table to pour two glasses. We toasted. The beer was ice cold.

"Thanks for the beer," I said.

"Yeah, I thought a beer might help," Glória replied, smiling. "And some Benito di Paula!" Glória jumped up from her chair and went into the adjoining room to put on a CD of Benito di Paula, one of her favorite samba musicians from the 1970s.

When she came back into the kitchen, she told me matter-of-factly, "Yesterday you had your first day in Jardim Gramacho."

"What?" I asked, assuming I had not heard her correctly. At this point, I had been living in Jardim Gramacho for nearly two months and had come there twice before.

"Your first day," she repeated. "You had your first day in Jardim Gramacho."

Noting the confused look on my face, she continued: "When I saw you arrive last night, I took one look at you and I knew that you had had one of those days in Jardim Gramacho. When nothing goes right, when everything seems too much to bear, when it rains, and the truck is late and you are very tired, and all you can think about is everything you have to do when you get home—wash your dump clothes, make dinner, prepare your backpack for the following day, take care of your kids, you know, in my case."

Glória paused to take a drag of her cigarette.

"Then you think about how you will have to get up at five, in just a few hours, to face another day on the dump. You feel so hopeless [*desesperado*], that you can't endure it anymore [*não o agüenta mais*]. And you find yourself asking: 'My God, what did I do to deserve this? What did I do in life to deserve this?'"

In the weeks that followed, I kept pondering Glória's words. Her interpretation of the day I broke down as my "first day" in Jardim Gramacho made me wonder what constitutes arrival to the dump. I had spent so much effort during those early months of fieldwork trying to be "tough," trying hard not to be overwhelmed or nauseous or shocked, that I had failed to recognize that at times catadores also reacted to the dump in these ways. This was especially true for "novices" (*novatos*), newcomers to Jardim Gramacho who were still learning how to work as a catador—how best to carry material, how to distinguish through feel and smell which bags to open and which to leave alone, how to time the movement of trucks and tractors, when to ask for help and when to rest. When I began asking catadores what they thought of the dump when they first came to Jardim Gramacho, nearly everyone responded that they were shocked (*me estranhei*), cried, could not eat, thought they would never stay, or found the work so difficult that they hardly filled a single sack. By calling the day that I cracked my first day, Glória was in part drawing a connection between my expressions on that day and those of new catadores. It was like she was telling me: This is what it feels like to be a novice. This is what it means to arrive.

I knew that my struggles on the dump in my often feeble attempts to carry out the ethnographic method of participant-observation were not commensurate with Glória's lifetime of helping her parents and seven siblings and then caring for her own child as a single mother by working as a catador. Rather, I took Glória's statement about my first day to be a moment of recognition, like the time I put aside a knapsack that I had found in the garbage to take home later and drew the attention and approval of catadores around me. In this case, what I began to recognize was the dump not as a *place* of work but as an ontological experience of labor. That is, by maintaining that I had not yet come to Jardim Gramacho even though I had been physically present there for several months, Glória called into question the assumption, often critiqued by phenomenologists, that the world exists apart from one's experience of it (Desjarlais and Throop 2011: 88). To arrive on the dump was to enter into a shared experience of its conditions. But what was this experience? If, as Robert Desjarlais (1994: 887) has argued, "experience is not an existential given," then how was the experience of the dump constituted, through what historical, material, and social processes? Was there even such a thing as *an* experience of the dump? Or was that experience always a multiplicity, always ambivalent, always changing?

BECOMING A CATADOR

That weekend I went to visit Brenda, a catadora who had recently befriended me on the dump. When Brenda pulled back the plywood door of her shack, I realized that she had been sleeping. I told her I would return another time, but she insisted that I stay. "Go sit with Liliana and Inês," pointing to two of her neighbors whom I did not know, who were seated on a couple of buckets in the middle of the path between the two rows of shacks. "I'll go take a quick shower." Brenda headed off to what I assumed was a communal bathroom at the end of the row.

When I approached Liliana and Inês, they told me that they had heard all about me from Brenda. Inês seemed a bit shy but Liliana quickly launched into a series of questions. She wanted to know where I was from, how I had ended up coming to Jardim Gramacho, what I thought of the place. I responded as best I could and then returned the questions. Had they always lived in Jardim Gramacho?

"Not me," Liliana replied.

"So when did you come here?" I asked.

"It was after I had my last child. I had separated from my husband after ten years of marriage. My son was only six months old at the time—no, eight months. Anyway, we separated. And I was all proud. I didn't want to depend on him for anything. So, I went to live with my sister—with four children and unemployed."

Liliana paused momentarily to make room for Brenda, who was back from the shower, and Inês's mother. Several children had also gathered around.

"So then," Liliana continued, "one of my sister's friends, Carla, said to me: 'Liliana, let's go to Jardim Gramacho. I'm going to take you to a *depósito*.'"

The word *depósito*, which can be translated as depository, warehouse, or any kind of storage yard, had a specific meaning in Jardim Gramacho. It referred to scrapyards. A depósito was a place where catadores sold their material and where they often acquired work vests and bought other supplies for collecting, such as burlap sacks. I counted over a hundred such enterprises in Jardim Gramacho, four of which were registered, formal businesses and the others very small-scale, makeshift operations. Most of them consisted, literally, of just a yard—with a baler and a very rickety old truck.

"But when she said 'depósito,'" Liliana continued, "I thought she was talking about a warehouse like the kind I'd worked at before, like the L'Oréal factory. Ah, it must be a firm, I thought. Let's go!

"Boy, when I arrived here, when I saw that depósito—I said, 'Why did you bring me here? You said it was a depósito!' She was like, 'This *is* a depósito.' To which I replied, 'A depository of what? Of garbage?'"

Everyone broke out in laughter. Liliana was laughing so hard she could barely continue her story.

"I said: 'I'm not going to work here, no way!' I cried. I started to cry."

"You started to cry?!" Brenda exclaimed, still laughing to the point where tears formed in the corner of her eyes.

"I did!"

"But you stayed?" I asked.

"I stayed that day," Liliana replied, regaining composure. "Just watching people picking up garbage. I had come wearing high heels! My hair done up. The same clothes I had on to work. One guy said to me, 'You sure you are ready for this?' I said, 'Look, they told me it was a depósito. I thought it was a depósito!'" More laughter ensued.

"I vomited everything when I saw people picking up garbage. I vomited. I couldn't take it. So, I left. I arrived home and said: 'Mom, I don't want to stay at that place.' She replied, 'My child, why not? It's work like any other. Carla has worked there for years. It was there that she managed to build her house.' I said, 'Heaven forbid! For the love of God! Put me in the street. I'll become a beggar!'" Liliana started laughing again.

"So then, the next day, Carla came to get me again—to come here. I took one look at her." At this point in her story, Liliana rolled her eyes and gave us a look of utter exasperation.

"Man, you should have seen the expression on my face!" she continued. "Every day, Carla insisted. I was like, what an affliction this woman is! She ought to be killed!" More laughter.

"I left the house at four o'clock in the morning. I came dragging my feet. I dragged myself here. I wasn't used to waking up at four o'clock in the morning. Not even when my children were little did I get up that early. I arrived home exhausted. Everything swollen. I would go shower. I used everything that had bleach, disinfectant, alcohol, anything like that. My sister was like, 'What are you doing?' I said, 'That place is garbage. I am going to die contaminated. I'm serious, people. I'm going to buy everything with disinfectant that I can. I'm not going to breastfeed my son like this.'

"I put so much alcohol on my breast, so much, so much that it looked like it was taking off the skin. And the smell that I thought was on me! My mom kept telling me, 'You don't have any smell. You smell good.' I was like, 'Mom, I stink. Mom, I want to shower all the time.' And my little one, crying, wanting to nurse. I didn't even want to leave the bathroom. It was hell, I tell you. That is, until I got used to it. Oh, and I didn't eat. Not here, not at home. I vomited all the time. When I found a dead rat in the garbage—Girl! I didn't want to eat ever again. My God!"

At this point, Liliana was interrupted. Her reference to the dead rat led everyone to chime in with their own story of something grotesque that had been found in the garbage—stories I return to below.

LILIANA'S NARRATIVE OF HER first day on the dump could be read as an experience of what psychoanalyst Julia Kristeva (1982) calls "abjection." A visceral repugnance and revulsion, abjection is experienced when there is a threat to one's sense of self or to the distinction between self and other. Kristeva offers various examples of what could be the abject: filth, dung, sewage, garbage, a piece of food one cannot stomach, a pus-filled wound, a cadaver. The abject, however, is not a particular, definable object. Something becomes abject only by virtue of being rejected and expelled in the effort to establish the self. "Refuse and corpses *show me*," writes Kristeva, "what I permanently thrust aside in order to live" (3). Kristeva argues that to see a cadaver is to be faced with the materiality of the body and with one's own death. Similarly, for Liliana, the leaky, smelly, infecting qualities of garbage disrupted her sense of corporeal integrity. She thought she would die "contaminated." Her body swelled as if absorbing the surroundings of the dump. She showered constantly in an effort to remove the smell from her skin. Smell, as Anna Tsing (2015: 46) has noted, "is a sign of the presence of another," and I would add here that by inhaling odor through the breath, smell becomes the presence of another *in me*. This resonates with Kristeva's insight that abjection occurs at the border of one's being: "I experience abjection only if an Other has settled in place and stead of what will be 'me'" (10).

This notion of the abject shares affinities with Mary Douglas's (1996) structural analysis of dirt as that which is eliminated in the creation of order. For both Douglas and Kristeva, the presence of dirt/the abject threatens identities, boundaries, and social systems. This is why Kristeva defines the abject as the ambiguous in-between and adds to her list of potential sources of abjection the shady business or sinister crime that operates in the gray areas of the law. From this perspective, it is not surprising that remote areas of Jardim Gramacho sometimes served as a dumping ground for the charred remains of stolen cars, or that the work of catadores was often stigmatized by others as synonymous with criminality and begging. Garbage, theft, and vagrancy disturb the normative social order and it is this commonality—their shared status as sources of abjection—

that lead to their (erroneous) conflation. However, Kristeva departs from Douglas by conceptualizing the abject not as a socially constituted, structural category, but rather as a "braid of affects" (1). That is, for Kristeva, abjection is a visceral response. It is felt, bodily, instinctual, reactive. Liliana cried when she first arrived in Jardim Gramacho, she vomited at the sight of people picking up garbage, she refused to eat after discovering a dead rat in the refuse. Kristeva argues that reactions like crying and vomiting show that abjection involves not just the rejection of the loathed item but also the expulsion of the self—here, in the form of tears and bile—that occurs in the effort to reestablish the self. The harder Liliana worked to wash away what she perceived as the smell of garbage on her body, the more her scrubbing appeared to remove her own skin. The experience of abjection, Kristeva writes, "places the one haunted by it *literally beside himself*" (1; emphasis mine).

Yet while theories of the abject help illuminate several elements in Liliana's story—particularly, her shock upon arriving to the dump—they fail to explain the storytelling itself. Liliana's narration was downright funny. At every turn, it prompted choruses of laughter from her audience, not to mention her own bouts of laughter that made it nearly impossible for her to continue telling her tale. This was not an account narrated in a somber tone of horror and hardship, but rather a story told comically, with irony, light self-ridicule, and amusement. Such laughter signaled a disconnect between the way Liliana first experienced the dump and the way she (and her audience) experienced it now. That is, the very reason it was humorous that Liliana reacted in shock to her discovery that a depósito was a scrapyard, that she arrived to work in Jardim Gramacho wearing high heels, that she cried and then vomited when she saw people picking through garbage, and that she insisted (for the love of God!) on never returning to the dump was that none of these reactions were those of a seasoned catador. Something changed for Liliana. And this change meant that garbage is not always or necessarily experienced as the abject (Hawkins 2006). In other words, the relationship between the self and waste is not a psychological given, as Kristeva's theory of abjection implies, but rather transforms through social and material processes.

One such transformative process was the seemingly simple act of returning to the dump. It was often the case, as in Liliana's story, that the person who introduced a catador to the dump played an active role in ensuring that he or she went back. Carla, Liliana's friend, had to show up at her door at four o'clock in the morning and drag her out of the house for Liliana to have a second day in Jardim Gramacho. With the exception of catadores who had worked previously on other city dumps, this initial dependence on a more seasoned catador was so common that I soon learned it was possible to ask catadores who it was who (literally) had brought them to Jardim Gramacho. They always had an answer: a relative, neighbor, friend, former coworker, friend of a relative, friend of a friend. These experienced catadores not only accompanied a novice to the dump but also took it upon themselves to teach the new catador how to dress appropriately, acquire supplies, hop a truck, arrange their burlap sacks, negotiate with scrap dealers, load a flatbed, time the traffic of trucks and bulldozers—and most importantly, how to recognize and distinguish materials in the waste.

This recognition, which is essential to the very labor of catadores, requires learning to see the dump differently, not as an overwhelming mountain of garbage but as a rich assemblage of things. Catadores often described the initial moment this recognition occurred as transformative. The first time they managed to fill and sell their own sack, or the first time they carried home bags of perfectly fine foodstuffs turned the shock they experienced upon arriving to the dump into amazement or even excitement. One catadora, for example, related that when she first came to the dump, she kept asking herself, "My God, what am I doing here?" until she filled three sacks of plastics worth R$70 and discovered in the garbage several packages of rice, beans, dried beef, and sugar. "I became ecstatic [*fiquei doida*]," she told me. It is notable that, in contrast, Liliana spent her first day in Jardim Gramacho at a distance, "just watching people," and referred to what they collected as "garbage" and not anything in particular—not paper, not plastics, not cardboard, not cans. If the abject is "a 'something' that I do not recognize as a thing," as Kristeva (1982: 2) argues, then garbage ceases to provoke abjection the moment perception shifts from the amorphous mass of detritus to its identifiable contents. This suggests that abjection stems from a refusal to engage with the materiality of garbage, a materiality that has the potential to constitute the self in new ways. Liliana gestures toward such self-transformation in her passing comment that she (of course) "got used to it"—a deceptively simple phrase catadores commonly used to index the complex learning process and adaptation involved in *becoming* a catador.

The shift in experiences of the dump over time did not mean that the garbage stopped smelling or that the toxicity of rotting matter became of no concern for catadores. What changed was that the garbage no longer prompted a generalized feeling of disgust. Instead, learning to recognize the dump as an assemblage of things led to the perception of its real and specific dangers. As any novice quickly learns, oncoming bulldozers— which do not stop as they plow through giant heaps of garbage—are far more dangerous and terrifying than the putrid waste itself. Furthermore, the potential harms that do come from handling the discarded on the dump are often caused not by garbage per se but by a particular object in its contents, such as the protruding iron rod that made me trip on my "first day." The dump is grueling because of the odors, gases, and leachate produced by putrid matter, but also because of the unrelenting sun, dust and mud, lightning strikes in summer storms, the activity of machinery and trucks, the crushing weight of a full barrel of recyclables, and the exhaustion from it all.

Liliana's story of her first day in Jardim Gramacho expressed an ontological experience of the abject. However, her storytelling indicated that this was not her only experience, that arrival to the dump was not a discrete event, but rather a gradual process of transformation. Over time I gathered dozens of stories like Liliana's, which I came to think of as entry narratives—accounts of the factors that led catadores to Jardim Gramacho and of their initial days on the dump. I noticed, though, that catadores told me these stories because I asked them to. When I listened instead to the stories that arose spontaneously in conversations among catadores, I found that other kinds of narratives circulated. These tales, which were told and retold with varied details, often contained grotesque elements similar to the dead rat that appeared in Liliana's story. Yet these tales were narrated in ways that belied an experience of abjection. They were also tales that addressed not so much the question of what it is like to first come to Jardim Gramacho as the question of what it means to arrive on the dump, day after day.

VITAL LIMINALITY, OR THE STAKES OF ARRIVAL

"Did you hear about the time a group of catadores made soup at night?" asked Dona Marta, a veteran catadora. She was waiting along with several catadores for ACAMJG's truck to arrive; it had broken down again, and they had started up a conversation about the relative dangers of collecting on the rampão versus the rampinha. Dona Marta's story was set on the rampão.

"They gathered *podrão* [food found in the garbage]," she continued, "and they made a huge soup. Everyone ate until they were full. The next morning, when it was light again, they looked into the large can that had contained their soup. At the bottom of the can, there were human hands."

A few weeks later, I heard another catador tell the same story, this time adding that the catadores who ate the soup did not notice that it contained human hands because they were drunk on *cachaça*, a type of rum.

When I first heard this story, it reminded me of a common form of humor and storytelling in Brazil that Robert Stam (1997: 242) has described as a "carnivalesque aesthetic." This aesthetic invokes Brazil's pre-Lenten celebration of carnival, which has traditionally been analyzed as a ritual of subversion and revelry that embraces the obscene, absurd, and grotesque.[16] The elaborate floats, colorful costumes, and scantily clad samba dancers in Rio's televised carnival parades have tended to associate the event with its more festive and sensual elements. But Brazil's carnival has long involved such practices as throwing dirty substances such as mud or motor oil on passersby, attaching exaggerated body parts, and crying out in celebration of death (Scheper-Hughes 1992). While stories that focus on body parts and repugnant aspects of life and death are considered "bad taste" by elites outside of carnival, such an aesthetic often permeates the everyday worlds of Brazil's lower classes (Goldstein 2003: 11). For example, in his study of plastic surgery in public hospitals in Brazil, Alexander Edmonds (2010: 97) describes how patients commonly gave graphically detailed accounts of surgeries that went wrong—a detached nipple or a misplaced belly button—calling such stories a "kind of medical grotesque." The jokes that fill the pages of Donna Goldstein's (2003) ethnography of laughter among Rio's poor similarly relate gruesome events, including assault, rape, and death. This black humor, she argues, constitutes an oppositional discourse of the poor in Brazil's deeply unequal society.

However, in this case, to explain the story of the soup solely as an example of a carnivalesque aesthetic in Brazil fails to do justice to the details of the story. Why, for example, was there an emphasis on soup? And why, no matter the version being told, was the discovery at the bottom of the soup can human hands and not some other gruesome thing like maggots or a rat? What is striking about the story is not just that it recounts a grotesque incident but that it does so while referencing an otherwise enjoyable event in the form of a shared meal among friends. Soup made collectively from reclaimed vegetables and meat—still in good condition or not yet expired—is a tangible sign of the bounty of the dump. It suggests that the contents of the dump can nourish the body and generate sociality through an evening spent eating and drinking together. The story of the soup with human hands thus expresses an ambivalent experience of the dump. The dump is nourishing but also toxic. It can sustain social life but also contain traces of violence and death. And as the catadores who ate the soup discovered the next morning, the line between the two is not always clear.

It was not unusual for the tales that circulated among catadores to reference dead bodies and death specifically, as in the case of the soup containing hands, conceivably of a cadaver. On the afternoon when Liliana recounted her first days in Jardim Gramacho, the conversation eventually evolved into a tale about a ghost who was said to haunt the entrance to the dump at night. Inês began the story:

"They say that every night there is a white woman, like a ghost, who . . ."

"Ah, come on," Brenda interrupted. "Are you going to start telling fairy tales too?"

"What? You haven't heard?" Inês replied.

"What with all the people who have died on the dump," Liliana added. "Think about it."

"She appears to this day," Inês continued. "A white woman who waits at the corner. There is no way for people to go up [to the top of the dump]. They say that when someone arrives, she beckons the person."

"Yeah, it's just like people say about hospital waste," Brenda responded. "That in the area for hospital waste, you hear the cries of children. I never heard anything. I used to work there secretively at night, collecting syringes.[17] I never heard anything like that. Once I did see a dead guy fall from an unloading truck. It was horrible, so swollen and his stomach full of bullet holes, everyone trying to pull him out from the garbage by his legs."

"I've seen a lot of things on the dump," Liliana interjected. "Getting down from a garbage truck in the morning, a corpse almost at my side. Once, there was this woman. She was all tied up. They'd left a stick in her business. She was brought from Caju.[18] She was still dripping, all tied up with wire. A beautiful girl. With long, thick hair. I wanted to cut her hair so that I could make hair extensions for myself. I said, 'Hey, give me some scissors, a knife, a glass bottle so that I can cut the hair off this corpse. What big hair!'

"My sister was like, 'You're nuts. I am going to smack you.' So I went over to [my friend] Adriana real fast. I said, 'Adriana, come on, there are damn good locks that I found on the dump.'"

THE CORPSE, ACCORDING to Kristeva (1982), is the quintessential abject. Yet the stories of cadavers falling into the midst of catadores do not depict experiences of abjection. No one vomits or cries. Though sometimes described as horrible, a dead body found in the garbage does not cause paralysis nor prompt an act of rejection or expulsion. If anything, the stories are about drawing near. Catadores *approach* the corpse, pulling it out of the garbage with their own hands. Liliana—the same person who vomited the first time she arrived on the dump—races to cut the locks off a dead woman so as to braid them into the hair on her own head.

These stories are thus not about the ontology of the garbage and the abjection it inspires. It took me a long time to see that instead, these stories of ghosts, swollen corpses, and severed hands speak to the ontology of the dump as a burial ground.[19] That is, the stories of catadores speak to the very nature of what a garbage dump is—a world constituted not by the mere presence of waste but by the way it is disposed of like the dead in a graveyard. Dumps and landfills are first and foremost places where the discarded is interred, literally placed "into the earth." The Jardim Gramacho dump did not have the pre-dug and lined cells—much like burial plots—that are typical of sanitary landfills, but its engineers did follow standard industry practice of covering deposited waste with dirt. Each day, bulldozers on the dump worked relentlessly to spread and compact piles of waste left behind by unloaded trucks. Once a layer of waste was formed, it was capped with dirt and arriving garbage trucks moved on to another area of the dump. Over time, the dump became a massive grave mound that concealed everything it contained. This was the point, after all. Dumps and landfills are places where society's discards are made invisible and meant to be forgotten.

In the case of Rio de Janeiro, this concealing work of the dump includes the effects of urban violence. In the late 1970s and 1980s, as Rio de Janeiro became a key node in an expanding Latin American trade in cocaine, the criminal organizations that came to power saw Rio's hillside favelas as optimal sites from which to run their operations. These favelas are close to middle- and upper-class neighborhoods where a wealthier customer base resides, yet have historically been excluded from state services and regular policing. Their steep entryways and winding alleys also make it easier to control access, and the relative lack of decent employment for young residents of favelas has made them a recruiting ground for "soldiers"—those low in the hierarchy of the drug trade who perform the everyday labor of running errands and keeping watch, and who therefore are often most at risk of being arrested or killed (including by police). It was not coincidental that in nearly all the stories of corpses found in the garbage, the body was of a young black or brown man, sometimes hardly an adolescent, and bore the marks of gunshot wounds.[20] The corpse was not the only sign of violence buried in Jardim Gramacho. When taking the back route between the dump and the Polo, I sometimes stumbled across the charred metal carcass of a stolen car that had been burned and then abandoned after being used in an armed robbery, weeds already growing up through the empty cavity. These charred remains and the dead bodies that fell from unloading trucks were potent signs of the way the dump functioned as a graveyard, but, of course, they were not its only deposits. *Everything* that arrived on the dump was intended to be buried.

The experience of the dump expressed through the macabre stories of catadores was thus an experience of being at the border of life and death, or what I have come to think of as vital liminality.[21] This liminality emerged from the ambiguous status of the dump as a place of burial that was simultaneously, for catadores, a source of sustenance. I call this liminality "vital" both in the sense of the Latin word *vita*, meaning "life," and in the sense of high stakes, as when something is vital or life-and-death. By vital liminality, I am interested in what it means to labor at the edge of life, which implies the presence or possibility of death—not necessarily one's own. That is, vital liminality does not refer to an individual life hanging in the balance, as in the case of a comatose person on life support who is not quite alive but not yet dead. Nor is it a threshold in Giorgio Agamben's (1998) use of the concept, in which modern state power reduces certain human lives to bare life or mere survival—the "living dead," as Agamben puts it, epitomized in the figure of the slave, prisoner, or refugee. Rather, the life I aim to capture is that of vitality, a force present not only in human existence but also in nonhuman and even inorganic matter (Bennett 2010). To collect on the dump meant having to contend on a daily basis with energy-rich plastics easily buried by the blade of an advancing bulldozer; with bruised tomatoes that might become soup or rot; with used syringes that at one point might have saved a life and now might generate income or infection or both; and in the most extreme case, with a corpse usually bearing the marks of a violent death. Even in this last case, the line between life and death is not clear. Liliana saw the dead body of a young woman as "beautiful," with her voluminous, cascading hair, often considered a sign of vitality and youth. And in all the stories I heard, catadores always worked to pull the discovered corpse out of the garbage—initiating a judicial process in which the death could be counted and the body might be identified and returned to the family, generating a new social life in death.

This vital liminality produced by the dump-as-burial-ground made the dump not a place of work but an ontological experience of labor. That is, arriving each day on the dump meant entering into a labor condition in which the stakes were fundamentally life and death. Some of the stories catadores told—not of corpses that came from elsewhere but of injuries and fatalities that occurred in their midst—expressed in a literal sense this meaning of arrival. One frequently recounted story was of two catadores crushed by a trailer that overturned at night.

"The trailer caught two catadores who were at my side," recalled Rafael, a catador who was in his early twenties and had been collecting for only five years.

"They had been collecting together. The man slipped and fell. And the trailer—it was tumbling down. The woman saw him fall and she ran to free his foot that had become entangled in a plastic bag. When she went to pull his foot loose, the trailer fell and there she stayed, at his feet. She was his wife. The man was buried beneath the garbage that had spilled from the overturned trailer. Another woman beside me began digging, and then everyone was helping, digging, digging, digging, digging, looking for him. We found him and he began to breathe. It took about five minutes to look for him beneath the garbage, digging. There was a lot of construction debris. We cleaned him off. When we tried to pull him by the arms, he told us that he was stuck. The trailer had trapped both of his legs along with his wife. His wife's whole body was below the trailer, whereas just his legs were trapped. She had ended up at his feet, and his feet were trapped at the edge of the trailer. Emergency workers then came and pulled him out with a machine. They arrived later, right? It was only *after* the trailer was lifted upright that one could see how things were: the man's wife had already died and he had to have his two legs amputated.

"The guards didn't allow any reporters to go up to the top of the dump—no one. And so it was just us—the catadores—who saw [what happened]."

I FOUND IT DIFFICULT for a long time to see elements of Rafael's story and the many others that circulated on the dump beyond their graphic details and what felt at times like the surreal. This despite the fact that an example of nearly all the types of events recounted in the stories occurred at some point during my time in Jardim Gramacho. Three times I saw a large, orange trailer of a semi-truck tipped over on its side, the metal beam that had raised it mangled and crushed. In all three cases, everyone was able to get out of the way before the container collapsed and no one was injured. Twice, a corpse was found in the garbage. Both were bodies of adolescent boys who had been killed by gunfire. And just two weeks before I was to complete a major period of my fieldwork, a catador was killed by a tractor on the dump. It was the morning that I was to present my research to waste management staff. I waited in the office for the manager to return from handling the situation. I watched the ambulance slowly go up to the dump. "They must know that he has already died," the secretary commented. Twenty minutes later, the ambulance drove past the office, its siren silent.

It was only after returning innumerable times to Rafael's story that I began to notice its other qualities, such as the emphasis it placed on the labor prompted by the accident. Rafael repeats the word *digging* five times as if each utterance represented another layer of waste removed in the work of excavating the buried catadores. This enormous effort was collective—everyone helping, Rafael stresses—and it occurred long before any emergency workers arrived. To reclaim in this instance was literally to revive. It also involved the work of recognition, making visible what was unseen by others, including by emergency workers who were late to the scene and by reporters who were refused entry to the dump. Rafael's story reveals how vital liminality—the experience of being at the border of life and death—is itself a form of labor. Reclaiming on the dump entailed the work of resurrection, of first recognizing the life in things that would otherwise be buried.

By telling and retelling this story and many other macabre tales, catadores shared what it meant to arrive on the dump, day after day. The gruesome events they recounted, however, did not depict an experience of abjection prompted by exposure to revolting garbage. Rather, these stories spoke to the ontology of the dump as a world of burial that one must enter into physically and existentially in order to do the work of reclaiming the discarded. When catadores hopped aboard a truck with a bundle of sacks ready for a day of work on the dump, they did so knowing full well what was at stake. This recognition made their returns to the dump, as we will see, all the more significant.

2 · The Precarious Present

"I found a job!" Rose snapped open a can of beer and quickly reached for my glass to catch the foam that poured down its sides. It was a quiet Sunday afternoon in Maruim, an unpaved section of Jardim Gramacho that bordered what remained of the mangrove swamp. I had stopped by Rose's house for a visit and the two of us had taken to lounging on overturned wooden crates in a yard that was brown and barren except for a few scattered plastic bottles and tin cans. Though I first met Rose and her husband, Carlos, while collecting on the dump, I got to know them particularly well because they were frequent customers at Deca's bar. Each time they arrived, Rose would call out for me to join them from the gate behind the bar—too afraid of my neighbor's crazed rooster, which would chase anyone who entered and peck at their feet, a problem given that nearly everyone wore flip-flops. I came to expect Rose's shouts for me to join them, especially on Sundays when they liked to splurge on a plate of Deca's rotisserie chicken. On this Sunday, however, they had invited me over to their place. Rose had good news to celebrate. I had picked up some chicken wings and sausage along the way, which Carlos was now arranging on the charcoal grill beside us.

Indeed, Rose's new job seemed like a cause for celebration. Like other catadores, she had insisted many times that she would leave the garbage if she could. "The dump is pure suffering," catadores commonly said. Or, "In the garbage, there is no future." I thought of Seu Marcão, a rather eccentric catador with over twenty years on the dump, who would spontaneously shout over the clamor of unloading trucks: "Pay to enter and pray to leave!" an expression taken from the Portuguese-translated title of the horror film *The Funhouse*.

However, Rose's new job meant more than an exit from the garbage dump. For the first time in her life, she had acquired employment with a signed worker ID (*carteira assinada*), a document guaranteeing a minimum wage, benefits, and the recognition of a regularly employed worker in Brazil. She told me that she would receive the equivalent of twice the monthly minimum wage[1]—as much as if not more than she was presently making on the dump. She would be cleaning the house of a couple who lived a relatively short twenty-minute bus ride away, and she was due to start that Monday. After Rose shared the good news, I lifted my glass to propose a toast to her new work. No, not just work (*trabalho*), she corrected me— this was a job (*emprego*).

I was therefore surprised when, after a few weeks, I asked Rose how she was finding her new job and she replied with a brush of her hand, "Oh, I quit." Rose's employer insisted that she stay at work until seven o'clock in the evening even though she easily finished all of her cleaning tasks by two in the afternoon. The requirement to remain at work while not working struck Rose as absurd. Her three children would already be dismissed from school and she would rather be home with them.

A few days later I saw Rose back on the dump. She waved to me from across a pile of recently unloaded waste—balancing a barrel of plastics on her right shoulder as she carefully stepped through mud that oozed puddles from the drizzling rain.

LIKE ROSE, MOST CATADORES repeatedly insisted that they would leave the dump instantly if another work opportunity appeared. And yet those who did find work outside Jardim Gramacho often came back to the dump within a few weeks or months. Their departures and returns inflected life in Jardim Gramacho with a generalized quality of transience, captured in the common expression, *vou e volto, vou e volto* ("I go and return, go and return," as in the idiomatic phrase in English, "I come and go"). Sometimes I would not see a catador for weeks on the dump and, almost without fail, the person would reappear—often with a story of a family visit to another part of Rio or a story of employment very similar to Rose's.

In what follows, I explore how the comings and goings of catadores—as they moved in and out of other jobs—emerged from competing desires and demands in their lives. On the one hand, formal, stable employment was upheld by catadores as a dominant cultural value. In addition to regular income and employment benefits, a formal job with a worker ID brings the status of a respected *trabalhador*, a worker. Yet on the other hand, the very regularity and stability of a formal job comes into conflict with the fragile conditions of urban poverty in Rio de Janeiro. Borrowing Ben Penglase's concept of "everyday emergencies," I consider how disruption and insecurity not only suspend but can also constitute "normality" in Rio's favelas (Penglase 2009). While Penglase considers everyday emergencies in the specific context of drug trafficking, I reflect on multiple forms of insecurity that destabilize daily life: health vulnerabilities, makeshift housing, environmental hazards, debt, incarceration, and crime and violence. My aim is to show how, paradoxically, the deeply painful and precarious work that catadores continually returned to on the dump enabled them to contend with insecurities in other dimensions of their lives.

The comings and goings of catadores thus illuminate the *relationship* between precarity as a labor condition and precarity as an ontological experience (Neilson and Rossiter 2008).[2] A translation of the French word *précarité*, the term *precarity* began circulating heavily in the early 2000s as a way to capture both the tenuous conditions of post-Fordist labor as well as states of anxiety, desperation, unbelonging, and risk experienced by temporary and irregularly employed workers. In discussions of precarity, work as a source of insecurity is usually traced to the rise of neoliberal economic theories in the 1980s that emphasized the "free" market as the guarantor of human well-being (Harvey 2005). Trade liberalization, the privatization of public enterprises, attacks on organized labor, and cuts in social spending, among other social and economic policies, resulted in the systematic dismantling of the expectation of full employment along with state benefits and protections for workers, which had defined the post–World War II period in the industrialized world. Downsizing, outsourcing, and various forms of "flexible" (meaning temporary, part-time, or subcontracted) employment became commonplace, leading the French sociologist Pierre Bourdieu to propose by the late 1990s that "job insecurity is now everywhere" (1998: 82). Indeed, many of these same neoliberal theories were first implemented as structural adjustment measures attached to World Bank and International Monetary Fund loans to countries in Latin America and other parts of the so-called developing world as early as the 1970s.[3] This led many of the first social scientists who embraced the concept of precarity to perceive it as a worldwide symptom of neoliberalism. Some theorists of late capitalism have gone so far as to argue that insecure employment is an increasingly shared condition that is merging the destinies of the Global North and South.[4]

However, to see precarity as a shared condition misses how the articulation between precarious labor and precarious life depends significantly on the specific history and experience of capitalism in a given location, both in the sense of a geopolitical site (e.g., Brazil) and in the sense of a social position (e.g., urban poor in the periphery of Rio). The term *precarity* was initially adopted by social-movement activists in postindustrial societies of Europe, North America, and Japan—places where Fordism was strongest in the twentieth century and which therefore have been most affected by its unraveling (Allison 2012; Neilson and Rossiter 2005). In many countries of the Global South, in contrast, precarious work has arguably *always* been a part of the experience of laboring poor. Rose's grandparents were seasonal agricultural workers in Brazil's arid northeast, a region marked by the uncertainties of drought and hunger. Her parents, part of a wave of rural–urban migration to Rio in the 1960s, worked as itinerant street vendors at downtown bus stops. In her own life, prior to her brief stint with a worker ID, Rose moved between a range of irregular forms of employment: selling garlic on the streets, cooking for a luncheonette, and eventually reclaiming recyclables from city garbage. Though Fordism might have existed as a dream, aspiration, or incomplete project in Brazil and other countries of the Global South (Muehlebach and Shoshan 2012), full employment nonetheless remained the exception.

Moreover, for workers who identified as middle class in places where Fordism was strong in the postwar years of the twentieth century, work provided not only an income but also social belonging, a public identity, a sense of well-being, and future aspirations (Muehlebach 2011). Consequently, the dismantling of full-time, lifelong employment under neoliberal regimes had the effect of disintegrating social ties and eroding the sense of having a place in the world. In such post-Fordist contexts, therefore, we can understand the relationship between precarious labor and precarious life as one in which "unstable work destabilizes daily living" (Allison 2012: 349).

In contrast, the continual returns of catadores to the dump suggest that many urban poor in Rio experience this relationship in reverse: unstable daily living destabilizes work. That is to say, the fixed conditions of waged employment often stand in tension with the uncertainties and disruptions that punctuate life in Rio's periphery. As a result, catadores experienced the garbage dump not only as a source of hardship but also, as they claimed, a "refuge"—a place to which they could turn in difficult times and which afforded them greater autonomy in their everyday lives. Here, autonomy is conceived not in the liberal sense of the sovereign, independent, self-reliant individual, which fails to account for the ways "the self is always in relations with others" (Han 2012: 20). Rather, the returns of catadores reveal what I call "relational autonomy," showing how a relative degree of control over work and time enables catadores to sustain relationships, fulfill social obligations, and pursue life projects in an uncertain everyday.[5]

"The dump has a good side and the dump also has a bad side," catadores often told me. I begin with this seeming contradiction, unpacking the ways catadores experienced and narrated their world of work. The particular characteristics of reclaiming material from city waste that emerge in these narratives suggest the need to better differentiate forms of post-Fordist labor that are frequently folded into categories of informal, irregular, or precarious employment. I then turn back to Rose's story. How can we understand her decision to quit what seemed a coveted job, to return to the garbage and her work as a catadora? This question leads me first to consider the symbolic value that the worker ID held for Rose—the desire for a possibility that never became realized. I then explore how catadores perceive their experience of the dump as an inner transformation of the self. This new worker subjectivity is one in which catadores, in their own words, "can no longer adapt" to conditions of waged employment. Finally, I consider how this inability to adapt to waged employment is further compounded by the everyday emergencies that disrupt life in Rio's periphery.

As I pieced together these different parts of Rose's story, I realized that what mattered most for Rose were not so much the conditions of her labor but the ways these conditions intersected with daily rhythms, embodied habits, social ties, and the ability to pursue different life projects. In short, it was only by perceiving the collection of recyclables not just as work, but as a form of living, that I began to understand why Rose returned to the dump.

Though I was stunned when Rose told me she had quit her job, I knew that it was not out of the ordinary. The work histories of catadores were filled with numerous moments like this—a month working as a maid in a hotel, twelve days as a seamstress, a week as a deliveryman for a household appliance store, seven months at a cleaner's, two weeks as a housekeeper, nine months as a street sweeper, a few weeks at a local recycling plant. None of these jobs seemed to last. At first I tried to decipher whether a catador quit the job or was fired or laid off by the employer. I soon learned, however, that the difference between quitting and being let go was murky. Those who held a job with a signed worker ID commonly *asked* their employers to fire them when they wished to quit so that they could access a state-managed job security fund that is only paid to a worker in the case of an unjustified dismissal.[6] When catadores were indeed fired, they often described this moment more like quitting, as no longer conforming to the structures or demands of the job. Miguel, for instance, told me that after nine months working as a street sweeper, he simply "left and returned again to the dump." But when I asked why, he told me that it was because he was "restless" and unable to habituate to a job with a carteira assinada. He frequently left the worksite during his dinner break, which was considered against the rules. One night his manager caught him in the act and fired him on the spot. For Miguel, whether he effectively quit his job by leaving the worksite during his breaks or was fired for the same reason was inconsequential. "I always go back to the dump," he told me. "It's a kind of refuge."

Anthropologists have often explained the decisions of laboring poor to quit regular jobs as a form of resistance to degrading or onerous aspects of wage labor. I found it difficult, however, to apply these explanations to the ways catadores experienced their work. For example, in his study of crack dealers in East Harlem, Philippe Bourgois (1995) argues that the refusal of the drug dealers to take menial service jobs is a form of oppositional politics to demeaning, minimum-wage work. Dealing in East Harlem brings status, respect, and an affirmed masculinity utterly lost in "the humiliating interpersonal subordination of service work" (141). For catadores, working in and with garbage—far from bringing respect—is a type of work that is stigmatizing even within their own social worlds. Catadores who lived in another favela of Rio would carry with them extra clothes, rent tiny shacks as changing rooms, and purchase body lotions and creams to mask lingering odors so that their neighbors, and in some cases their family members, would not know what they did. Even catadores who proudly affirmed that they worked as a catador were aware that others perceived their work of reclaiming objects from garbage as not "real" work, as not any different from being a beggar or vagabond.

Others have argued that underground economies provide an alternative to strenuous employment, as in the case of undocumented Haitian workers in the Dominican Republic's underground tourist economy, who seek to escape their only other option of hard labor in the sugar industry (Gregory 2007). But, as poignantly expressed in the macabre stories that circulated on the dump, catadores endured brutal conditions of work. They also risked injuries, some of which could be fatal: a hospital needle that punctured a catador's worn boot, a tossed rod that split open the forehead of an elderly catador, a tractor whose driver failed to see a catador slip in front of his path. Injuries were so common that I stopped asking *if* a catador had ever been hurt on the dump. The answers often involved a catador removing a glove, pushing down a sock, or lifting a shirt sleeve to reveal a scar.

However, the dump as "pure suffering" existed in tension with other ways that catadores perceived their place of work. For many catadores, the garbage dump was a constant, one of the most stable sources of income in their lives. Trucks unloaded at the dump twenty-four hours a day, every day of the year, allowing catadores to work day and night or to not work at all for several days or weeks. The few impediments to access to the dump enabled catadores to leave Jardim Gramacho for stretches of time without concern that they would lose their right to work in this place, as can sometimes occur for street vendors who must maintain their claim to space (Anjaria 2011).[7] Scrap dealers paid catadores at the point of sale and catadores decided when to sell their material. They could therefore wait to return to the dump until their previous earnings ran out. Or, in the case of an unexpected expense, a catador could work continuously on the dump, day and night, knowing that she would have immediate payment in hand. There was a shared sense in Jardim Gramacho that the dump is always there, that work could be taken up when needed or desired. "The garbage never ends," I commonly heard.

I do not mean to suggest that collecting on the dump is stable work in the sense usually invoked by this term. No prevention or compensation existed for the injuries that catadores suffered, and life itself was at risk on the dump. Rather, catadores experienced the dump as a stable refuge in one particular way that stands in tension with other dimensions of their work. In short, catadores could decide when and how much to work. And it is this characteristic of their work that distinguishes it from full-time waged employment, as well as from other forms of post-Fordist labor marked as such by their very contingency. Temporary, part-time, or piecemeal workers must contend with the unpredictability of work and wages. This distinction points to the importance of disentangling forms of precarious labor that hold very different relationships to a worker's experience of the everyday.

THE WORKER IN BRAZIL'S MORAL ORDER

As I tried to understand Rose's return to the dump, I realized that her story began not at the moment she quit her job but rather with her initial excitement at having acquired a job with a signed worker ID. Though such enthusiasm does not seem to require any explanation, Rose's response takes on added significance when considered in relation to the symbolic value of the formally employed worker in Brazil's historical and political context. Unlike in other Latin American countries, most notably Argentina, the image of the worker in Brazil has not always functioned as a primary source of identity and citizenship.[8] Brazil's history of slavery and the continued power of the oligarchy following abolition in 1888 had the effect of devalorizing manual labor. Many anthropologists have pointed to the middle and upper classes' avoidance of household work and to the historic separation between service elevators and entrances in buildings from those used by residents as manifestations of this perceived indignity of labor (Goldstein 2003; Holston 2008). Others have suggested that the figure of the *malandro*—the trickster or hustler—that became exalted in samba lyrics in the 1920s expressed in a different register this disdain for work (Oliven 1984a, 1984b).

In the 1930s, Brazilian President Getúlio Vargas sought to radically transform the position of labor in Brazil by making working-class employment the basis and emblem of Brazilian citizenship. Vargas passed a series of labor laws that positioned the state as the sole arbitrator between capital and labor. This functioned as a state technology to control the labor organizing that developed in conjunction with Brazil's industrialization at the beginning of the twentieth century and with the high levels of European immigration that brought to Brazil anarchist and communist influences. Through these labor laws, the state began regulating work organizations, defined what legally counted as a profession, granted rights based on one's status as a worker, and instituted the carteira assinada—the worker ID that Rose pointed to as the most important element of her newfound employment.[9] However, despite (or rather because of) the rights and benefits that workers gained through the carteira assinada, Vargas's labor reforms produced a new kind of unequal citizenship in Brazil (Holston 2008). On the one hand, labor became valorized for the first time in Brazilian history, and workers could access rights on the basis of their labor; on the other hand, those who were not employed in legally regulated professions were excluded from this new citizenship status. In short, by exalting "the worker" as the model Brazilian citizen, Vargas created a worker–criminal dichotomy that continues to function in Brazilian society's moral order.

In recent years, the symbolism of "the worker" has acquired new meaning in the context of drug trafficking, violence, and the fear of crime among middle and upper classes in Brazil's major cities. Rather than associate favelas with the working-class poor, Brazilian elites have increasingly come to perceive favela residents as *marginais* (marginals), a word now signifying criminals and drug traffickers rather than the poorest of the poor.[10] This semiotic shift has furthermore justified extreme forms of police violence targeting favela residents and street children, as well as the elite's disregard for the everyday struggles of Brazil's lower classes, no longer deemed the hard-working, "deserving" poor.[11]

In this context, favela residents themselves have taken up the *trabalhador–marginal* (worker–marginal) or *trabalhador–bandido* (worker–drug dealer) dichotomy as a way to distinguish themselves from criminality in the eyes of the state and the broader society. This is especially the case for poor, black, male youth who are frequently the targets of police abuse.[12] For example, I observed one adolescent catador, who was stopped and shoved by police, plead his innocence by taking out his boots, gloves, and water bottle to try to prove that he was an honest worker. In such instances, *trabalhador* invokes the Vargas-era valorization of the "worker of Brazil" and becomes synonymous with law-abiding citizen. It also echoes strategies to avoid police harassment during the period surrounding Brazil's abolition of slavery, when vagrancy laws became a mechanism for addressing a severe labor shortage on plantations in the Brazilian northeast.[13] If the rural poor who flocked to cities at this time could not demonstrate to police that they had "honest" employment, they could be sent to agricultural penal colonies tied to the sugar industry. Brazilian anthropologist Leticia Veloso (2010) has argued that in the contemporary context, this slippage between worker and law-abiding citizen in Brazil has led to the fetishization of the worker ID. During her fieldwork among poor youth in Rio, she observed several adolescents, who had acquired formal jobs through an NGO program, flaunt their worker IDs at every opportunity (Veloso 2012). Even though their employment consisted of minimum-wage jobs with no possibility of advancement, it provided them with the status of worker and the ability to demonstrate this status through their signed IDs. The carteira assinada, according to Veloso, became more important than the actual job, because the worker ID "proved" that these young men worked and therefore were not bandits.

Rose's initial excitement about obtaining a job with a worker ID must be understood within this larger moral order situating the worker in contradistinction to the criminal or low-life *marginal*. Andrea Muehlebach and Nitzan Shoshan (2012) have argued that we find a post-Fordist affect in places like Latin America and South Africa that takes the form of a nostalgic longing for Fordist promises that never quite materialized. In certain respects, we can see the fetishization of the worker ID as an affective attachment to Fordism that in the Brazilian context became enshrined in the social rights and state protections bestowed on formally employed workers in Vargas's populist, paternalist state. I would add to this insight that, for many Brazilian poor, Fordist attachments are inflected with other anxieties and desires. The significance of the worker ID for Rose entailed not only the guarantee of full-time employment. It also, and perhaps more importantly, held the promise of shedding the stigma of an activity associated in the wider social imaginary with crime, drug addiction, alcoholism, and begging—a stigma that can carry violent consequences. However, as we will see in what follows, this aspiration clashed with other values and pressures in Rose's life.

LOST LIVELIHOOD

The city square known as Praça XV borders the historic Palácio Tiradentes, now the seat of Rio de Janeiro's legislative assembly, and is known for having been the site where, on May 13, 1888, Princess Isabel declared the abolition of slavery in Brazil. I knew Praça XV mostly through a few antique resellers who had stands in the square's Saturday market and who regularly came to the dump to purchase vintage items—like old coins, books of stamps, or jewelry—that catadores might have stumbled across while collecting their recyclables. For Rose, though, Praça XV held other meanings. On a trip into downtown Rio to collect empty beer cans during the pre-Lenten festivities of *carnaval*, Rose pointed out the Praça as we passed by.

"You see that square?" Rose asked, gesturing toward the far side of the street. "Every time I come here, I remember when my father abandoned us in that square."

Despite all the time I had spent with Rose on the dump and at Deca's bar, I realized I knew very little about her childhood. I asked her what had happened.

> I was four years old. My brothers and I were playing in the square. I used to love *churros*, you know, those pastries that have *doce de leite* in the center, that they sell in street carts. I loved those things. My father bought a few churros and told us, "Stay here. Your mother will come get you." He then went to one of those shops that sell propane canisters, fans, televisions and sold everything we had while my mother was working. He grabbed the money and left. He abandoned us all in the square. When he arrived at the bus station, just before the bus was scheduled to depart, he called my mother and told her: "Leave now because your children are all in the square and have been there since nine o'clock this morning." My mother arrived at three in the afternoon.

When Rose's grandparents learned the news of her father's sudden departure, they came to Rio de Janeiro from their home in rural Paraíba, in the northeast of Brazil, to fetch Rose. They were fond of Rose, the youngest of the three children, and they were concerned that Rose's mother would have to leave their granddaughter in the care of others while working at her job in a small boarding house. Rose eventually returned to Rio to join her mother at the age of fourteen, and it was at this time that Praça XV took on renewed significance in her life. Unable to adjust to living with her mother, Rose moved out and began supporting herself by selling garlic as a street vendor (*camelô*) in downtown Rio. She sold garlic along Rio's busy thoroughfare, Avenida Rio Branco; near the Uruguaiana metro station; and in the public squares of Cinelândia, Candelária, and Praça XV—where only ten years before her father had abandoned her with the parting gift of a churro, purchased from one of the numerous vendors in the area.

Like Rose, the work histories of many catadores began on the streets or in other public spaces of the city. João shined shoes at busy transportation hubs. Funabem sold snacks on the commuter trains that funnel workers into downtown from Rio's outskirts. Tatiana preferred to work on Rio's busiest streets, particularly when they were clogged in a traffic jam. Interweaving among stopped vehicles, she sold water and Coke when it was hot; candy, cookies, and popcorn; and even the odd household item like flannel cloths for cleaning windshields and furniture—two for one *real*. Fabinho similarly sold a variety of merchandise near the metro station on Uruguaiana, an area Rose described as "heaping with street vendors." Dona Helena carried bags for customers at an open-air market, peddled juice on the beach, and sold mints at the entrance of a movie theater. Together, the former routes of these ex-camelôs—now catadores—traversed many of the central thoroughfares, stations, and public squares of Rio de Janeiro.

But things began to change in the mid-1990s, Rose told me. "A new mayor took office and the *guarda municipal* (a police force) began taking our merchandise on the street. We had to run from them. You must have seen this on television. How the *rapa*—we call them the rapa—come and take vendors' merchandise."

I had indeed seen this from time to time on the early evening news—scenes of police dressed in khaki shirts and pants, pouring out of white vans, waving batons at street vendors as they scrambled to gather their vegetables, clothing, pens, batteries, CDs, DVDs, or other products and run. The officers usually chased them down.

Soon after the crackdown on street vendors began, Rose quit selling garlic on the streets. The loss of merchandise was too high a price. As I pieced together this part of her work history, I began to see it as telling a larger story of how the politics of urban space in Rio de Janeiro has increasingly eroded the possibilities of self-employment. The mayor she mentioned was Cesar Maia, an economist and right-wing politician who was elected mayor of Rio de Janeiro three times. During his first term (1993–96), Maia launched a series of urban reform projects that implemented a new politics of bringing order to what he described as Rio's "urban chaos."[14] In contrast to urban planning in Rio de Janeiro in the 1970s and 1980s, which emphasized large-scale solutions, Maia's intervention focused on targeted, relatively short-term projects with immediate results that became known as "urban acupuncture."[15] These projects aimed to beautify the city so as to improve Rio de Janeiro's image as a global city that would be attractive to international capital and tourism. Inspired by Mayor Rudolph Giuliani's "broken windows" approach to crime in New York City, Cesar Maia also saw the aestheticization of city space as a way to address issues of security and violence.

Maia's initial project, Rio Cidade, targeted the streets as a priority for urban reform. The planner responsible for initiatives in the central business district of Rio, Augusto Ivan, referred to his efforts as "straightening up the house" and "cleaning the landscape."[16] This "cleanup" involved burying telephone and electric lines, relocating bus stops and mailboxes, and removing ambulant vendors, street children, and the homeless from highly visible spaces of the city.[17] Though Maia justified the removal of street vendors from major avenues on the basis that they impeded the flow of traffic, geographer Márcio de Oliveira (2008) has shown how this campaign merely freed up these vacated spaces for commercial businesses. Bars, fast-food joints, cafés, and lunch counters extended their dining areas onto the sidewalks. The city government also allowed kiosks to be built—all with the same style and size—in public squares and pedestrian-only streets that had previously been the selling spots for ambulant vendors. Thus, Maia's project had far less to do with opening up streets and sidewalks than with controlling who could occupy these areas and what activities were permissible within them. The end result was the privatization of public space.[18]

To enforce this spatial politics, Maia furthermore instated a new police force, the guarda municipal, during his first term.[19] This police force was based on an article in Brazil's 1988 constitution that granted municipalities the right to organize a guarda municipal that would be responsible for protecting the city's patrimony—its parks, squares, gardens, beaches, and monuments.[20] It did not specify, however, the manner in which the guarda municipal would carry out its responsibilities. Such ambiguity enabled Maia to extend the duties of the guarda municipal to the repressive policing of street vendors operating within public spaces, actions further spurred by anxieties in recent years over pirated and counterfeit goods.[21] Though officers of the guarda municipal do not carry firearms, they make use of clubs, handcuffs, and in some cases attack dogs when detaining vendors and confiscating their goods. Catadores who had previously worked as street vendors told numerous stories of losing their merchandise in raids by the guarda municipal. Though this cost was usually the reason they stopped selling on the streets, many also spoke about the humiliation of being treated like a criminal. Fabinho, for example, told me that he kept trying "to resist," but eventually gave up after having "received a thrashing" (*ter apanhado*) too many times. "I was handcuffed," he said, shaking his head. "I had to pass through the center of Rio, in handcuffs, as if I were a bandido. Just because I wanted to work."

As an alternative to ambulant vending, Maia inaugurated several popular markets (*camelódromos*), including one on Uruguaiana where Rose had once peddled garlic. Built on land that remained after building the Uruguaiana metro station, this covered market was designed in a grid with evenly divided stalls, each bearing a registration number. Vendors who wished to sell goods in the public market had to acquire a license from the city, remain in their designated stall, and operate their business according to the fixed hours of the market (closing at two o'clock in the afternoon on Saturdays and closed on Sundays). In her study of a similar campaign to regulate unlicensed vendors in Lima, Daniella Gandolfo (2013: 285) incisively notes that the assumption underlying such efforts is that individuals, if given the chance, "would formalize in a heartbeat." And yet, similar to the vendors Gandolfo encountered in Lima, neither Rose nor any of the other catadores who formerly worked as camelôs turned to state-run public markets as an alternative. Instead, Rose worked a few odd jobs—none with a signed worker ID. She served as kitchen help for a woman with a lunch counter on Uruguaiana, whom Rose had met during her many years as a camelô in the area. The woman soon passed away from a heart attack and the restaurant closed. Rose got a job at another lunch counter but did not like the owner and quit. She found work sweeping the classrooms of a school, but shortly after became pregnant with her third child and again quit her job. It was at that point that one of Rose's friends introduced her to the dump.

For several months, I forgot about the moment Rose and I passed by Praça XV. It was only when trying to understand her return to the dump that I recalled her story about her time as a street vendor and the subsequent jobs that did not last. I went back to my notes on that day. I played the recording of Rose's account, still untranscribed, listening for answers. What connections, if any, were there between Rose's movement between jobs after stopping work as a camelô and her later departure from and return to the dump? Why was it that the crackdown on street vendors seemed to lead not only Rose, but also many other catadores, to the dump in the first place? Perhaps it mattered that both street vending and collecting recyclables were forms of wageless work. But how? What bearing did the experience of work as a street vendor have on Rose's later experience as a catador?

"I CAN NO LONGER ADAPT"

Ironically, it was the rare catador who had consistently held jobs with a signed worker ID who helped me understand the transience in Rose's work history. Alessandra was one of these. I met her the first time I came to the dump and she quickly took to schooling me in the ways of Jardim Gramacho. Though gregarious and kind, Alessandra always had a frank, no-nonsense attitude about her. She liked to ask questions that she would answer before anyone had a chance to respond, as in: "You know what they call that? Well, I'll tell you. . . . You know why? Because, like I said. . . ." She also tried to disabuse me of notions that she thought were erroneous beliefs of other catadores, like the common saying that money earned on the dump is cursed. "Ah, that's just a popular superstition," she told me. "I don't believe that at all." It was almost as if Alessandra felt that she, too, was still an outsider to Jardim Gramacho. Even after working for fifteen years on the dump, she continued to live in a neighboring municipality that required her to take two buses each way. When I asked her once if she had ever considered spending the night in Jardim Gramacho to cut down on her commute, she looked at me with wide eyes. "What?!" she exclaimed. "Never. Heaven forbid! There are rats here!"

Alessandra's story was relatively rare in Jardim Gramacho because she had *only* worked in jobs with a signed worker ID before coming to the dump. A native of Rio de Janeiro, she grew up in the favela of Nova Holanda, in Rio's industrial North Zone. This area later became one of the most dangerous battlegrounds between rival drug gangs and police, but during Alessandra's childhood in the late 1960s and 1970s, it was a community she described as calm. Both of her parents were employed with signed worker IDs, her father as a furniture maker and her mother as a manicurist in a nail salon. Together they earned enough income to enable Alessandra and her seven siblings to focus on their studies without having to work. "We had a real childhood," Alessandra recounted. "Because for me, childhood means going to the beach, going to Quinta da Boa Vista [a city park], going to an amusement park. My father took us on all kinds of outings. I even saw Santa Claus in the Maracanã Stadium."

Alessandra was on track to finish high school, but in her second-to-last year, she became pregnant and had to stop her studies. Her partner at the time continued to support her. It was only a couple of years later, when her partner broke his leg in a soccer game, that Alessandra began looking for work. By this point, she was twenty years old. A friend helped her get a job as a seamstress at a clothing factory, where she stayed for four years before moving on to work for another three years at a day care center—both jobs with a signed worker ID. Wanting desperately to buy her own house, Alessandra eventually decided to quit her job at the day care center (asking her employer to fire her officially) so that she could access her job security funds. She found a house that she could afford, but it was in São João, another municipality on the outskirts of Rio, where Alessandra knew no one. With few contacts, she struggled to find another job. Eighteen months passed without any work.

"So what did you do?" I asked Alessandra as she came to this point in her story. She had stopped by my house on her way back to São João in the late afternoon. I had made us a fresh thermos of coffee and then suggested we sit at the table in the open-air kitchen at the back of the house to catch a little of the afternoon breeze. "It was a difficult phase of my life," she replied.

I didn't have money, groceries were running out, I was broke. When my situation had already become critical, I had a friend—she is still a friend—an older lady, Dona Solange. She said to me: "My dear, I am going to take you to a place that is very good, where there falls all kinds of things from the supermarket that you can help yourself to. Come on, let's go." And I said, "All right, then, let's go."

It was a Saturday when I came. I stared at the sign: The Metropolitan Landfill of Jardim Gramacho. It all begins there. I was frightened the first day that I went up to the top. Frightened because I never imagined myself in garbage. I thought that I wasn't raised for this sort of thing, to end up in a place like this. I asked myself, *What am I doing here?* I kept thinking. *My God, what am I doing here?*

Dona Solange told me, "You have to wear long pants, put on knee-high socks, protect your feet to go up to the top. Let's go."

When I arrived at the top, a large semitrailer was unloading and a bag of cookies fell out. When I saw all those people tearing open a bag of cookies, I became scared. I thought I had come to the ends of the Earth. That's how I arrived. It was a Saturday. And now it will be fourteen years that I have worked here. I entered on that day and until this very day, I have not left.

Alessandra paused to refill her glass with coffee, asking if I had any extra sugar—I never made the coffee sweet enough. I wanted to ask her why she had stayed all those years. But before I had a chance, she began describing catadores who first befriended her on the dump. There was Pernambucano, an elderly man whom she met on that first Saturday—a "damn good person" (*gente boa para caramba*), as Alessandra put it. He let her use a few of his own burlap sacks and plastic barrels before she acquired the necessary supplies for collecting. Later, when Alessandra wanted to start collecting on the rampão (where semitrailers from transfer stations unload), he told her to look for a catador named Zumbi when she arrived. He explained that Zumbi would already be expecting her.

"When I arrived," Alessandra recalled with a laugh, "I went around calling out: Who is Zumbi, who is Zumbi? Finally! Zumbi appeared."

Zumbi taught Alessandra to pay attention to the back door of an unloading trailer, not to stand too close, to collect along the sides. When the trailer starts to back up—that's the moment to approach, and quickly. If she did all that, Zumbi explained, she would quickly fill her sack.

At the time, no one was buying PET, only thick plastics. And I thought to myself: My God, how am I going to collect much of anything? What am I doing here? But damn, on that day, Kathleen, I filled three sacks. Today those three sacks would be worth R$70. The next day I went back. And I got used to it. *Me acostumei*. I was no longer able to work a formal job—no way. I couldn't get used to it. *Não me acostumei*. And here I am to this day.

"You never left?" I asked, making sure I understood.

I got used to the dump. I tried to work formal jobs since, but I'm not able to adapt [*não consigo me adaptar*]. I worked as a maid in a hotel. I tried. I stayed one month at the hotel. It was so tiring! My boss was always saying, "Straighten up this room! *Do this! Do that!*" On the dump, this doesn't happen. You don't have a boss. You don't have a schedule. You don't even have days that you have to work. You make your own salary and your own schedule. The catador gets used to doing what he wants, when he wants. He gets used to not having orders. I got used to this too. So, I said, "Do what? I am going back to my dump, because there no one is trying my patience and pestering me."

Was this the only time, I wondered, when Alessandra had left the dump? In fourteen years? It seemed so unlike her—someone who always kept a little distance from Jardim Gramacho, someone who had held a signed worker ID. And so I pressed her: "What about other jobs, other than in the hotel?" Alessandra shook her head.

> I'm not able to. I know that I'm not able to. I've worked as a cleaning lady. They told me, "Look, I'll pay you R$70 for the day." But it was a matter of working one day. I went, cleaned the house, and then left. I don't want anything tying me down. I also put up a refreshment stand at my house. This works well for me, because I am working for myself. I can no longer adapt to working as an employee of someone else. I'll do anything else. I make flower arrangements; I make tablecloths to sell. But for me. To work as an employee of someone else—that I can no longer manage.

As I listened to Alessandra's story, I was struck by her use of the term *to adapt* (*adaptar-se*) or its synonyms such as "to get used to" (*acostumar-se*, *habituar-se*). I had come to expect this turn of phrase in the entry narratives of catadores, who often told me that, following an initial shock, they gradually adapted to the dump—to the smells, to the nauseating fumes of methane gas, to the movement of trucks and tractors, to the feel for distinguishing types of materials. Often it was the guidance of friends, like Dona Solange, Pernambucano, and Zumbi in Alessandra's case, that helped a novice catador through this process of adapting. What surprised me in Alessandra's story was not so much her emphasis on becoming accustomed to the dump, but rather the connection she drew between her experience of adapting to the dump and the reason she could now "no longer adapt" to regular employment. Unlike Rose, who had long worked outside relations of wage labor, for Alessandra the adjustment to work on the dump also involved the habituation to conditions of self-employment.

One of these conditions, I soon learned, involved time. When I asked another catador named Cordeiro why he had left a formal job for the third time, he told me that there comes a time when you can no longer adjust to a job with a signed worker ID because of its different temporality. "In a job like that, you have your shift and you have to clock in and out. And as catadores, we are used to a different rhythm of life—to not having a work schedule—and we just don't adapt." Miguel, the catador who had lost his job as a street cleaner, insisted that the reason he was fired was because he was "restless"—not that he *felt* restless, but that he *was* restless, using the Portuguese "to be" form (*ser*) that suggests an ongoing or intrinsic quality or state. It was as if the rhythm of life experienced through work on the dump had a way of "reaching into the body" (Munn 1992: 111).[22] Rose's primary explanation for quitting her job similarly suggested a kind of restlessness. She did not complain about the workload or an overbearing employer, but instead deplored the five hours she had to stay at work with nothing to do. For someone used to working hard and then taking a break, hanging out with friends, or going home, the requirement to remain at work without working struck Rose as absurd.

In his social history of industrial capitalism, E. P. Thompson (1967: 57) shows how the transition to wage labor entailed "a severe restructuring of working habits" and the creation of a "new human nature." The emergence of a new time-sense oriented by the clock, the moralization of regular work patterns, and a clear division between "work" and "life" were some of the values and dispositions instilled in workers through what Thompson argues was a process of *making* workers into proper waged employees. When catadores spoke of their adaptation to the dump, they similarly expressed how the cumulative experience of a particular form of labor can remake inner processes and ways of being in the world. Catadores commonly described their inability to adapt to wage labor as a consequence of their lived experience of an alternative way of organizing work and life, a process that changed their desires and habits in ways incompatible with regular employment. Cordeiro pointed to his experience of working without a schedule on the dump as instilling in him a new orientation to time that conflicted with the regularity and stark divisions between working and not working in wage labor. Alessandra perceived the ability of the catador "to do what he wants" on the dump as a reason for her stress when working for someone else, for feeling a loss of control in formal jobs. Finally, Rose—someone long accustomed to coming to and going from work, first as an itinerant street vendor and later as a catadora on the dump—expressed intolerable frustration at the demand to remain at work when she had nothing to do.

Just as the transition to wage labor in industrial capitalism entailed the creation of new worker subjectivities, the transition to precarious labor in contemporary capitalism is also a process involving the transformation of desires, values, and forms of living. In other words, like wage labor, work on the garbage dump was a site of subject-making, which catadores experienced and expressed as transformative of their inner dispositions. Over time, I began to see Rose's return to the dump as emerging from a worker subjectivity fashioned under conditions very different than those of her job with the worker ID.

LIFE DISRUPTED

I also began to see the inability of catadores "to adapt" to regular employment as compounded by the precarious conditions of life in Rio's periphery. Ironically, this became clear in Rose's response to what was an offhand question I asked her on the day we sat in her yard and she shared the news of her new job. Throughout that afternoon, several of Rose's neighbors stopped by to chat, and as I later watched two boys fly a kite across the street, I asked Rose where else she had lived in Jardim Gramacho. I knew that she had moved to the area known as Maruim relatively recently.

During her first nine years in Jardim Gramacho, Rose recounted, she lived in Chatuba, an area of the neighborhood sandwiched between the dump and what remained of the mangrove swamp. She built a shack there for herself and her three children, having already separated from her first husband, whom she referred to as simply "the good-for-nothing" (o traste). "I had nothing," Rose told me. "Some clothes, a small wooden table. That was it." Then the shack caught fire. Everything burned. Rose felt fortunate that no one had been injured in the fire, since she knew the stories of others who had not been so lucky. Her friend Ana Carla, for example, lost her grandmother and a younger brother when a leaking propane canister caught fire in her childhood home. It was early morning and everyone was asleep except for her younger brother, who was five years old. He saw the fire and was scared and so he hid in a cabinet. When the rest of the family awoke to the flames, no one could find him.

After the fire, Rose lived with another friend while she built a new shack. She gradually began to acquire some household goods—her brother gave her an old television, she bought a secondhand refrigerator, she found a small kitchen cupboard that she brought back from the dump. She had also acquired a washtub that she lent to everyone. One day, when Rose had a pile of dirty clothes that needed to be cleaned, the washtub broke. It seemed like such a small thing, but she couldn't take it, Rose told me. "I kept crying, thinking that I had all these clothes to wash and nowhere to wash them."

By this point, Rose had met Carlos and he had moved in with her. Carlos tried to calm her down, insisting that they would figure something out. Carlos had just returned from a day of collecting, but he suggested that they go back to the dump and collect as long as they needed to have the money for a new tub. "It's always something," Rose sighed. A few months later it was the rain. Whenever it stormed, water would enter the shack; this time it filled up to their knees. Most of Chatuba, I had learned while recording data for a neighborhood map, was located below sea level. I remembered being astonished the first time I downloaded the elevation measurements and saw numbers in the negative digits.

After the flood, Rose decided to move. She borrowed money from a friend for the first month of rent, moved into a crowded building at the edge of the neighborhood and then later into a small house in Maruim. There was less flooding in this section of the neighborhood, but other problems arose. One of these had to do with the lack of running water. The streets just beyond Rose's house were never connected to the water lines. Rose pointed to six or seven water jugs lined up at the edge of the yard. "I filled them for my neighbor, Michele's mother—the one I told you about," she explained. Rose had passed by her neighbor's house that morning and was shocked to find that Michele, who was four years old, had not taken a bath in two days. "You know," Rose said, "there was not a single drop of water in that house."

Over time, I began to see the forms of social, environmental, and economic precariousness that Rose described—the fire, flood, broken tub, empty water jugs—as constituting everyday emergencies. These everyday emergencies disrupted daily routines, stable living arrangements, and networks of care—straining families, especially women, with additional needs and obligations. Sometimes an emergency was the very reason a catador began working on the dump. This was the case with Ana Carla. After the fire, her mother could no longer cook the meals that she once sold, and so Ana Carla began collecting recyclables to help support her family. At times, it was not the physical infrastructure of life (or lack thereof) that produced an emergency but rather the politics of security, policing, and violence in

FIGURE 2.1. Puddles. *Photo by the author.*

Rio de Janeiro. One of Rose's closest friends, for example, stopped working altogether for a few months, relying on the support of friends in Jardim Gramacho, after her husband was shot and killed and her three-year-old daughter died of pneumonia within six weeks of each other. Less tragic everyday emergencies occur as well: buses break down, creditors arrive to collect debts, long waits stretch indefinitely at understaffed health clinics, police invade favelas and stop residents for questioning. Life in Rio's periphery can feel continuously interrupted.

At the time that Rose accepted the job with a worker ID, she was living with Carlos, his two children from a previous marriage, and her own three children. She had also informally adopted the child of a neighbor and friend who was dealing with an addiction to crack cocaine. Rose's oldest daughter, who was fourteen years old, had recently befriended a young man known for his involvement with drug dealers in Jardim Gramacho. Rose feared that her daughter's mere association put her in danger, and she furthermore worried about leaving the other children in her care. Prior to taking the regular job, Rose and Carlos had alternated the times that they worked on the dump so that one of them could always be home to keep a closer watch on their children. Rose gained the stability and status of a worker ID, but as a result she lost control over her schedule, and subsequently her ability to perform what she saw as important work of caring for kin.

As Rose's story makes clear, regular employment does not always fit easily into the precarious lives of urban poor. The returns of catadores to the dump—and their interpretations of these returns as the inability to adapt—point to the incongruence between their experience of the everyday and the demands of wage labor. In contrast, the ability to come and go from the dump allowed catadores not only to manage everyday emergencies but to pursue life projects amid these disruptions. Catadores often engaged in a "double shift" (*dobrar*), meaning that they worked day and night consecutively, in order to earn extra money to pay a debt incurred from a purchase they otherwise could not have made. For some catadores, especially those in their youth, the dump allowed a blending of intense work with an intense social life. Rose described her early years on the dump as a time when she alternated collecting with days spent barbecuing, drinking, dancing, and socializing with friends, many of whom have remained important figures in her life.

It might seem that the combined demand and desire for mobility in the lives of catadores echoes neoliberal logics that value flexible labor and flexible bodies (Martin 1994). However, the worker who is able to respond quickly to the changing needs of capital is quite different from the catador who moves between jobs or decides to work in a context with few controls on time and schedule in order, in Rose's case, to be present for her children amid tension and threats of violence. In the first case, the flexible worker becomes radically individualized; flexibility emerges from the worker's alienation from her social world. This dissolution of the social is one reason that many theorists have pointed to an emphasis on autonomy as a defining characteristic of neoliberal governmentality (Rose 1999). Autonomy in the neoliberal sense refers to individual empowerment, entrepreneurialism, and self-help, and to the conception of the self as an economic resource requiring investment, management, and care that the subject then brings to social transactions.[23] The neoliberal subject is autonomous, Ilana Gershon (2011) argues, insofar as the self is conceived as existing prior to relationships.

I suggest instead that we read the returns of catadores to the dump as a way of claiming what I think of as relational autonomy. By calling this autonomy relational, I seek to emphasize how the desire for mobility among catadores was tightly woven into other desires—for sociality, intimacy, and relations of care. The boredom that prompted Rose to quit her job—the way she experienced the demand to stay at work while having nothing to do—became wrapped up with her desire to be attentive to her children at a perilous moment in their lives. Rose's autonomy, manifested in this instance as her ability to come to and go from work as she pleased, emerged not from investment in the self but rather from immersion into relations of care. We might also see Rose's involvement in a vibrant party life with friends during her early years on the dump as similarly an entanglement of autonomy and sociality. By relational autonomy, I do not mean to index relational labor per se, such as caring for children or elderly parents, but rather to underscore how autonomy, for catadores, is always already woven into relationships and forms of social belonging.[24]

My understanding of autonomy among catadores, therefore, resonates more with an alternative meaning of this term that has emerged from social movement struggles *against* neoliberalism. Ranging from the struggles of indigenous movements in Latin America to antiglobalization activism in Europe and North America, these movements share an affirmation of autonomy as a way to distance themselves from certain forms of power.[25] Autonomy for these activists refers to the relinquishment of state power as an end, to a withdrawal from capitalist markets and modes of consumption, and to the carving out of spaces in which other forms of sociality and coexistence can flourish. Rather than a technique of neoliberal governmentality, autonomy in this sense is an aspect of liberation (Williams 2008). And rather than the freedom of an atomistic self, the liberation that comes from autonomy is about the "ability to create new communities and ties of mutual dependence" (Graeber 2009: 266).

The desire for autonomy among catadores does not emerge from a professed, deliberate political project as it does for the social movement activists mentioned above. That is, catadores express their autonomy not in terms of a political ideal to be achieved or enacted, but as their inability to adapt to regular employment—an inability that stems as much from alternative worker subjectivities as from the everyday emergencies that disrupt their lives. However, autonomy for catadores is similar to the political autonomy sought by antiglobalization movements in that both constitute a distancing, withdrawal, or release from particular relations of power. This parallel leads us to see Rose's return to the dump as an act of turning away from the employment contract and from relations of wage labor. By relinquishing the carteira assinada, Rose gained greater self-determination in her everyday labor—to reconfigure her work rhythms, to modify the length, frequency, and intensity of her labor, and to interweave multiple dimensions of her working and nonworking life. Moreover, Rose's experience of relative autonomy in her labor enabled her to attend to everyday emergencies and thereby sustain her social world. Relational autonomy can thus also be conceived as an art of living through the precarious present, as that which makes possible a continued, shared existence in delicate times.[26]

THE POLITICS OF DETACHMENT

For a long time, as I strove to make sense of Rose's story, I kept revisiting the writings of the historian E. P. Thompson. Describing a very different moment in the history of capitalism when industrial wage labor was in its infancy, Thompson (1963) documents a host of objections among workers in eighteenth- and nineteenth-century England, including resentment toward the factory bell, the demand to maintain a regular pace of work, and the monotony of the workday. Such grievances did not center on wages or "bread-and-butter" issues, but rather referenced the disruption of more fluid work–life rhythms (203). Thompson furthermore maintains that workers expressed a sentimental attachment to a previous golden age not because they believed material life was better prior to the industrial revolution, but because they were nostalgic "for the pattern of work and leisure which obtained before the outer and inner disciplines of industrialism settled upon the working man" (357). In short, the first struggles of factory workers were struggles over arts of living (Thompson 1967).

If there is anything that Rose's return to the dump makes clear, it is that work cannot be understood apart from modes of inhabiting the everyday. Much like the grievances of the factory workers that E. P. Thompson describes, Rose's reason for quitting her job did not cite its compensation or even its content, but rather how its structure prevented her from interweaving work with other demands and desires in her life. The labor of collecting recyclables on the dump thus emerged as something more than a means to generate income. It became for Rose a form of living—that is, it helped forge a particular way of being in the world or, as Cordeiro put it, "a different rhythm of life."

When seen in this light, Rose's return to the dump exposes the limits of survival and resistance as common analytical frameworks for interpreting the precarious labor of the urban poor. The figure of the unemployed worker sifting through refuse on a city dump certainly evokes what Mike Davis has termed *informal survivalism* (2004a: 24). While an understanding of precarious labor as a strategy of survival draws attention to the everyday emergencies that unsettle life in Rio's periphery, this account overlooks the aversion catadores expressed to conditions of waged employment as well as the fuller life projects and forms of sociality enabled by their work on the dump. Yet neither is this a story of resistance, which fails to capture the tension between Rose's desire for a "real" job with a worker ID and her desire for what I have described as relational autonomy. Perhaps even more importantly, the concept of resistance suggests an oppositional stance that does not resonate with the affective register of catadores' returns. Rose's nonchalant brush of her hand when she tells me she quit her job or Alessandra's remark that she just can't adapt to formal employment are expressions that convey detachment, not defiance or even refusal.

Instead, Rose's return to the dump is better understood as an act of release—in the sense of a relinquishment or withdrawal from particular conditions of labor. In the moment that Rose leaves her job to go back to the dump, she lets go of the employment contract and of the organization, subjectivities, and relations of work that it entails. I see in this act of release a politics of detachment that is quite different from the politics of precarity inspired by what Guy Standing has called the precariat's "four A's—anger, anomie, anxiety, and alienation" (2011: 19). Especially in the post-Fordist contexts of the Global North, these affective states and the politics (or antipolitics) of hopelessness that they activate emerge from the continued attachment to an imagined good life, promised by capitalism, that can no longer be realized (Berlant 2011). In contrast, Rose's act of quitting her job entails a rupture with normative forms of capitalist labor that opens up the possibility of other ways of fashioning work and life.

The politics of detachment is thus not only about departure. Turning away from something involves turning toward something else—in Rose's case, a re-*turning* to the dump and to the forms of living and relationality that it enables. Far from a politics of disinterest or disengagement, this movement of detachment entails loosening certain normative ties so that other attachments can be retained. The precarious labor of catadores allows relationships to be woven, life projects pursued, and social worlds reproduced amid the disruptions of the here and now. The garbage dump becomes, then, not an overdetermined end for Rio's poor. Rather, the returns of catadores to the dump constitute a politics of detachment that enables life to be lived in the precarious present.

3 · Life Well Spent

Eva was late. This was unlike her, and my impatience turned to worry as I called her cell phone several times with no answer. I contemplated going ahead without her so as not to keep ACAMJG's truck driver, who had agreed to give us a ride, waiting for us at the entrance to the dump. But just as I grabbed my backpack and boots, leaving behind a pile of dried mud flakes in the corner of the room, I heard the front gate squeak open and then slam shut. I opened the door to find Eva smiling, but I noticed immediately that her grin seemed forced. "I have to talk with you about something," she told me, bypassing any greeting. "We can talk about it on the way."

As we crossed the street, Eva unfolded four sheets of paper stapled together and handed me a document that read CORPO DE DELITO in bold letters across the top. Noting my confusion, Eva told me that she would explain everything, emphasizing the word *everything*. She began by recounting a fight that she had had with a neighbor who accused Orlando, Eva's eleven-year-old son, of theft.

"Orlando doesn't even go as far as the gate!" Eva told me earnestly. "How could he have stolen from her? But there she is, calling him thief, thief, thief."

Eva finally decided she had had enough. The previous day, she had gone over to her neighbor's house to implore the woman to stop calling her son a thief, but the neighbor continued repeating the accusation. In response, Eva hit her.

At this point in Eva's story, I stopped walking. An eighteen-wheeler rumbled by us, kicking up a billow of dust that caused me to cough. I now realized the significance of the document that Eva had showed me—a criminal report documenting the injuries that she inflicted on her neighbor during their fight. I also realized that the accusation of theft in a community where bandidos were often called upon to resolve disputes must have terrified Eva, whose affable nature made her more likely to evade a confrontation than to seek one out.

Eva told me that she was in real trouble, that she could go to prison for three months because of the fight.

"But your neighbor hit you too, right?" I pointed out. "She was pulling out your hair. You were defending yourself."

"Yeah, but she is an elderly woman," Eva told me.

"What do you mean? How old?"

"Seventy." Eva replied.

"Seventy?"

"Don't laugh," Eva pleaded, as she strained to hold back her own laughter. "Everyone is making fun of me for getting beaten up by an old woman." As Eva said this, her stifled chuckles broke into open laughter and I joined her, wondering how a situation could simultaneously feel so grave and so absurd.

After we regained our composure, Eva turned to me and said, "Look, do you think you could lend me something? I don't have enough for bus fare and I need to get back to the police station in Caxias to fill out a form, to have proof of *my* injuries, otherwise I don't know what will happen. . . ." Her voice trailed off.

I realized that Eva's story was partly meant as a prelude to this request, a way to demonstrate that she was only asking me for money because her situation was dire. Over time in Jardim Gramacho, I became accustomed to such requests for loans—some repaid, some forgotten. I often observed catadores ask to borrow money from other catadores or from family members and friends (requests were almost always framed as loans, never as gifts or for money outright). Eventually, as I became more deeply involved in the lives of a few catadores—not only as a researcher but also as a friend, neighbor, or work partner—I began to receive such requests myself.[1]

Before Eva said anything further, I unzipped my pouch and pulled out a R$10 bill that I always brought with me for incidentals: water if we ran out, a snack if we got delayed, new gloves if one ripped. "You should go ahead," I suggested. But Eva offered to stay and collect with me for a couple hours before going to downtown Caxias. The police station wouldn't be open at this early hour anyway, she reasoned. And she needed to collect as much as possible.

By this point, Eva and I were close to the dump's entrance, and so we dropped our sacks and sat on the curb to wait for ACAMJG's truck, hoping that we had not already missed it. I kept thinking about everything Eva had told me. The alleged theft, the fight with her neighbor, the criminal report, and now her financial stress felt both sudden and familiar—another compounding series of everyday emergencies. That her story culminated in a request for a loan seemed to emphasize that such emergencies disrupt not only work but also the planned management of money. Unexpected troubles can cause unexpected expenses.

Yet something did not quite add up. Though Eva's request for a loan did not surprise me, I was struck by the implication that she was broke. I was with her on Friday when she was paid R$300 (roughly equivalent to what it cost monthly to rent a small, one-bedroom house in the area). And it was only Monday morning. How could she possibly have spent all that money in just two days?

As I sat on the curb, I thought of other times I had asked this kind of question. It was common for catadores to be broke when collecting on the dump even if—as in Eva's case—they had recently been paid. In response, catadores insisted that earnings from the dump simply "vanish." When I asked why, I only received what felt like cryptic answers: "Money enters one hand and goes out the other," I was often told. Others claimed that money vanished because it was "cursed." But what happened when money vanished? I kept wanting to know. *Where did it go?*

It was only much later that I realized that vanished income had far less to do with the question of how money was spent than it did with the question of how to spend one's life. Or rather, as I worked to trace the money that disappeared, these two questions—of spending money and spending a life—became inseparable. They also helped me see that vanished money and being broke offered another explanation for why and when catadores returned to the dump.

IN THE *NICOMACHEAN ETHICS*, Aristotle (1985: 19) maintains that the highest purpose or ultimate aim—what he calls "the good"—in all human action is "a sort of living well." He notes that while most people concur that living well is synonymous with happiness, there is a great deal of disagreement about what happiness is. Rather than reduce happiness to pleasure, Aristotle argues that living well requires cultivating certain dispositions or "virtues" that are instilled through habits and that orient one's actions in particular circumstances toward a mean between deficiency and excess. Generosity, for instance, is considered a virtue by Aristotle insofar as it is an intermediate state between wastefulness and stinginess. Thus, from the perspective of one of the founding figures in Western philosophy, living well is a lifelong project of doing the right thing in the right way with the right desire and the right intention. In short, for Aristotle, the good life is the virtuous life.[2]

While not necessarily invoking the concept of virtue, much contemporary scholarship in the human sciences on "the good life" posits that notions of living well are often, as with Aristotle, ideas about the *right* life. In her critical inquiry into the emphasis on happiness in Western society and the moral work that this performs, Sara Ahmed (2010) insightfully shows how the ideology of happiness often serves to reinforce normative ways of living. In self-help literature, positive psychology, and other studies in what Ahmed calls "the new science of happiness," there is an assumption that acting a certain way and being a certain sort of person are what lead to happiness. And usually, Ahmed argues, these ways of being reflect liberal, bourgeois, and heteronormative ideals of middle-class life. For example, in her discussion of Toni Morrison's novel *The Bluest Eye*, Ahmed notes that the socially oppressed and deviant family depicted in the book is narrated in terms of misery and lack: "This family is *not* white, *not* middle class, where 'being *not*' means being unhappy" (80; emphasis mine). The conflation of the good life with particular middle-class ideals is one of the reasons Lauren Berlant (2011) argues that it can become a source of "cruel optimism." That is, she maintains that the continued attachment to the fantasy of a successful and stable career, upward mobility, a durable marriage, and a beautiful home—at a historical moment when neoliberal capitalism is eroding for many in the Global North the economic opportunity and state guarantees that followed the Second World War—means that the pursuit of the "good life" can actually impede its acquisition. In both these discussions of contemporary aspirations for well-being, the good life appears as a powerfully conventionalizing force that shapes subjects in the "right way" of (middle-class) living or, if those qualities are lacking or unattainable, excludes them from the possibility of any alternative form of living that could be deemed good.

It might therefore seem odd to contemplate what the vanished income of catadores has to do with the question of what it means to live well. Populations like catadores, whose conditions and forms of living diverge radically from middle-class social norms and ideals, tend to be invoked in discussions not of the good life but of bare life. Such "bare life," as first proposed by Giorgio Agamben (1998) in his theory of sovereign power, is life devoid of its political significance. The modern state governs, Agamben argues, through the power to reduce populations to bare life that can be abandoned or killed with impunity. The emaciated detainee in the Nazi concentration camp is paradigmatic of bare life for Agamben. But there are also other, less extreme forms of bare life in modern politics, which scholars drawing on Agamben's work have identified, such as the figure of the "disposable" worker, discarded by capital, who is left to eke out an existence on the margins of society.[3] It is important, furthermore, to note that in developing the concept of bare life, Agamben draws on a distinction in ancient Greek between *zoē*, which referred to the mere fact of living common to all beings, and *bios*, meaning a particular, qualified way of life. Given that *bios* is fundamentally about *how* one lives, it is also necessarily about the good life. This is why, as Agamben notes, Aristotle used the term *bios* and not *zoē* in his discussion in the *Nicomachean Ethics* about which form of life—the life of gratification (*bios apolaustikos*), the life of political activity (*bios politikos*), or the life of study (*bios theōrētikos*)—leads to happiness. In contrast to *bios*, bare life is mere survival. It is the remnant—a word belonging to the semantic field of waste—of a life stripped of the specific characteristics that gave it social, cultural, and political value. Bare life is thus the antithesis of the good life. It no longer raises the question of *how* one lives, just that one lives. Another way to put this is to say that bare life is no longer a form of living.

Vanished money or the state of being broke is usually understood as a condition of lack, and as such feeds easily into narratives of bare life. But such narratives preclude the possibility that even in apparent situations of deprivation and dearth, what is at issue is not mere living but good living. As I strove to answer the question that stumped me on the morning Eva asked for a loan—*How could several hundred bucks disappear so quickly?*—I began to see that vanished money was not just an economic problem of material needs, earnings, costs, and expenditures. These concerns, while important, were wrapped up with other considerations such as experiences of enjoyment, forms of sociality, and orientations to work. Moreover, the fleeting earnings of catadores revealed how spending often became a form of relationality—a way of working out how to be kin, friend, or neighbor to others in conditions of radical uncertainty. By shifting my inquiry into vanished money from a question of want to one of desire, I began to consider how the state of being broke emerges from an existential reckoning with the relationship between work, wealth, and well-being. As a result, I frame the spending of catadores not through scarcity and excess, as is common in accounts of urban poor, but rather as a moral argument about what constitutes a good life.

By invoking the term *moral* here, I am not referring to morality as a set of rules or prescriptions distinguishing between right and wrong behavior. Nor am I using moral in the sense of the normative, as evidenced in the middle-class fantasies of the good life examined by critical theorists such as Ahmed and Berlant. Notions of well-being were diverse in Jardim Gramacho, as we will see, but rarely did any of them map neatly onto dominant social ideals. Rather, my use of the term *moral* is meant to capture ideas about what is of value in life. That is, I am interested in how money, on the one hand, and notions of what makes life livable, on the other, constitute different dimensions of value. This focus on the interlocking dynamics of economic and moral value draws inspiration from David Graeber's (2001: 2) observation that value in the economic sense (as in the price one is willing to pay for something) and value in the sociological sense (as in the moral or what is seen as good in human life) are "refractions of the same thing." Namely, they both speak to questions of the desirable. I find this insight useful, because it suggests that the question of how money is spent and the question of how life is spent are not distinct inquiries. By emphasizing desire, it also shifts focus away from the morally right as the normative and obligatory and toward the morally good as what enhances human existence. That is, when I say that the spending of catadores constitutes a moral argument, I mean to draw attention to the ways this action expresses their own understandings of what is meaningful, worthwhile, and beneficial in life.

My approach to vanished money diverges, then, both from popular notions of urban poor as profligate spenders and from critical perspectives in the social sciences that examine the poor's relationship to money primarily in terms of scarcity and debt. The former, with its roots in Oscar Lewis's

(1961) concept of the "culture of poverty," portrays the poor as incapable of budgeting, saving, and rational economistic behavior.[4] Extreme versions of this view hold that if the poor spend money on anything other than their most basic needs (such as on alcohol, electronics, or brand-name clothing), they are being wasteful or even irresponsible. The latter perspective—often appearing in critical social research on unemployment, microfinance, debt, and urban crisis—emphasizes political-economic conditions to the exclusion of questions concerning pleasure, excess, and desire.[5] Instead, if the economic and the moral (in the sense of what is desirable and good) are understood as two expressions of value, then it becomes possible to ask how spending—even in conditions of extreme poverty—is not just a pragmatic concern but also a philosophical one: *What does it mean to live well?* In what follows, I approach the vanishing money of catadores as a way of grappling with this question within the precariousness of life in Rio's periphery and within their own particular social worlds.

CURSED MONEY

I first met Eva because of a loan. She stopped by Glória's house one night when I was still living there to ask if she could borrow a few reals. I was busy arranging my supplies for an early morning start on the dump the following day and failed to catch the circumstances of Eva's request. Eventually I went into the kitchen, where Eva and Glória were talking, to fill a two-liter plastic bottle with water to take with me the next day. Glória introduced us and told Eva that I was currently collecting on the dump. Immediately, Eva suggested that we collect together. She had been away from the dump for nearly a year and had been wanting to go back. A collecting partner (*truta*) was just what she needed to motivate her.

I would later learn that Eva wanted to resume collecting on the dump because she needed to pay a credit card bill that her husband refused to pay. Hector had supported her and their youngest son for the last few months when she had been sick, suffering from chest pain, and unable to work. But their relationship, which had been conflictual over the years, had recently reached a breaking point. Hector began insisting that he see the credit card statement before giving Eva money for the bill, which was a problem because she occasionally bought items for their two older sons, both of whom were estranged from their father. Eva rarely spoke about the discord that propelled her sons to leave home when they were still adolescents, and

I was not comfortable discussing the matter with Hector. Despite all the time I spent with Eva, I never got to know her husband well. "He has back pain," Eva told me the first time I visited their home in Ibarié—the result of a motorcycling accident. When we arrived, Hector was lying in a hammock, staring off in the direction of the neighbor's parched yard. Eva called out to him to leash their pit bull, concerned that the dog would frighten me, but Hector seemed to ignore her. When we passed by the hammock, he did not look up.

Eva's goal of paying down her credit card was never far from our minds in those first few weeks we collected together. Yet it was only when another catadora, named Letícia, told me directly that money is "cursed" that I began noting the entanglements of money and the dump. Eva and I had run into Letícia—a longtime friend of Eva's family—while collecting on a particularly hot summer day. The noon sun was scorching the cracked surface of the dump and many catadores were resting in any shade they could find—under beach umbrellas pulled from the garbage or in the shadows cast by tall, filled burlap sacks. Eva and I had plopped down in a shady spot to eat lunch, not too far from where Letícia was busy smashing plastic bags into what looked to me like an already full sack. As I passed a container of rice and beans to Eva, she called out to Letícia to join our meal.

Letícia shook her head. She told us that she could not stop working, because she didn't have "a single cent" from her previous week's earnings. When I asked what had happened, she sighed, "Money that comes from the dump is cursed."

"Cursed?" I asked.

Letícia explained that money comes into your hand quickly, but then leaves just as quickly. She told me it was because dead bodies were buried beneath the garbage. I wanted to ask more at the time but she went back to the tedious task of compacting plastic bags.

After Letícia introduced me to the idea of cursed money, I began to notice this expression in conversations among catadores, frequently given as an explanation for why someone was broke. Cursed money evokes notions of decay, lifelessness, and ruin—qualities that Letícia directly referenced in her connection between money that comes from the dump and the dead bodies beneath its surface. This expression also grants agency to the money, not to the spender whose hands cannot grasp or hold on to it. Here, money does the moving. It comes into one hand and leaves from the other. It appears and disappears as if on its own.

For a long time, I remained puzzled by the responses of catadores that their income vanished or that the money that came from the dump was cursed. I kept wanting to get to the bottom of things. Did catadores really believe that their earnings were cursed, that money was tainted by the death and decay buried beneath the dump's surface? I thought of the work of economic anthropologists who have documented numerous qualifiers of money—beliefs that certain kinds of money can be "barren," "baptized," "dirty," "bitter," "hot," or "burning."[6] In certain respects, the cursed money of catadores seemed to resonate with these other beliefs. Similar to Michael Taussig's (1980) description of "barren" money among Colombian peasants whose wage-labor earnings—seen as being made through a pact with the devil—would not bear fruit, the cursed money of catadores could not be saved, accumulated, or invested. It simply vanished too quickly. In this way, cursed money seemed akin to earnings made from the sale of sapphires that Malagasy miners perceive as too "hot" to hold on to (Walsh 2003) or the remittances of Sri Lankan migrants that have a tendency to "burn like oil" (Gamburd 2004).

Yet in other ways, the cursed money of catadores was distinct. Earnings from the dump could be spent on any desired good, whereas anthropological accounts of barren, dirty, and bitter money describe prohibitions that prevent such tainted money from being spent on crops, livelihoods, marriage contracts, or other transactions oriented toward long-term social reproduction.[7] Even more importantly, these beliefs are often theorized as a moral critique of the way such money was earned—such as through bribery, gambling, or stealing (Gamburd 2004), or even, as Taussig (1980) argues, through participation in the capitalist system of wage labor. In contrast, the belief in cursed money among catadores never implied that the act of collecting recyclables was morally suspect. If anything, catadores linked cursed money to the actions of others—to those who discarded the things and even the lives (in the case of "dead bodies") that were buried beneath the dump's surface.

The more I sought to connect cursed money to other anthropological analyses of money's symbolic representation, the more it seemed a mystery. This was partly a result of the way such analysis focuses on the content of beliefs rather than on their use. It was only when I stopped trying to determine *what* catadores believed about cursed money and instead explored the practices surrounding this belief that I began to see it not as a truth claim about the world, but as a way of living within it. That is, to borrow an insight from Michael Jackson's (2013: 35) reflections on the "pragmatic efficacy" of beliefs, the veracity of the belief in cursed money was far less important than what this belief *does*. What was this effect? How did the belief in cursed money become "true"? Answering these questions meant tracing the movement of money as it passed out of the hands of catadores and into relations of obligation and debt.

TO SPEND IS TO SAVE

On that early Monday morning Eva and I spent waiting on the curb for ACAMJG's truck, I decided to ask her if she could recall each expenditure she had made since Friday. I pulled out a pen and small notebook that was stuffed between a pair of stained cotton gloves in the pouch I used to carry my supplies while collecting on the dump. As Eva recounted her expenditures over the previous two days, I made the following notes:

R$130—CREDIT CARD: The last installment that Eva owed on her credit card. She had charged groceries for Maicon (her sixteen-year-old son who moved out of the house because of conflict with his father).

R$20—RITA: For shampoo that Eva had bought from her friend, Rita, to treat lice that Eva believes she caught from "*as crianças da Chatuba*" (children who live in Chatuba, the part of the neighborhood closest to the dump).

R$15–DRESSER: Eva's old dresser fell apart. She is making four monthly payments of R$15 for the new one.

R$10—BUS FARE FOR MAICON: So that Maicon could make the trip from Jardim Gramacho to her home in Ibarié to visit her on Sunday.

R$50—DRUM SET: Eva bought a drum set from the pastor of her church for Orlando (her eleven-year-old son). His MP4 was stolen when they went to stay at Orlando's house during a fight with her husband. She feels that it is her fault that Orlando's MP4 was stolen, which is why she bought him the drum set. The drum set costs R$200 total. She had already paid R$100 on it and gave the pastor another R$50.

R$20—MOTHER-IN-LAW: Eva paid back her mother-in-law, from whom she had borrowed money to go to a doctor's appointment.

R$13—PIZZA: On Saturday night, Eva came to Jardim Gramacho to look for Adílson (her oldest, nineteen-year-old son). Adílson's wife had called Eva to tell her that Adílson had not come back to their home in several days and she was worried that he was on a drug binge in Jardim Gramacho. Eva went to his shack to see what he was up to. He was not there, and when she asked others, they told her that he had gone up to the dump to work. It began to rain and she waited out in the rain for Adílson to return, eventually falling asleep. When she woke, she felt extremely hungry and craved pizza. She went to a stand in the neighborhood plaza and bought a whole pizza—*não uma individual, mas aquela da família* (not a personal pan pizza but a large). She also ordered a Coke. She said that her husband had not taken her and Orlando to eat pizza in a long, long time. She felt bad that she had splurged on pizza when Orlando was not with her.

R$2.50—WATER

R$5.00—CIGARETTES

R$17.50—LUNCH AT THE POLICE STATION: She bought lunch for herself, Orlando, and Hector during their trip to the police station the previous day.

R$2—LOAN TO ADÍLSON

TOTAL: R$285

The total left R$15 unaccounted for, though as I glanced back over my notes, I saw that Eva did not include any bus fare that she must have spent on the trips she made to Jardim Gramacho and to the police station in downtown Caxias. I also noticed that nearly all of Eva's expenditures arose from circumstances that were unexpected or unplanned. She bought shampoo to treat a case of head lice—a relatively minor issue but the kind of ailment that was ubiquitous among catadores given their constant exposure to toxic materials. Over time, I acquired my own collection of over-the-counter medications that catadores suggested I buy to treat a series of recurring skin infections. Eva also bought a new dresser to replace one that periodically became damp in rain storms and finally rotted through and broke. And then there were the multiple expenditures related to ongoing domestic tensions. As fights with Hector escalated, Eva considered leaving home, and she occasionally spent nights at her mother's house or at one of her sons' houses. However, Eva declined to stay more than a few days with a relative, because she felt that she would only be a burden. The list of expenditures in my notebook condensed in just a few lines the various forms of insecurity that intersected in Eva's life: toxicity, erratic health care, conflictual domestic relations, unstable housing, legal issues. All of these became entangled with the financial accounting on the page.

When I looked up from rereading my notes, Eva asked for my notebook. With an index finger on the page, Eva pointed out, one by one, all the expenditures that were not for herself—the groceries for Maicon, the drum set for Orlando, the bus fare for Maicon, the loan for Adílson. I later noticed that, with perhaps the exception of the water and pack of cigarettes, the pizza was the only purchase Eva had made exclusively for herself and it was the one she took the longest to explain. It would be tempting to read the guilt that Eva expressed for buying the pizza as echoing dominant ideologies that distinguish between "responsible" and "wasteful" spending of the poor. But Eva's regret had less to do with the pizza itself than with the fact that she had consumed it alone. In fact, her response to the pizza seemed to resonate with comments I often heard catadores make about what it means to be a *pessoa ignorante* (know-nothing). When I first heard this phrase, I asked a catador, Rafael, if he could explain it to me, and he replied that a *pessoa ignorante* is someone who accumulates money, is afraid of spending it, and only buys material things for himself. As a result, the *pessoa ignorante* never goes out with others, never has fun, and so never enjoys (*curtir*) the "good things in life." I began to see Eva's response to the pizza as a different way of expressing the critique of the *pessoa ignorante*. That is, her regret seemed to reinforce the idea that good spending is at least in part about enjoyment shared in the company of others.

As I finished tallying Eva's expenditures, I noted that there was yet another way her spending was directed toward others: as payments on debts that she owed. Of the R$300 she took home that Friday, R$235 were already claimed by others. A substantial portion of this debt (R$130 worth) came from a store credit card issued by Carrefour, a big-box store that sold everything from socks to sacks of rice. Foodstuffs were more expensive at Carrefour than at other grocery stores in the area, but because Carrefour offered credit, Eva would shop there whenever her shelves were empty and she was low on cash. She was particularly concerned about making the payments on this credit card because she had already defaulted or "dirtied her name" (*sujou seu nome*) at Casas Bahia, a furniture and appliance store geared toward low-income customers. As a result, her name was now blacklisted in the System of Credit Protection (Sistema de Proteção ao Crédito), preventing her from acquiring new lines of credit for another five years.[8] However, despite the significance of Eva's credit card payments, this was not the only debt that she owed. She had also borrowed money or acquired credit from her mother-in-law, neighbor, and church pastor. At the same time, she had made loans to others; the credit card debt, for example, was actually the result of a purchase she had made on behalf of her son. Eva's simultaneous borrowing and lending made it difficult to adopt debt as a straightforward explanation of vanished money. Far from an opposition, credit and debt were intertwined.

Like other residents of Rio's favelas and peripheral neighborhoods, catadores contend with a constant barrage of financial needs and requests within their social worlds. However, catadores negotiated such demands in particular ways as a consequence of immediate payment on the dump. Paid in cash by scrap dealers at the point of sale, catadores were able to earn money each day they collected. Those who knew catadores—their family members, friends, and neighbors—knew that when catadores arrived home from working on the dump, they most likely had money in their pockets. This made it difficult for catadores to deny requests for loans: they knew that others knew that they had just been paid. Similarly, when catadores owed money, it was difficult for them to evade paying their debts. For example, Eva's credit card debt had originated in a loan to her son in the form of groceries she bought on the card. The morning after I made the list of her expenditures, Eva suggested that we stop by her son's shack on our way to the dump, knowing that Maicon would be returning home from the dump around that time (since he worked at night). Sure enough, we arrived as his door just moments before he came winding down the muddy path that led through tilting wooden structures. Before Eva even had a chance to greet him, he cried out, "Ah, mom, I'll pay you Sunday when I come over!" Eva shook her head. She knew he had the cash to pay her and there was no reason for him to wait. He reluctantly handed over several folded bills.

In a social world disrupted by everyday emergencies, the temporality of payments among catadores weaves webs of credit and debt.[9] Eva simultaneously owed and was owed by others. And as her son found out to his dismay, one's earnings could be reappropriated far too quickly. Ironically, the best way to "save" one's money is to spend it—instantly.[10] I began to see signs of this immediacy all around me: the clustering of bars at the entrance where catadores first come off the dump or a parent's hurried command that a child dash off to the market to purchase whatever staples were running low. There were unusual signs as well. One of these was a bar made of red bricks that stood out among shacks lining the pathway that Eva and I regularly took on our treks between the dump and ACAMJG. The owner was a former catadora named Dona Lorena, who others told me had built the bar while collecting on the dump along with her husband. One day, I stopped to ask Dona Lorena how this was possible, how she and her husband were able to save their earnings to build the bar. "Hah! We never saved a single cent," she replied. It was impossible to save money, she insisted. Something would always arise—one of their children would get sick and need medicine. The savings would disappear. Instead, each day she and her husband left the dump, she went directly to the brickyard and bought as many bricks as their payment allowed. When they had enough bricks, they started buying the bar's inventory, bottle by bottle, each day that they worked. And that, she told me, was how they built the bar.

IN HER STUDY of markets in northern Cameroon, Janet Roitman suggests that debt "represents a moment when particular truths about social relations are revealed" (2003: 214). The same could be said for expenditure more broadly. Eva's single purchase of the drum set, for example, laid bare unequal power relations with her husband; the ways she both depended on and sought to care for her sons; her ties to social institutions that included an evangelical church; and her position within larger relations of insecurity in Rio's periphery, crystallized in the incident of the MP4 theft.

However, Eva's list of expenditures or Dona Lorena's pile of bricks seem to suggest more than this—that spending is not only a reflection of social relations but a means of working through them. If spending reveals anything, it is that relationality is never given, stable, or complete. Rather, each moment of expenditure—whether in granting a request for a loan, purchasing a pizza, paying back a debt, or adding bricks to a bar—involved some kind of accounting of who one is in relation to another. This accounting, of course, always depended on the particular state of affairs that happened to arise in the flux of everyday life and thus could never be predetermined. Sometimes loans were given and other times money was spent hurriedly so that it could be "saved."

FIGURE 3.1. Saving bricks. *Photo by the author.*

After Dona Lorena explained how she built her bar, I began to see the spending of catadores as a form of existential labor, as a way of working out how to live well within a fragile social world. If money vanished, I realized, it did so in part through ongoing efforts to construct life projects in and amid one's obligations to others.

RESIDENTS OF THE GARBAGE

Cursed money was only one explanation I encountered in Jardim Gramacho for why the earnings of catadores seemed to disappear so quickly. The other common reason given was addiction. I heard social workers, waste management personnel, other residents of Jardim Gramacho, and even some catadores attribute vanished earnings to the consumption of alcohol or drugs. Many of these explanations centered on crack cocaine. In 2005, when I first lived in Jardim Gramacho, crack was virtually unknown in the neighborhood and in Rio de Janeiro more broadly.[11] By the time I returned in 2008, crack use had proliferated in Rio and other cities of Brazil, part of what many Brazilian public health officials have described as a "crack epidemic," comparing its sudden rise to the expansion of crack in U.S. inner-city neighborhoods in the 1980s.[12] In just five years (2006–10), police seizures of crack cocaine in Rio de Janeiro increased by 365 percent (Vallim 2012).

In Jardim Gramacho, many catadores who once consumed marijuana or powder cocaine began buying rocks (*pedras*) of crack for R$10 apiece. Crack was said to increase a catador's energy and intensity when collecting, though also to consume all the earnings a catador made through this frenzied labor.[13] In many ways, crack was considered a more intense and dangerous drug; several catadores told me that they were afraid of crack and so only used *pó*, powder cocaine. But in other ways, crack was similar to other substances, or what catadores called *vícios*, at least in its relationship to earnings. A catador whose "money does not make it past the entrance" referred to someone who leaves the dump and goes directly to the bars clustered near the base of the dump or to the *boca de fumo*—whether to buy liquor, marijuana, powder cocaine, or crack.

Fabinho was one of the first catadores I heard explicitly draw a connection between addiction and vanished earnings. "I've used crack," Fabinho told me. "One hit makes you want another [*craquar outro*], makes you want another, makes you want another. So long as you have money in your pocket, you continue using crack [*craquando*]." I first met Fabinho when Eva introduced me to a group of catadores known on the dump as *moradores do lixo*, literally "residents of the garbage." Though I found that Fabinho and other moradores shared in the same kinds of circulations in and out of Jardim Gramacho—intermittently leaving the dump to visit family or to pursue an amorous relationship—these catadores effectively lived on the dump. They built makeshift camps of reclaimed tarps and umbrellas that they relocated each time the unloading zone moved to another area of the dump. They made shared meals from *podrão*, a term derived from the root word *rotten* that referred to expired food found in the garbage, and cooked collectively in metal cans over open fires.[14] And as Fabinho explained to me on our first meeting, they would only go down to the base of the dump to replenish their supplies of water, *cachaça* (sugarcane liquor), marijuana, powder cocaine, and more recently crack—most of which they would then take back to consume on top of the dump.

Eva had struck up friendships with several moradores a few years previously when her adolescent son had a fight with his father, left home, and began working and living on the dump. Worried about her son's rumored

FIGURE 3.2. Resting. *Photo by the author.*   FIGURE 3.3. Soccer. *Photo by the author.*

drug use, Eva started spending nights on the dump with the moradores, who had welcomed her son into their camps, so that she might "pull him out of that life," as she put it. Her efforts were partly successful. Though her son still worked as a catador, he had since married and lived with his wife near the base of the dump. Eva's friendships with the moradores might seem strange given their founding circumstances, but I gradually understood these relationships as part of an ethos of tolerance in Jardim Gramacho. Eva enjoyed the company of the moradores, and the moradores seemed to understand and respect a mother's project to extricate her adolescent son—whom they affectionately nicknamed Craquinho (Little Crack)—from the life of a morador.

On the day that Fabinho explained vanishing money as a consequence of an addiction to crack cocaine, it was raining. It was not a hard rain but the kind of steady drizzle that gradually soaked through each layer of clothing, leaving the skin cold and clammy. Eva and I were collecting plastics on the rampão, and as we raced to catch up to a semitrailer that had just pulled in, I heard someone shouting my name—not Kathleen but Azul do Mar (literally, "sea blue"), the nickname that the moradores had given me when we first met, a reference to the color of my eyes. I turned and noticed Fabinho and another morador, Vidal, on the perimeter of the unloading zone. They had taken shelter beneath an oversized yellow beach umbrella that was propped up in a sack filled with plastic bottles. When I pointed out the moradores to Eva, she suggested we go join them.

When we approached, Fabinho got up to grab a couple of large metal cans that were piled next to one of his sacks, turned them over, and invited us to take a seat. He also came back with a blue rain umbrella. When Eva opened it, a couple of the rusted spokes ripped away from the fabric, leaving it limp and dripping on one side. "It's not getting you wet, is it?" Fabinho asked. I told him it was fine.

"Oh, Nega.[15] Oh," Vidal stuttered, trying to get Eva's attention. "Last night you missed our pizza," he declared, stretching his arms wide, as if to indicate the size of the pie.

"You ate a pizza?" Eva sounded impressed.

"Damn! At that time we were looking for you two. We grilled a pizza. We put it over there," pointing to a rack suspended across two large, square cans similar to the ones we were now using as stools.

"Remember our soup?" Vidal asked me. "You ate our soup, didn't you, Nega?"

I told him that I certainly remembered the soup that Vidal and four other moradores had shared with Eva and me on a previous afternoon on the rampinha. That afternoon Vidal had invited us "to come take a *breque*" [pronounced bráy-kee] with him and several of his friends.[16] The term *breque* had a particular meaning among catadores in Jardim Gramacho. In general Brazilian Portuguese, this word, derived from the English homonyms *break* and *brake*, is used in the sense of a coffee break at a conference (written in English in an event program), in reference to break dancing, or to signify a car's brakes. Among catadores, the word *breque* referred instead to a wide range of objects including a cigarette, alcohol, a meal, a rented shack, and even a person. "Give me a breque of a cigarette [*me dá um breque dum cigarro aí*]" was a request to bum a cigarette. "Did you rent a breque down below? [*vocês foram alugar um breque lá embaixo?*]" was a way to ask others if they rented a shack at the base of the dump to have a place to wash up, change clothes, and rest after working. "He was a strong breque [*ele foi um breque forte*]" was used to describe a catador named

Paulo who joked around a lot, sometimes sitting in the path of the tractor that flattens out the piles of unloaded garbage; he would cross his legs, hold a newspaper in front of him, and shout at the tractor driver that he was a "pussy" (*babaca*). Though these usages can seem disparate, they all refer to some kind of diversion, fun, play, joking, and relaxation. Activities associated with the breque, such as playing music or kicking around a soccer ball, often occurred in the midst or alongside the work of reclaiming recyclables. And a breque was usually a collective affair—much like the soup that Vidal had invited Eva and me to share.

Served in old butter containers, the soup contained pieces of beef, sausage, tomatoes, collard greens, onions, peppers, potatoes, and carrots—all reclaimed from the waste around us. What most stuck in my mind was the coffee that followed. Vidal had poured it into the cut-off bottoms of clear bottles, made from a type of plastic called "crystal" in the jargon of the recycling industry. He kept insisting between chuckles that we be careful with his "crystal" glasses, that they could easily break. But for us, Vidal added, he would only use crystal.

Vidal laughed again when I mentioned the crystal glasses. And then, noticing another catador who was smoking pass by, he called out: "Hey, Nélson, you don't have another cigarette, do you?" Nélson shook his head.

"No problem, no problem," Vidal replied.

Simone offered to fetch a few aluminum cans from our sacks. She often set them aside for Vidal and Fabinho when she came across them on the dump—a rarity since most aluminum, one of the highest-priced materials, was reclaimed by street catadores long before bags of trash made their way to the dump. The cans never amounted to much, but some of the moradores still liked to collect them. A bag was usually enough to buy a pack of cigarettes.

As Eva left to get the cans, Fabinho pointed out that the cans probably would not be worth much. The price of aluminum had dropped once again, reaching a low of one real per kilo.

"All the prices have fallen," Vidal added, referring to the slump in the value of recyclable materials that followed the 2008 global economic recession.[17] When I asked by how much, he began pointing to burlap sacks of different sizes that were scattered across the staging area of the dump, reciting what each of them was worth before and after "the crisis." A sack that used to bring in twenty-five reals now earned only ten. Another sack that used to receive twenty reals was now worth only eight.

"They're not paying right," Vidal shook his head. "No, not like before. We made money—fifty reals a day, sixty. Now everything decreased, everything decreased. In those days, we used to collect, spend, get high with that money. We had money for two days, three days on the dump. Just living. Wasn't it so, Fabinho?"

Fabinho was slouched against the sack beneath the yellow umbrella. The baseball cap he always wore backward was now covering his face. I thought he had gone to sleep, but he replied with a barely audible "eh."

I asked Vidal if they ever had money left over in the good days when they earned so much more.

"*Puxa*, Nega, I spent a lot of money at Ricardo's."

Ricardo operated a bar at the base of the dump that served for some time as the boca de fumo. Vidal began reminiscing about good times at Ricardo's—listening to music, playing the slot machine, lounging on Ricardo's big sofa. Fabinho rejoined the conversation at this point, telling me that it doesn't matter how much you have. You spend all the money in your pocket on a night smoking crack.

"Everything?" I asked. "How much is that?"

"If you have R$500, you spend R$500," Fabinho replied.

"If you have a R$1,000, you spend R$1,000. . . ."

A few moments passed—the soft pattering of raindrops filling our silence. And then Vidal added, "Once a friend found R$18,000. It was Leão, wasn't it Leão?"

Vidal looked over to Fabinho but he did not answer. Fabinho had put the baseball cap back over his face and seemed to have dozed off.

"Damn," Vidal said as if to himself. "Leãozinho found 18,000 and he spent it all."

MY CONVERSATION WITH Fabinho and Vidal seemed to lend support to the argument that the earnings of catadores vanished because many were addicts. This explanation, however, not only echoed moralistic concerns around the profligate and destructive behaviors of the poor; it also missed a much more complex and fraught relationship between the dump and substance addiction. Over time, as I came to know Fabinho and Vidal, I gradually began to see the dump as a refuge in an additional sense: as a place where life with addiction can be lived. The ability to have cash in hand every day protected moradores from withdrawal and relieved them from the anxiety of not knowing how to obtain their next hit. And though binges and deadly overdoses were enabled by the dump's reliable bounty, these were not the only possibilities. For some, sustaining life with addiction on the dump allowed other potentials to take shape. Vidal introduced me to an ex-morador, Gilberto, who come to Jardim Gramacho as an alcoholic after having lost his job as a professional welder. He spent many years on the dump in a cycle of collecting and binge drinking until he befriended a scrap dealer involved in Alcoholics Anonymous, an encounter that sent his life on another trajectory.

Cash earnings were not the only way the dump provided the resources with which moradores could sustain their daily existence and care for each other. Meals were another clear example. Ingredients were assembled from whatever each morador happened to find in the garbage, which was why soup was their most common meal. And as illustrated in Vidal's use of "crystal" glasses, moradores repurposed an assortment of containers retrieved from the garbage as cooking pots, bowls, plates, and cups. These meals were collective in part because they had to be. "Even without wanting to, one makes friends here," Fabinho told me, "because each one depends on the other." These friendships seemed fragile, as moradores came and went from the camps. However, there were also ways they accounted for each other. When Eva had not seen Vidal for several weeks and worried that he might have overdosed or fallen, in a stupor, in front of one of the dump's bulldozers, the other moradores reassured her. They knew that Vidal was visiting his "old lady" (coroa) in Petrópolis. He would be back within the next few days.

The entanglements of the dump and addiction furthermore laid bare the familial, social, and institutional failings from which many of the moradores sought refuge. "I left that life," Vidal told me, "and I don't ever want to go back! Ask me if I want to go back. I don't want to." The life Vidal referred to was one in which he lost three older brothers in the drug wars that followed the 1994 assassination of Orlando Jogador, a leader of the faction known as the Red Command. Vidal was young at the time and was involved in an evangelical church (Vidal would still occasionally sing church hymns on the dump). But he eventually left the church when he was twenty-two years old—"because of a woman" was all he said. One of Vidal's other brothers, who was still alive, worked in the drug trade, mixing cocaine with baking soda and repackaging it. Vidal joined him, and his use of cocaine soon followed. "It helps you stay awake when you are on watch on the night shift," he explained. "A bandido cannot fall asleep."

Prison was the reason Vidal gave for why he was now on the dump. He worried that if he "went back out there" and stole something, he would end up back in prison, and this was one of his greatest fears. "I suffered there, in prison," Vidal told me. The food was what he most remembered. It had often gone bad—turned sour—prompting everyone to start yelling in protest. Eating was done quickly, and when there was not enough food, portions had to be divided with those who had none. But this was all part of the past for Vidal. To collect on the dump and to camp with other moradores was to fashion a form of living that made a new existence possible. Making meals from wasted food, exchanging cans for cigarettes, cutting plastic bottles into "crystal" glasses, and building a shelter from umbrellas and overturned metal cans were all transformative acts that Vidal saw as ultimately transformative of the self. It was in the garbage, Vidal explained, that he became a different person: "And here I am. I was once a gangster, I was once a thief, I was once everything and here I am, in the garbage. I'll say this much: God took this guy [tapping his thumb to his chest] out of a crazy life. And here he is, thanks be to God."

ADDICTED TO THE DUMP

A few weeks following my afternoon with Fabinho and Vidal, a conversation between Eva and a friend of hers, named Mariana, profoundly shifted how I understood the relationship between addiction and the dump. Eva and I had stopped by Mariana's house on our way to the Polo on a rainy afternoon. Thoroughly drenched and spattered with mud, we had gratefully accepted Mariana's invitation to come inside, dry off, and warm up with a late lunch of pasta and beans that she was preparing. As we waited for the beans to finish cooking, Eva started to tell Mariana about her latest family troubles, which involved a quarrel with her brother over a request to borrow R$100 for groceries. After listening to Eva for several minutes, Mariana shifted the conversation from Eva's specific difficulties to the general problem faced by all catadores whose earnings on the dump are "cursed."

"But why does the garbage make this money cursed?" I asked, even though I had asked this same question many times before.

"Because it's easy money," Eva responded. "I've always said that the money that comes from this garbage is cursed. It comes into this hand here and it goes out the other."

"Look," Mariana said turning to me. "You go up to the dump, you put in a quick stint, you grab that money, and you go off to do some drug or to buy some [cooking] gas."

"Even if you don't use any drugs," Eva added. "Let's say Mariana lives here. She goes up to work in order to maintain her house here. But the money she earns doesn't amount to anything. You don't see any profit. Understand?"

"But why . . . ," I started to ask.

"Because it's difficult," Mariana replied. "Look, thousands of people have worked on the dump. And I can say that there are maybe two people who built a grand house by working on the dump. One example is Seu Marco."

A much-loved catador and founding member of ACAMJG, Seu Marco had passed away suddenly on New Year's Eve from lung cancer that had long gone undiagnosed. On multiple visits to the clinic for chest pain, Seu Marco was tested repeatedly for tuberculosis (the results continued to come back negative) or was told that he had pneumonia and sent home with antibiotics. By the time a doctor performed an X-ray on his chest, a tumor had grown so large in his lung that the doctor said he was astonished that Seu Marco was still alive. In the weeks that followed, the subject of Seu Marco's death arose frequently in conversations among catadores. Some pondered his ability to work on the dump until nearly the day he died, wondering whether Seu Marco knew that he was sick. Those who were closest to him said that they had noticed times when Seu Marco was not feeling well—that he would stop momentarily, drink some water, swallow a painkiller, and then go straight back to collecting.

"But Seu Marco had ambition from money," Eva interjected. "What destroyed Seu Marco was ambition from money, from money that he wasn't even able to enjoy. Because he was up on the dump from Sunday to Sunday, under the sun and under the rain. Seu Marco didn't live. He lived for the garbage."

"He wouldn't even stop to talk," Mariana remarked.

"Seu Marco doesn't stop. Just for coffee and a cigarette. . . . He didn't stop even to eat. The man didn't even eat right. You understand? He let the garbage dominate him. This also exists [on the dump]: the spirit of ambition. He picked up ambition, ambition of garbage. What did the ambition of the garbage do to him? He only wanted money, money, money, money, and he practically lived on the dump. He wasn't a *morador do lixo*. But he was a *consumidor* [consumer]. He just wanted to stay there, to stay there and work, work, work, money, money, money, money . . . something that he never enjoyed."

"But didn't he use money to . . . ," I again started to ask.

"To do what, my dear?!" Eva exclaimed. "He stayed—"

At this point Mariana interrupted, talking over Eva. "Seu Marco built his house. He furnished his house."

"But what does it matter if you build something that you never enjoy?" Eva insisted.

"Sure," Mariana replied, "Seu Marco could have said to himself: *Puxa*, I've already built my house. So now I'm just going to work between Monday and Friday, work three times a week."

"Three times a week generates enough money."

"He could have slowed down, taken care of his health. "You know. . . ." Mariana stopped stirring the pot of black beans. "I think he died of cancer."

"Seu Marco did die of cancer. It was lung cancer," I told Mariana.

"Is that so? Well, there, you see. I think that the garbage ate his lung. . . ."

IN THE WEEKS that followed his death, catadores often pointed to Seu Marco as an example of someone "*viciado na rampa*"—addicted to the dump. Like the moradores, catadores who are considered to be addicted to the dump spend most of their time in the garbage. They are perceived as always being on the dump, Sunday to Sunday, in the sun and in the rain, regardless of their physical condition, and most importantly, regardless of their present need for income. They do not live on the dump, as Eva implies when she states that Seu Marco was not a *morador do lixo*. But the implication in Eva's comparison is that Seu Marco could easily be thought of as living on the dump since it seemed "he just wanted to stay there." However, unlike the moradores who cycle between periods of intense collecting and periods of "just living," as Vidal calls it, addicts of the dump *only* collect. The *viciado na rampa* is seen as someone who works constantly, who becomes obsessed with making money each day, but who ironically can never enjoy the money that he earns. At first I assumed that the phrase *viciado na rampa* originated in an association of the dump with substance addiction, that a slippage had occurred between those who depend on the dump to sustain a substance addiction and those who become dependent on the dump in pursuit of more earnings. Only later did I realize that catadores rarely referred to alcoholics or drug users as addicts. Fabinho and

Vidal were not called *viciados*, but rather *moradores*—residents, or "those who *live*" on the dump. The *viciados* were catadores who seemed only to work.

In his genealogy of the spirit of capitalism, Weber (1958) describes the attempts of modern employers to incentivize agricultural laborers to work longer and to work harder by raising their piece rates. Yet this incentive, Weber tells us, produced the reverse effect. Rather than working more to increase their earnings, the workers responded by working less. That is, they preferred less work (that earned them the same amount sufficient for their needs) to making more money. Weber argues that the "immensely stubborn resistance" of this attitude on the part of workers became one of the most important obstacles in the rise of a modern capitalist ethos (60). If workers could not be incentivized to labor more intensely through the appeal of higher wages, then work had to be promoted as a value in and of itself. This analysis led Weber to his famous thesis that the development of modern capitalism relied in part on the rise of a new conception of work that emerged in the Protestant Reformation—the conception of work as a moral good, "an absolute end in itself, a calling" (62).[18]

Though Weber's origin story of modern capitalism has been challenged on its empirical grounds, it remains useful for the ways that it denaturalizes the conception of work as an end, not just a means to sustaining human life. From this perspective, we might see Eva's assertion that Seu Marco "lived for the garbage" as a meditation on the relationship between work and life. Both Eva and Mariana claim that Seu Marco should have worked less, that he should have worked only to the extent necessary to provide for his needs. We see a similar logic in Vidal's description of the good days when he made enough money to spend two or three days on the dump "just living." The implication in these arguments is that one only returns to work when broke. Work is a means here, not an end. Of course, it could be argued that, for Seu Marco, work on the dump was a means to accumulating money and increasing consumption. However, for Eva, the problem is not that Seu Marco made lots of money or built a large house, but that he never paused to enjoy the wealth that he earned. Many scholars have interpreted Weber's conception of the work ethic as an ascetic denial of wealth and consumption. But as Kathi Weeks points out, Weber argues that wealth only becomes a problem within the work ethic when it leads workers to no longer see the need to continue working (2011: 50). "The real moral objection [to wealth]," writes Weber, "is to relaxation in the security of possession, the enjoyment of wealth with the consequence of idleness" (1958: 157).

The comparison between the addicts who *live* on the dump and the "addicts" who *work* (continuously) on the dump allowed me to see how vanishing money became wrapped up with other values in catadores' lives: pleasure, enjoyment, relaxation, "just living." Money is cursed, as Eva and Mariana first suggested, because of the immediacy of the concerns that lay claim to their earnings—whether this takes the form of withdrawal from a drug or of an empty container of cooking gas. Yet as their discussion of Seu Marco's life and death brings into relief, being broke is as much a function of quick spending as it is of living well. Seu Marco was one of the few catadores who managed to save and accumulate his earnings. But rather than a story of success, Eva and Mariana narrate a story of tragedy. It is a story of how work ended up consuming a life.

THE MICROTEMPORALITY OF RETURN

Ultimately, the vanished money of catadores sheds light on the question of why they returned to the dump. I initially explored this question in cases of an extended absence—when catadores worked elsewhere for several weeks or months, only to then quit and come back to the dump. In contrast, it never occurred to me to ask catadores why they returned to the dump on a day-to-day basis. That is, I never directly asked catadores why they went up to the dump on two days in one week and six in another, or why they went on certain days and not others, even though there was clearly no set schedule on the dump. Catadores came and went. They could work as little or as often as they saw fit. I assumed for a long time that catadores returned to the dump as much as they could.

As I sought to answer the question of why money vanished, I also answered the question that I had never thought to ask: catadores usually returned to the dump when broke. In other words, they returned to work on the dump at the moment when their previous earnings ran out, or at a moment when a new expense arose. With few exceptions that tended to highlight the norm—Seu Marco being one of them—few catadores worked every day of the week or in excess of what they thought would provide for their needs and desires. This is not to say that catadores were unconcerned with saving and planning for the future, or that they expressed what anthropological studies of marginalized groups have often described as a primary orientation to the present.[19] As Dona Lorena's story made clear, immediately spending one's earnings, paradoxically, can be a way to develop long-term projects in conditions of precarious living. This is also not to say that catadores were not "hard-working"—an attribute commonly cited in culture-of-poverty discourses that posit moral distinctions between the "deserving" and "undeserving" poor.[20] The descriptor of "hard-working" hardly does justice to the intensity of labor involved in poring through several thousand tons of rotting refuse, nor does it capture the ways catadores blended work with other dimensions of social life.

The microtemporality of returns to the dump revealed the qualities of what catadores described as a different rhythm of life—a rhythm of collecting, spending, and "just living," as Vidal put it. This was a rhythm that denaturalized the valorization of work. It was a rhythm that emerged through efforts to live a life well spent. I have suggested that to return to the dump after an extended absence was to return to a particular form of living. Here I would add that the comings and goings of catadores on a day-to-day basis actually gave shape to this form. The rhythm produced through these comings and goings was certainly one aspect of this form of living. What were others? How else did this form of living come into being? How else did it take shape? As I pondered these questions, I began to focus more closely on the form of work itself, a concern I take up in the chapter that follows.

4 · Plastic Economy

In a single week in September 2008, the price of cardboard in Jardim Gramacho plummeted. At ACAMJG, cardboard began the week at twenty cents per kilo, then dropped to eighteen cents, then sixteen cents, then ten. By the following Monday, I was the only one still reaching for the half-smashed cardboard boxes that tumbled loosely from the backs of unloading trucks. Until that point, I had only collected *dry* cardboard—boxes that by some miracle were still crisp and unblemished despite falling out of trucks between layers of rotten vegetables and grimy plastic bags. Dry cardboard was much lighter than sodden cartons, making it easier for me to hoist a full barrel of cardboard onto my shoulder and carry it back to the staging area. But its lightness also made it less valuable. In my first few weeks on the dump, catadores I did not know continually approached me to explain that it would be better to collect the wet stuff, that it weighed more, and that scrap dealers paid by the kilo. Despite my protestations over the amount of weight I could lift and carry, several catadores took to "instructing" me by occasionally tossing soaked cardboard at my feet. Now that *no one* was collecting cardboard, I felt even more ridiculous bypassing the damp boxes that were strewn everywhere I looked. As I reluctantly picked up a soggy piece of a box, a catador next to me suggested that I collect something else.

He explained that the price of cardboard had fallen and that most scrap dealers had stopped buying it altogether. The box I was holding was no longer "material," he said. "Cardboard has turned into garbage [o papelão virou lixo]."

When Eva suggested late in the second week of the price slump that I collect plastic with her, I agreed. The price of plastic—particularly, polyethylene terephthalate or PET—was still relatively stable compared to cardboard, paper, or scrap metal. Glória thought this was because of high oil prices. PET is a petroleum product, she explained, and so its price depends in part on the price of crude oil and natural gas. Glória told me this on the morning of September 17, 2008, the day following one of the most precipitous drops in U.S. stock prices in history.[1] As we made our way to ACAMJG, we stopped at a corner store so that she could buy a pack of cigarettes. The front page of the newspaper O Dia, which displayed a large diagram of plummeting stock markets from around the world, caught her attention and she added a copy to her purchase. As we walked, Glória began to read the report aloud, adding her own commentary. She noted the depreciation in shares in the Brazilian mining company Vale, the world's largest producer of iron ore. "This means that the price of scrap iron is going to drop," she told me. Noting that the Brazilian real had fallen against the U.S. dollar, she reasoned that there would be more exports of cellulose and that the price of cardboard would rise. (Unfortunately, Glória did not anticipate the sudden drop in the Chinese demand for packaging that sent the scrap paper industry worldwide into a near total collapse in the last quarter of 2008.)[2] She also observed that shares in Petrobras, the Brazilian state oil company, had fallen and that oil prices were in decline. However, this decline was from an all-time high of US$145 a barrel in July 2008.[3] By mid-September, the price of oil had tumbled to US$91 a barrel but was still high enough to make virgin plastic more expensive to produce than recycled plastic.[4] At least for now, Glória assured me, the price of PET would stay the same.

I took this as good news but struggled to switch from cardboard to PET. On the first day that I gathered PET alongside Eva, I realized that collecting plastics required a different set of skills, techniques, movements, and muscles. Chief among these was the ability to decipher the contents of opaque garbage bags before one of the bulldozers arrived to flatten them out. The key to distinguishing quickly between different kinds of plastics, Eva explained, was to do so by feel and sound rather than by sight. She taught me how to choose which garbage bags to rip open by first squeezing them to feel for any plastic containers inside. Once a bag was open, I could then identify the type of plastic by its resistance. What Eva called "thick plastic" (*plástico grosso*, or high-density polyethylene) remained rigid when pressed. In contrast, PET bottles could be dented but did not easily bounce back into shape. The exception to this was a kind of transparent PET bottle called "crystal" (*cristal*) that readily flexed back and forth. It also made a crackling sound when squished that other PET containers did not. Then there was a kind of plastic called *carina* (polyvinyl chloride or PVC) that was found in a wide assortment of objects ranging from flip-flops to medical IV bags. Carina tended to bend like rubber rather than crumple like a can. The way to determine if an object was made from carina was to fold and then release it. If it slowly unfurled rather than snapped back into position, it was carina. Eva demonstrated with a faded pink flip-flop, bending back the toe to meet the heel, letting go of the toe, and then waiting as the sandal gradually straightened. Of course, Eva added, the easiest plastic to identify was "thin plastic" (*plástico fino*, or low-density polyethylene)—the material that garbage bags were made of. Though many catadores collected plástico fino, Eva hated it and suggested we stick to PET. The problem with plástico fino was its smell. The skin seemed to absorb the fetid film that formed on the surface of black garbage bags. Catadores who collected plástico fino often rubbed lotions into their hands in an attempt to mask the odor, but it never completely went away.

On our way home from the dump in the late afternoon, Eva and I stopped to let a flatbed truck pull out from one of the scrapyards along Monte Castelo, Jardim Gramacho's main street. The truck was laden with bales of PET that were stacked four rows high. I had seen trucks like this innumerable times before, but this time I marveled at the shape of the plastic—each bale was a perfect rectangular cuboid. I thought back to the jumble of variously shaped and sized bottles that Eva and I had just assembled. It was difficult to imagine our bottles one day emerging, all flattened and fused, as one of these blocks.

Weeks later, after moving into a house on Monte Castelo, I would sometimes sit at my neighbor's outdoor bar in the evening and watch the trucks carrying PET pass by. On one of these occasions, two of the trucks pulled over in front of Deca's bar and the drivers came over and ordered beers. I asked them where they were headed, and they told me Santa Catarina, a coastal state located six hundred miles to the south of Rio de Janeiro. "You're

FIGURE 4.1. Plastic bales. *Photo by the author.*

not from here," one of them said, as much a question as a statement. I told them about my research and interest in recycling. "You must be familiar with Arteplas, then," the first driver suggested. I had heard the name but did not know much. They explained that their two loads of PET were going to Arteplas, the largest recycler of PET in Latin America. Arteplas made mostly ropes, but for all kinds of purposes—cattle ranching, construction, camping, sailing. Its proximity to the port of Itajaí in Santa Catarina, I later learned, made it easy for Arteplas to export its rope all over the world. Though most of its exports went to other South American countries (Chile, Peru, Bolivia, Venezuela, Uruguay, and Colombia), Arteplas was increasingly expanding into U.S., Canadian, and European markets. When I went back to the United States, I found that it was possible to order Arteplas products on eBay or on one of several outdoor and sporting goods sites.

If I had a hard time imagining the PET bottles that Eva and I collected turning into solid blocks on a flatbed truck, it was even more difficult to envision those blocks as shiny threads braided into rope on a distant yacht. In short, I was struck by the plasticity of plastic. As PET changed shape, it also moved from the dump to scrapyards to recycling companies—traversing the so-called informal and formal economies. The constellation of events, markets, and relations that forced me to switch from collecting cardboard to plastic in the wake of the 2008 U.S. financial crisis made it clear, as economic anthropologists have long argued, that formal and informal economies do not exist as separate spheres. But the plasticity of plastic seemed to suggest more than this—that what we have long conceptualized through the binary of the formal and the informal is instead the quality of changing form. The difference between a PET bottle and a PET rope, I thought, is not their essence but their shape. What would it mean to envision not only the materials catadores collected but their work itself as plastic? What might the concept of plasticity illuminate about a wider range of economic practices and relations that we would not otherwise see?

PLASTICITY, CATHERINE MALABOU PROPOSES (2008: 5), is a concept that has two meanings: "It means at once the capacity to *receive form* (clay is called 'plastic,' for example) and the capacity to *give form* (as in the plastic arts or in plastic surgery)." In her philosophical work on plasticity, Malabou draws inspiration from Hegel's development of the concept as well as from neuroscientific research on the brain, which has shown that neurons and synapses are modifiable throughout the life of an individual. The brain is shaped and imprinted by its early development and genetic program. But it also eliminates, creates, modifies, and repairs connections and neurons as an individual interacts with the external world. Malabou argues that this dual movement of receiving and giving form is what makes plasticity distinct from flexibility—a term that has become common in neoliberal capitalist discourse. Though plasticity and flexibility appear to be synonyms, flexibility only captures the first part of plasticity's meaning. To be flexible, Malabou observes, is to bend or to fold to circumstance; it is to receive form but not to give form. Or as Marc Jeannerod puts it in his forward to Malabou's work, "plasticity is a mechanism for adapting, while flexibility is a mechanism for submitting" (2008: xiv).

I find Malabou's conceptualization of plasticity useful for the ways its emphasis on *both* giving form and receiving form disrupts enduring dualisms in social science's representations of economic life. In particular,

I adopt plasticity as a way to depart from the binary of the formal/informal economy, which has dominated social science's approach to nonnormative forms of work for over four decades. Most genealogies of the informal economy trace the origin of this concept to a paper that anthropologist Keith Hart delivered at a 1971 conference on urban employment in Africa in which he argued that many poor migrants in Accra, Ghana, were not unemployed or underemployed but rather engaged in a range of "informal" income-generating activities.[5] Hart's paper was certainly groundbreaking in providing a new language for development economics. However, I would argue that the emergence of the informal economy dates back prior to Hart's first use of the term—that the idea of an informal economy arose as a proposed solution to problems generated by what Timothy Mitchell (1998) has described as a mid-twentieth-century project that imagined and constructed the economy as a totalizing object and self-contained sphere. It was only relatively recently, in the years surrounding the Second World War, Mitchell maintains, that the meaning of economy shifted from a principle of frugality to its contemporary usage as a "structure or totality of relations of production, distribution and consumption of goods or services within a given country or region" (84). This invention of *the* economy as a totality (it now made sense to add the definite article) required delineating its boundaries. It involved counting some things as part of the economy and excluding others deemed not to belong—such as the myriad activities of urban farming, trading, transporting, divining, cleaning, and hustling that Hart observed among migrants in Ghana.

The birth of the informal economy can thus be read as an attempt to capture certain exclusions created in the making of the economy as an object. By the time Hart was conducting ethnographic fieldwork among migrants in Ghana in the 1960s, the idea of the economy as a totality or system that could be measured by indicators such as gross national product (GNP) was a taken-for-granted understanding of the term in both social science and popular conceptions. The problem that quickly arose in development economics, however, was that measurements of the economy of a country like Ghana left out a large portion of its productive activities. This prompted Hart to argue that, in places where informally produced goods and services are pervasive, their exclusion from economic analysis is "unwarrantable" and that this exclusion ultimately "allows economists to equate significant economic activity with what is measured" (1973: 85, 84). Concerns over measurement subsequently became a running theme in the literature on the informal economy. In an effort to correct for the perceived inaccuracy of GNP figures and to demonstrate the scale and significance of the informal sector, many scholars studying informality sought to create novel methodologies to measure it.[6] This was no easy task. Most informal enterprises are not registered, nor are their activities recorded on tax forms, licenses, or other state documents, making it difficult to count them. Still today, informality is often defined as that which "eludes measurement" (Goldstein 2016: 18). Though this attention to what is and is not counted in GNP, employment rates, and other economic measurements raised important critiques of mainstream economics, such critiques were fundamentally arguments over where the borders of the economic sphere should be set. They did not question the sphere as such. In other words, the concept of the informal expanded the edges of the economy, but in doing so it reinforced the very notion of the economy as a bounded object.

As a result, informality necessarily produced a binary. If the economy is understood as a self-contained sphere, then the inclusion of productive activity that had once been omitted meant that the whole now had two parts: the formal sector and the informal sector. This dichotomy quickly emerged as a problem that has yet to be resolved, fueling nearly all debates on the informal economy for nearly a half century. In the 1970s, scholars accepted the binary but disagreed on what exactly separated the two sectors. For Hart (1973), the degree of rationalization of work was the most important distinction between the formal and informal. Drawing on Weber's use of "formal" to describe the rationality of modern capitalist enterprises based on regularity, abstraction, and calculation, Hart classified all productive activities that did not operate according to this rationality as "informal." Others emphasized instead the relationship to the state—the informal referred to unregulated or unprotected activities.[7]

By the 1980s, critics of this early dualist framework began challenging the idea of two separate sectors by examining the linkages between them. Debates shifted from the question of what divides the formal and informal to the question of what connects them. Structuralists like sociologists Manuel Castells and Alejandro Portes (1989) argued that informality was incorporated into the broader capitalist economy through an exploitative relationship: the informal economy reduces the costs of labor, absorbs a labor surplus, and provides low-cost goods and services to those formally employed, thereby subsidizing wages.[8] Those who became known as the legalists, most notably Hernando de Soto (1989), countered this perspective by arguing that the relationship between formality and informality was not about exploitation, but rather bureaucracy. The "informals," de Soto maintained, were competitive entrepreneurs who would flourish if only the state eliminated its costly and onerous bureaucratic regulations. Clearly, scholars such as Portes and de Soto approached the study of informality from vastly different theoretical frameworks—the former rooted in a Marxist analysis and the latter in a neoliberal perspective. Yet despite important differences in the specific arguments of these debates, the very terms of the debate continued to reproduce the formal–informal binary. After all, even the emphasis on linkages between the formal economy and informal economy presupposes an originary divide.

An additional problem with analyses that focused on the articulation between the formal and informal is that these two categories are not so much linked as they are blurred in everyday practice. Take Jardim Gramacho as an example. Catadores collected recyclables as self-employed workers—an activity usually defined as "informal"—on a garbage dump that was owned and operated by Comlurb, a semipublic waste-management company. Comlurb, as I discuss in more detail below, engaged in everyday efforts to manage the work of catadores and scrap dealers and was thus very much involved in the "informal" activities at the dump. Furthermore, most scrapyards were unlicensed enterprises (hence, "informal"), but their daily business involved interactions not only with catadores but also with registered and regulated recycling companies, like Arteplas, that sourced material for their products from Jardim Gramacho. The licit and illicit also merged in Jardim Gramacho. Scrap dealers paid bribes to enter the dump at certain times of the day and paid both bandidos and police to allow them to operate in peace. Even the dump itself was technically illegal, violating Brazilian environmental laws that prohibited waste dumping in waterways and that established mangrove swamps as protected areas.[9]

I am not the first to point out that the boundaries around formality and informality dissolve in practice. Most studies of the informal economy today explicitly acknowledge conceptual problems with the formal-informal binary. Yet they do so while arguing that the formal and informal are categories we cannot do without.[10] In part, this is a consequence of the terms having entered into state and popular discourse. In contexts in which the terms formal and informal circulate, ethnographers who aspire to be faithful to the language used in everyday discourse must continue to engage this binary. Moreover, there is a shared sense that the formal–

informal framework has been around for too long, that it is ingrained in the social science and development literatures, and that if we were to abandon the concept of informality, it would become difficult or even impossible to discuss the actually existing, nonnormative kinds of work that the term was meant to describe.

These arguments raise important points about the entrenched and everyday usage of the formal/informal distinction. However, the continued adoption of informality is problematic not only because it reifies the notion of the economy. It also unintentionally lends weight to everyday uses of the term that justify the repression or differential treatment of practices performed by particular social groups. For example, Ananya Roy (2005, 2009, 2011) has shown how middle-class and elite housing construction in India often violates regulations just as much as squatter settlements, but only the latter is perceived by the state as "informal" and therefore illegitimate. Daniel Goldstein (2016: 23) similarly notes that "to classify one thing as formal and another as informal is to praise and reward the one and to marginalize, condemn, and 'illegalize' the other." It should not be surprising, then, that in the Brazilian context the category of informality was historically an elite invention that pathologized the urban poor (Fischer 2014). Though today the terms *formal* and *informal* still circulate in Brazil, I found it rare for catadores to use these terms. The closest they came to this language was the distinction commonly made between working with a signed worker ID (*carteira assinada*) and working without one.[11] However, unlike informality, the carteira assinada does not distinguish between different spheres of the economy nor between productive activities of an inherently different nature. Rather, it draws attention (often critically) to a specific legal mechanism that grants benefits, protections, and recognition to some workers and not to others.

While contemporary scholarship remains wedded to the conceptual language of the formal and informal, I draw inspiration from the ways those same studies have reconceptualized informality as a *mode* rather than a sector, status, or economy. This approach makes it possible to observe how various actors and institutions—not just urban poor, who have long been conflated with informality—engage at times in a way of operating that involves negotiating, sidestepping, or modifying norms and legalities. Indeed, even the state itself produces informality, suspending and violating its own laws and determining in which cases regulations will be enforced (Fernández-Kelly 2006; Goldstein 2016; Roy 2005).[12] This work has furthermore examined how actors and institutions oscillate between modes of formality and informality, a fluidity that Carolyn Nordstrom (2007: 211) represents through the use of a slash in her concept of the "non/formal." Daniella Gandolfo (2013) likewise suggests that the formal and informal are two opposing forces, the former driving toward regularity and efficiency and the latter toward excess and freedom. These two forces fluctuate, she argues, "coalescing and colliding in a frenzy of mimesis and contagion" (290).[13]

What I want to suggest here is that the mode such analysis has aimed to capture is not that of informality, but rather plasticity. As *both* the capacity to receive form and to give form, plasticity disrupts the dualist framework of the formal/informal in representations of "the economy," allowing us to see how systems and structures are molded in practice and that what appears unregulated or "disregulated" (Goldstein 2016: 7) produces its own order. It furthermore draws attention to the *interplay between* different forms of economic life—the "mimesis and contagion" that Gandolfo mentions. That is, plasticity necessarily implies a relationality in which different forms leave imprints on each other, impressions that can be remolded but never erased. This means that plasticity is not just a quality of labor performed by marginalized workers like catadores. As I aim to show below, it is also observable in normative institutions typically viewed as "formal," such as Rio's waste management company, Comlurb.

In a retrospective essay published roughly three decades after his seminal article on the informal economy, Keith Hart (2006) notes that by inventing this concept, he "sacrificed" ethnography to some extent. "The informal sector," he writes, "allowed academics and bureaucrats to incorporate the teeming street life of exotic cities into their abstract models without having to confront the specificity of what people were really up to" (28). This is partly due to the way the *in*formal is a negative construction, defining something by what it is *not* rather than what it is. In contrast, plastics and plasticity were all around me in Jardim Gramacho—as I learned to squeeze bottles or bend flip-flops to determine their form; as I listened to catadores explain how certain materials can leave imprints on the skin; as I watched jumbled piles of containers being transformed into monochromatic rectangular blocks; as I discovered that these blocks would take on yet other forms, such as that of rope, produced for other markets in other parts of the world; and as I traced the ever-changing relations between the city, waste, catadores, Comlurb, scrap dealers, police, bandidos, and recycling plants. In what follows, I explore this plasticity of economic life, focusing specifically on Comlurb's decades-long project of managing the actors and operations involved in the collection and exchange of recyclables in Jardim Gramacho. This story would usually be told as a project to formalize the informal economy—that is, to bring order to a seemingly unstructured world of work. Here I tell the story differently. My aim is to show that it is in the interchange between structures—in both giving and receiving form—that what we understand as "the economy" emerges.

THE PROFESSIONAL CATADOR

On an early August morning, I made my way to Comlurb's offices located at the entrance to the dump. It felt strange to be wearing dress slacks and a blouse rather than my usual rampa clothes—boots, cargo pants, an old T-shirt, and the requisite work vest. By this point, I knew the two security guards who worked the morning shift, and so rather than stop for authorization as a visitor would have to do, I headed straight for the cluster of buildings on the right-hand side of the entrance. Suddenly, I heard one of the guards shouting at me to stop. I approached him to explain that I had a meeting scheduled with Valéria, a social worker hired by Comlurb to attend to catadores. "Ah, Kathleen!" he replied. "I did not even recognize you!"

Though Valéria was one of the first people I met in Jardim Gramacho, this was only the second time I had been to her office—a small, concrete-block room plastered with posters from campaigns, events, and organizations related to catadores. Our paths usually crossed outside Jardim Gramacho at meetings or events involving the National Movement of Catadores (MNCR), such as the regional congress of catadores that is held annually in downtown Rio de Janeiro. Occasionally, I saw her in and around the gatehouse of the dump, resolving disputes between catadores and guards or walking between her office and the cooperative, Coopergramacho, which was located on the other side of the entrance. I never encountered Valéria while on top of the dump.

When I arrived, Valéria invited me to sit down on a folding chair opposite her desk. Noting her long stylish dress, matching shoes, and chunky jewelry, I was glad that I had dressed up. Before I had a chance to thank Valéria for meeting with me, she received a call on her cell phone and apologized to me as she answered it. Her phone continued to ring throughout our conversation; she later explained that she had arranged a meeting that morning between a couple of journalists and a few catadores, but the catadores had not shown up for the meeting. Valéria kept trying to reach Alessandra, one of the no-show catadores, who was not answering her phone, and the journalists continued to call back. Seemingly miffed, Valéria commented as much to herself as to me, "This just makes me look bad."

At the time of our meeting, Valéria had been practicing social work in Jardim Gramacho for over twelve years, dividing her time between working with catadores and teaching part-time at Rio's prestigious private university, PUC-Rio, where she earned a doctorate in social work in 2008. She first came to Jardim Gramacho in 1996 as part of a large-scale project to "remediate" the dump. Prompted by the first international Earth Summit, which was held in Rio de Janeiro in 1992 (ECO '92), Comlurb initiated efforts to address environmental damages caused by what was then an open-air dump that sprawled across an increasingly destroyed mangrove swamp and that polluted the surrounding Guanabara Bay. Catadores who collected on the dump in the 1980s and early 1990s also told stories of fires that spontaneously erupted from untrapped methane gas, produced by decomposing waste beneath the dump's surface. Some of the first remediation efforts involved creating a road to mark a border around the perimeter of the dump, constructing a piping system to release methane gas more safely, instituting the practice of covering deposited waste with dirt, and replanting part of the mangrove swamp that had been destroyed.

These engineering interventions constituted but one part of the remediation project. As Comlurb sought to shape the physical contours of the dump, the company also began efforts to reorder the catadores who worked there.[14] Conceiving of the remediation project as not just environmental but "socio-environmental," Comlurb brought three social workers to Jardim Gramacho. According to the original plan, the social workers would remain in Jardim Gramacho for eight months, during which time they would help remove catadores from the top of the dump by constructing a cooperative located near the dump's entrance. Over the years, two of the social workers left Jardim Gramacho, but Valéria stayed. "I was only supposed to be here for a short time," Valéria told me. "But that time kept going on, and to this day I'm still here trying to coordinate things."

I wondered what Valéria meant by "coordinating." I knew that she was still involved in the management of Coopergramacho, the cooperative that had been built by Comlurb in the hope that it would eventually absorb all

960 catadores who were registered by the social workers in the mid-1990s and thereby end collection on the dump. Coopergramacho was designed in such a way that select garbage trucks unloaded waste at the cooperative near a conveyor belt along which catadores picked out recyclables and tossed them into containers that were lined up behind them. The majority of catadores refused to join Coopergramacho, and by the time I arrived in Jardim Gramacho, its membership had dwindled to a few dozen catadores, most of whom were elderly and found the conveyor belt system less physically taxing than collecting on the dump. I was fairly certain, however, that the management of Coopergramacho was only one dimension of a wider set of responsibilities that Valéria had characterized as "coordinating." I asked if she could describe in more detail what was involved in doing social work in Jardim Gramacho.

"Here, it's not really about doing social work," she replied. "If you were to put a health post, a day care, a school, a hospital, a nightclub, a samba club all inside here [meaning on or near the dump], a catador would never leave. So our goal is not to offer social services. It is to create a *work environment*."

I had never heard that phrase before and was struck by Valéria's use of an ecological term (environment or *ambiente*) that I associated with the physical attributes of the dump: the garbage, the toxic leachate, the fumes from burning methane gas. These were all part of the labor conditions of catadores—conditions that catadores said they adapted to over time and which they also molded through their own acts of arranging the staging area, constructing makeshift camps, cooking communal meals, and especially sorting the discarded material around them. This process of adapting to an environment while simultaneously reshaping it partly constituted the plasticity of the *work* of catadores. But it seemed that Valéria was signaling something else. What did she mean by a work environment? I asked.

"For example," she replied. "You have to have a schedule. This can't be an open door that one can enter at any time. Otherwise, you won't create work relations." Valéria's cell phone rang again, and she apologized as she picked it up. She informed the person on the other end that she was unable to reach the catadores to be interviewed and suggested that they reschedule the meeting. She hung up.

"So, as I was saying," Valéria continued. "We needed to regulate the work hours of catadores. We held a meeting, talked with catadores, and even resolved to end the practice of catadores working at night. But this didn't stick. There was a revolution outside [the entrance to the dump]. The police came. It was a huge mess. So I went and allowed catadores to work at night, undoing the agreement. It was a setback in our work."

Instituting regular work hours was not the only matter that the social workers "disciplined," as Valéria put it. They excluded those who were too young or too old to be of working age when they registered catadores in 1996. They furnished registered catadores first with punch cards and then with uniform vests (*coletes*) that catadores were to use to enter the dump—a story I return to below. They instituted entry and exit times for the scrapyard trucks and inspected the mechanical conditions of those trucks. They held meetings in which they sought to "educate" catadores, among other things, in the separation of work from other activities of life. This came back to Valéria's goal of creating a proper work environment in which catadores would engage exclusively in the collection of recyclables while on or near the dump and undertake activities related to social reproduction and leisure elsewhere.

It would be tempting to interpret Comlurb's efforts to "discipline" catadores as a project to bring structure to a disordered field of action. Yet as Henri Bergson (1998) has argued, there is no such thing as disorder but only order configured differently. What we perceive as disorder, he writes, is merely "the disappointment of a mind that finds before it an order different from what it wants, an order with which it is not concerned at the moment, and which, in this sense, does not exist for it" (222). I kept thinking back to Valéria's insistence on needing to create a work environment on the dump, as if one did not already exist. What did it mean to imply that the collecting, sorting, and selling of recyclables, among other activities on the dump, did not constitute some kind of work environment? Perhaps what mattered here was the meaning of "work."

Before I left Valéria's office, she suggested that I read her dissertation (Bastos 2008). The thesis would contain details that she might have forgotten to tell me on the history of social work in Jardim Gramacho. A few weeks later I found her dissertation online and was struck by the word *profession* in its title, *Catador: A Profession: A Study of the Process of Identity Construction from Garbage Picker to Professional Catador. Jardim Gramacho, from 1996 until the Present Day.* I knew that the social and legal recognition of the work of catadores as a profession was one of the goals of the MNCR. In addition to gaining political and legal rights through the establishment of *catação* (collecting recyclables) as an official category of work, the professionalization of the work of catadores was seen as a way to overcome stigmas attached to this activity and enable catadores to construct a dignified, shared identity. But becoming a "professional" catador also meant adopting attitudes and behaviors that fit a particular, regimented conception of labor. It meant transforming in ways that would make catadores *recognizable* to the state and the wider society as "real" workers.

As I read through Valéria's discussion of the professionalization of the catador, I began to see the ongoing struggles that she had described in our conversation between Comlurb's project and the everyday practices of catadores as emerging from different construals of productive action. For Valéria, what catadores did on the dump was "work," and her goal was to make this work more professional—that is, to make it conform to a hegemonic model of work based on the capitalist wage-labor form. For catadores, their activities on the dump certainly involved work, but as I have argued, this work was understood more in the sense of a form of living, a means to sustain life in precarious conditions. Indeed, many of the qualities of work on the dump that made it a viable form of living for Rio's poor were precisely those that Comlurb, via the social workers, aimed to alter—the ability to come and go from the dump, to work at any hour of the day or night, to work as much or as little as needed, and to combine work with other dimensions of social life.

Comlurb's socio-environmental project unfolded as a process commonly understood as "formalization." As the dump and its contents were bounded, covered, contained, and fixed, so too was the work of catadores. Or at least this was the intent. Valéria's depiction of the "revolution" that ensued with the regulation of times for entry to the dump made it clear that the work of catadores retained a certain degree of plasticity, manifested here as the "refusal to submit to a model" (Malabou 2008: 6). However, to see *only* the work of catadores as plastic reinforces the notion of formalization—that Comlurb was the one acting in bringing order or giving form to a fluid, flexible world of work. Not only does such a framing present a problem in that the work of catadores already had its own order. It also loses the second meaning of plasticity—the capacity to give form and not just receive it—raising the question of how catadores molded the work of Comlurb. In other words, I began to think of plasticity in Jardim Gramacho as the interplay between forms—the interaction between Comlurb and catadores, or better yet, the interaction between the various actors in the recycling market, including the scrap dealers.

This interplay became especially clear as I sought to understand one specific policy that Comlurb sought to implement: the requirement that catadores wear work vests. I first became interested in the work vest because it appeared to be one of the few barriers to catadores returning to the dump. Guards stationed at the entrance to the dump would only permit catadores who were wearing one of these vests to pass. However, it soon became clear that the ways the work vest functioned in practice did not always conform to the official rule. As I tried to unravel this seeming contradiction, I also began to see the various uses of the work vest as threads through which it was possible to trace the relations between Comlurb, scrap dealers, and catadores. In what follows, I explore these interwoven threads.

THE SOCIAL LIFE OF VESTS

Eva and I were in the staging area of the rampão, chatting with one of her friends about the various prices of PET bottles, when I noticed a catador named Adriano pass by. That is, I thought it was Adriano. It had been nearly a month since I had last seen him—either on the dump or at ACAMJG, where he had long been a member. He was also wearing a fluorescent green work vest, the kind that scrapyards distributed to catadores. ACAMJG's vests were pumpkin orange.

It was definitely Adriano, though. When I called out to him, he turned around and came over to Eva and me, dropping a barrel of PET from his shoulder when he arrived.

Eva's friend wanted to know which scrap dealer Adriano was selling to and what price he was getting for the PET.

"You're selling to a scrapyard?" I asked, surprised. "What happened to your ACAMJG work vest?" Adriano explained that it had been several weeks since he stopped taking his material to ACAMJG, that he had become frustrated with its administration. This launched Eva and Adriano into a discussion about the internal politics of ACAMJG. I tried to follow their conversation, but I kept wondering about Adriano's seemingly quick acquisition of a new work vest. The policy of the work vest was something that had perplexed me for some time. Implemented by Comlurb in 2001, the work vest was a requirement to enter the dump during the day. Catadores who were registered by Comlurb in 1996 received an orange, numbered work vest directly from Comlurb. All catadores who came to Jardim Gramacho after 1996 (which, by 2001, totaled an additional 1,800) had to acquire a work vest from one of the scrapyards that were registered with Comlurb. These work vests were bright green and bore two numbers—one designating the registration number of the scrapyard and the other identifying the individual catador.[15] Though there were only forty-two scrapyards with registration numbers, I counted over a hundred located throughout the neighborhood when systematically collecting data to develop a map of Jardim Gramacho. If a catador managed to acquire a vest from one of the registered scrapyards, he was expected to sell his material exclusively to that dealer. Otherwise, the scrap dealer would repossess the vest. Yet none of this ever seemed to happen. Catadores certainly wore vests in accordance to the policy, but they rarely had any difficulty acquiring one. They also sold material to multiple scrap dealers—not necessarily the one who had furnished a vest—depending on their preferences and the dealer's price on a given day.

The conversation shifted back to the price of PET at various scrapyards, and I asked Adriano how he had acquired his vest.

"It was easy," he told me. "The vest is rented."

"Rented?"

"Yeah, rented from another catador." There were times, Adriano explained, when a catador did not need his vest, and he would lease it to another catador. Or sometimes a catador managed to collect multiple work vests from various scrap dealers and would rent out the extra ones. Adriano was paying R$80 a month for his vest. That price seemed high to me, but Adriano thought it was worth it. The registration number on the vest belonged to a scrap dealer who paid R$70 weekly to the guards stationed at the entrance to the dump so that they would allow his truck entry outside of Comlurb's officially scheduled times. The payment also ensured that the catadores who wore this dealer's vest were allowed to enter the dump on any truck at any time of the day. This made it easier, Adriano pointed out, to make and remake his own schedule as he pleased.

This was the first time I had heard of work vests being rented, though I knew that vests were sometimes sold. Fabiana, the owner of a scrapyard located along Monte Castelo between the dump and my house, told me about the sales during one of our chats. I had come to know Fabiana on my walks home. On particularly hot and muggy afternoons, she liked to stand outside her doorway to catch any breeze, and, after I had greeted her several times as I passed, we struck up a conversation. One of her drivers had seen me on the dump, she told me, and she was curious about what I was doing there. When I told her about my research, she began asking questions—about anthropology, my choice of study, the economic crisis, recycling in the United States—joking that she was interviewing me. Eventually, I asked Fabiana how she had become a scrap dealer. Was it difficult to enter this business?

Fabiana shook her head. It was not difficult—that is, if you have enough capital to start. I assumed that Fabiana was referring to capital needed to buy trucks, purchase or rent a plot of land for the scrapyard, and have a sufficient start-up fund to be able to begin buying material from catadores. I realized I had misunderstood her when Fabiana remarked that the going rate for a registration number had doubled in the last five years, since the time she and her husband had opened the yard. One of her friends had just bought a registration number for R$8,000, whereas it had only cost her R$4,000. The way it works, Fabiana explained, is that a scrap dealer who is closing goes to Comlurb and switches out their name with the name of the new dealer who wants to open a yard. They sell not only the registration number but the work vests as well—R$20 per vest, which amounts to a total of R$1,000 for a set of fifty. Fabiana pointed out that her friend must have needed at least R$9,000 of start-up capital to open her scrapyard. And if no scrapyard is closing at the moment? I asked. What does a new dealer do? Fabiana replied that sometimes dealers and even catadores purchase vests that belonged to catadores who died. Or alternatively, a dealer could buy material from catadores who work at night.

This is what Latinha did. The owner of a tiny plastics depot that doubled as the yard surrounding his three-room brick house, Latinha was one of the few dealers I met who bought only from catadores who collected at night. Latinha was also unusual in that he became a scrap dealer by way of first collecting as a catador. When working on the dump, he had noticed that catadores who collected plastics sometimes found a few stray aluminum cans and would set them aside to later exchange them at the base of the dump for a shower, a snack, or cigarettes. Latinha decided to purchase a small scale, the kind used for weighing fish in the market, and began to buy aluminum on top of the dump. Gradually, his business grew and he was eventually able to buy a run-down truck and to switch to buying plastics with the help of a larger scrapyard that loaned him the necessary funds. Latinha received his nickname (*latinha* meaning "small can") because of his beginnings as an aluminum buyer.

I found that Latinha's position as a scrap dealer with previous experience as a catador and with a marginalized status as nonregistered owner

FIGURE 4.2. Scrapyard. *Photo by the author.*

made his perspective on work vests particularly insightful. He often attended meetings that Comlurb held to discuss various issues with the scrap dealers even though, without a registration number, he was not officially invited. One afternoon, when I was visiting Latinha, he told me about a recent meeting that had troubled him to the point that he did not think he would ever go back. The issue that arose concerned workers' compensation, and at the center of the matter, for Latinha, was the work vest.

"I heard someone say—I won't say who. I'm not going to name names. But I heard people who represent Comlurb say that the catador does his job, Comlurb does its job, the scrap dealer does his job. That Comlurb does not have ties to the catador nor to the scrap dealer. That Comlurb won't pay workers' compensation to anyone [*não indeniza ninguém*]."

Latinha paused to scoot the plastic crate he was sitting on farther away from the side of the house so that his wife could pass with a basket of laundry. She began hanging clothes on lines that stretched between the house and the various piles of blue, green, clear, and mixed-colored plastic containers that filled the rest of the yard.

"There was one person in the meeting," Latinha continued, "who said the following: 'Look, there was a catador who wore one of my vests and never sold me anything. He had borrowed the work vest from another catador and went to collect with it on the dump. He arrived at the top and had an accident and died. Then his relatives took the work vest and came to me, wanting me to pay them workers' compensation. There should be a way of doing something to control this kind of thing.'"

I remembered that Valéria had mentioned that the work vest had introduced a whole new set of problems with catadores, chief among them workers' compensation. Comlurb registered the 960 catadores who were on the dump in 1996 and later provided them with numbered orange work vests as a way to control access to the dump. However, in doing so, Comlurb effectively legitimated the presence of catadores on the dump and therefore became legally responsible for them in the case of injury or death. Comlurb personnel only realized this retrospectively. Over time, as the numbers of catadores in Jardim Gramacho swelled, there were various "interests," as Valéria put it, to expand the allocation of work vests. Certainly, additional work vests would make things easier for catadores who had recently come to Jardim Gramacho and for the scrap dealers who stood to gain from an increased supply of material. But this could also benefit Comlurb. Catadores removed tons of material from the dump every day, thereby extending the life of the dump. The original forecast was that the dump would reach capacity and have to close by 1998; it remained open for another fourteen years. The only problem was that new work vests would make Comlurb responsible for more catadores. "So in order not to hurt other interests," Valéria had told me, "and also in order not to block access, things were worked out through other means." These "other means" involved producing more work vests but allocating them first to the scrap dealers, who would then distribute them to catadores. The idea was that these vests would tie catadores to the scrapyard, not to Comlurb.

Latinha told me that the refusal to take responsibility for catadores upset him. "I started thinking about what happens up there [on the dump]—that sometimes the bulldozer runs over someone, that there are people who have lost a leg, lost an arm, lost a life. And oftentimes it's the trailer of a truck that overturns and people end up waiting for the ambulance to come get them. Why haven't they created a first-responders unit there? Or why haven't the guards taken a first-aid course?"

Latinha proposed in the meeting that they solve the problem of compensation for catadores by starting a support fund with the bribes that scrap dealers paid to Comlurb—payments that Latinha said were never requested but given "freely" to guarantee a dealer's trouble-free access to the dump or access outside of certain specified hours.[16] Since this money was already collected, Latinha suggested, the fund would not constitute an additional expense for the dealers and could be used to pay for health care, medicines, funerals, or other aid in the case of a catador who was injured on the dump. I found it interesting that Latinha saw these payments not as personal incentives—that is, as gifts that were accepted in the individual interest of the receivers and therefore would be kept. Rather, these payments were part of the "system"—more like a tax that, while enabling rules to be bent, could be channeled toward the collective good.

"I spoke a lot at that meeting," Latinha sighed, "but it went in one ear and out the other." Compensation was not the only problem that Latinha saw with the complaint that the scrap dealer raised. By emphasizing that the catador who died never sold material to him, the dealer implied that the work vest constituted a contractual obligation. In other words, there was an understanding among scrap dealers that if a catador wore a dealer's work vest, then he was required to sell exclusively to that dealer.

"This is what happens," Latinha explained. "If a catador collects with a vest, the owner of the vest arrives on the dump. If a sack is worth fifteen, he will pay twelve. If the sack is worth ten, he wants to pay eight. Simply because he provided the means for the catador to work during the day. So he sees himself as the owner of the material, the owner of the work of that person, and in a way this becomes exploitation because he wants to earn more than what is normal to earn. Why? Because he provided the vest. So he feels like he has the right."

As I listened to Latinha's depiction of how the work vest began to function like an employment contract in the eyes of the dealers, I was reminded of one of the earliest studies of reclaimers, conducted by the anthropologist Chris Birkbeck in the late 1970s. In this study, Birkbeck (1978: 1174) argues that "garbage pickers" on a dump in Cali, Colombia, see themselves as self-employed but are actually "little more than casual industrial outworkers."[17] This argument is based on Birkbeck's observation that the pickers are dependent on the buyers of their material, and ultimately on the industrial market that controls the prices of recyclables. In the case of Jardim Gramacho, the work vest would seem only to reinforce this interpretation. By requiring that most catadores obtain a vest directly from a dealer, Comlurb effectively enabled dealers to treat catadores *as if* they were their own hired workers. Latinha even suggested that dealers saw themselves as purchasing the labor power of catadores through the work vest—that they were owners not just of the material but *of the work* of the catador.

Yet this kind of structuralist interpretation of the work vest left much to be explained. It failed to capture how vests were rented, borrowed, and otherwise exchanged. Furthermore, the rules surrounding the work vest never seemed to be upheld in practice. A catador who collected with a scrapyard's vest did not necessarily sell their material to that yard, as implied in the complaint about compensation in the meeting between Comlurb and the dealers. And then there were scrap dealers, like Latinha, who entered the dump and bought material from catadores even though they lacked a registration number and the accompanying work vests. The more I tried to establish or fix the meaning of the work vest, the more it continued to shift and transform.

TO FORM AND REFORM

On a quiet Sunday morning, I was awoken by the shouts of someone calling my name. I peeked my head out the window to find a catadora, Juliana, standing behind the gate that penned in my neighbor's chickens. I had invited Juliana for Sunday lunch, but did not expect her to come to my house so early. She told me not to worry—that she only wanted to let me know that she had come with Rose and Carlos and that the three of them would be outside at Deca's bar to keep cool on what was already a hot, muggy day. I should join them, she suggested, whenever I was ready.

Though I had not anticipated Juliana's early arrival, I was not surprised that she had brought Rose and Carlos. A tall, robust woman with a bellowing laugh, Juliana was one of the most gregarious and well-liked catadores on the dump, someone who was always surrounded by friends. I first met her at a barbecue that Glória suggested I host when I first moved into the house on Monte Castelo. Juliana introduced herself, admitting she did not know me but saying that she thought she heard the sounds of a party from the street and decided to invite herself. Rose later joked that Juliana could detect instinctively the location of a party from a hundred kilometers away. After getting to know Juliana at my barbecue, I frequently encountered her on the dump and became grateful for her regular offers to help load my burlap sacks on the truck at the end of a day of collecting. Juliana needed only to call out once for assistance for a half dozen catadores to drop their sacks or barrels immediately and come over to the truck to help us.

After purchasing the necessary groceries and preparing the lunch, I later joined Juliana, Rose, and Carlos at the bar. It was in the long hours of conversation on that Sunday, extending from the morning into the late afternoon, that I stopped thinking of the work vest as a rigid instrument of control and instead began seeing it as one of many plastic forms that were produced by and gave shape to economic life in Jardim Gramacho. The topic of the work vest arose when I asked Juliana when she had first started collecting on the dump. It was before the era of the work vest, she told me.

"At the time," Juliana explained, "we didn't have to wear a vest to enter the dump. When I first came here, you didn't need a vest."

"What happened?" I asked. "Where did the work vests come from?"

"From the scrapyards," Juliana replied.

Rose interrupted: "It was Comlurb, in order to reduce people's access to the dump."

"But it didn't reduce at all," Carlos pointed out. "It increased."

"Fine, but this was the *idea* at the beginning," Rose said.

"Except that it increased," Juliana repeated.

"Okay," Rose said. "Let's say I am a scrapyard owner. I get twenty vests. They give twenty vests to so-and-so. Those who don't have a vest lose the right to enter. In order to reduce access. But then everyone starting saying, 'No, no. . . .'"

"Let's say Carlos has a scrapyard and he gives you a work vest," I said, gesturing at Juliana.

"Uh huh," she replied.

"Do you have to sell to him?"

"You are obligated to sell to Carlos," Juliana answered.

"But the catador doesn't sell *only* to Carlos," Rose clarified. "He sells to another, sells to another." Juliana and Carlos broke out into laughter.

"But . . . ," I began to say.

"Really! Really!" Rose insisted. "And when Carlos arrives hunting for you, you hide inside a burlap sack."

"Inside a plastic barrel," Juliana added. "In the middle of the garbage."

"Then Carlos will ask around," Rose continued. "'Did you see Kathleen?' And people will say, 'No, I didn't see her.' He'll ask around: 'What happened to so-and-so?' Even more so if you are well known. But if you are not well known"—Rose brushed her hands together in a gesture much like a shrug.

"And when you *are* known," Juliana said, "then everyone hides you."

"You get it?" Rose asked.

"Yeah, all right," I said, a hint of uncertainty in my voice.

"But the *idea* behind the work vest was to reduce how many catadores are on the dump," Rose restated, as if this would help me understand.

"But this didn't work," Juliana interjected.

"It didn't work," Rose said.

"Because you are able to enter the dump without a vest?" I asked.

"No," Carlos replied. "It's that one catador comes down from the dump and gives his work vest to another."

"When the work vest was yellow, we matched the color," Juliana told me. "We'd go buy cloth."

"And then go to the seamstress," Rose continued, "and the seamstress would make an identical vest."

"With the number." Juliana said.

"So, there was like. . . ." Rose paused. "For example, 38–01. There were—"

"Five 38–01!" Rose and Jo exclaimed in unison.

"Sometimes there were ten!" Carlos added.

Rose offered an example: "Let's say I make three additional vests. I give one to you, one to my cousin, another to my neighbor."

"One meter of cloth made two vests. You'd buy one meter of cloth to make two vests," Juliana said.

"And then," Rose continued, "you'd all work it out: 'Okay, so-and-so, I am going to go up in this truck. You wait until three trucks pass by, then you go up.'"

"Ah, so the guards wouldn't notice?" I asked.

"Yeah," Rose replied. "And in this way, they lost the control."

As I listened to Juliana, Rose, and Carlos describe all the discrepancies between the "idea" or model of the work vest and the ways they reworked it in practice, I noticed that all their tactics relied on cooperation and a high degree of organized action. Catadores did not just hide from buyers "hunting" them on the dump; they hid each other. They made exact copies of vests, circulated them among relatives, neighbors, and friends, and arranged it so that two people with the same vest did not enter the dump simultaneously. To do this successfully required a network, planning, timing, and coordination. In short, it required an order, albeit one that was constantly transforming. Juliana, Rose, and Carlos's explanations of the work vest began to illuminate how the interaction of catadores with Comlurb's "formalization" program, of which the work vest was a part, was itself formalizing. It was an example of plasticity, not informality—of changing form, not its absence.

Catadores were not the only ones to alter the work vest. As our conversation continued, Juliana explained that Comlurb eventually replaced the yellow work vests with green ones, making the duplicates that catadores had created obsolete and requiring that they reproduce the vests all over again. A few months earlier, Comlurb had also installed a new system involving magnetic cards that scrap dealers were supposed to swipe when entering the dump.

"But no one swipes the card at the entrance anymore," Rose said.

"First, there were the badges," Carlos recalled. "You had to show a badge, to go up [to the dump]."

"Oh, yeah," Juliana said. "I remember. Those badges from the scrapyards. There was that."

"You had to get a badge from a scrapyard," Rose explained. "And with that, you could go up. But that ended. It didn't work."

"It didn't work out," Juliana added.

"Recently they put in the magnetic card system."

"And that also didn't work out." Juliana said.

"That also didn't work?" I asked.

"It didn't last three months," Rose told me. "Nothing lasts more than two months."

I vaguely remembered that Valéria had mentioned the badges and the more recent card machine. She had told me that the badges predated the work vests but did not directly explain why they had been eliminated, only commenting that the fluorescent work vests (unlike the badges) made catadores identifiable from a distance. The purpose of the card machine, she explained, was to quantify and record the number of people who entered the dump. Each scrapyard had a card with a bar code that they had to swipe in a machine for each catador who entered the dump. At the end of the day, the data from the machine was downloaded. The problem, Valéria told me, was that the data from the machine never corresponded with the numbers on the work vests of catadores or with the number of catadores who were known to be collecting on the dump. "We have tried innumerable actions," she said. "An entry schedule, badges, work vests, magnetic cards.

For everything that we create, someone creates a subcontrol, a counter-control to avoid, to jump over the order."

When I later placed Valéria's account side-by-side with that of Rose, Carlos, and Juliana, I found it difficult to say who was responding to whom. It is usually common in the social sciences to see the disciplinary or regulatory action by those in power as coming first, followed by acts of resistance or opposition by those subject to the rule. This approach is the way that Valéria narrates Comlurb's actions: a regulation is enacted to bring order to the dump and then a "counter-control" arises to circumvent the regulation. But this presupposes that catadores (as well as the scrap dealers) had not already constructed their own order on the dump, an order that existed prior to Comlurb's socio-environmental project. One could just as easily describe Comlurb's actions as a response to the presence of catadores on the dump, as various attempts to adapt the operations and management of the dump to contend with the labor of catadores and dealers. Comlurb's actions, furthermore, were a series of ongoing adjustments—one (failed) action replaced with another. All these adjustments necessitated a degree of malleability comparable to that seen in the various efforts of catadores to duplicate, share, and circulate vests while avoiding ties to a single dealer.

There is a tendency to see form or order as coming from the outside or imposed from above. Referred to as hylomorphism, this view has been critiqued in metaphysical philosophy for its assumption that matter is formless, that it lacks structure in itself. In his elaboration of a counterargument to hylomorphism, for instance, Levi Bryant (2012) offers as a metaphor the example of clay and a wooden mold. The clay is usually seen as lacking any form until it is placed into the mold and pressed into shape. But as Bryant points out, there are various ways that the clay already had its own form, such as in its structure of interlocking molecules or in its asymmetrical shape as a lump of earth. "What takes place between the wooden form and the clay," Bryant writes, "is not an imposition of form on the *formless*, but an encounter *between* structured matters that generates a new structure as a result of the interplay of *both* of the matters interacting with one another."[18] This interaction echoes Malabou's conceptualization of plasticity as not simply matter being shaped by form but as the "relationship between form and form" (Malabou and Vahanian 2008: 4).

Bryant seeks to debunk hylomorphism not only to make an argument about the ontology of matter, but more importantly to show how this line of thinking creeps into the human sciences in dangerous ways. For example, theories of the state that trace back to Thomas Hobbes's (1994) notion that human life without government would exist in a chaotic and warring "state of nature" posit that the state and its top-down institutions are necessary to create and maintain social order. Similarly, the structuralist approaches to society that dominated anthropology in the mid-twentieth century conceptualized culture as a system of hidden rules that are external to and imposed upon individual behavior. Of course, both of these positions have since been challenged in the social sciences.[19] The ethnographic study of war has shown that even in the midst of violent conflict when governmental institutions, regulations, and infrastructure break down, what results is not absolute chaos but instead the creative and collective effort of "ordinary" people remaking their social worlds (see Nordstrom 1997). Proponents of practice theory could likewise be read as offering critiques of the hylomorphic logic in structuralist theories by arguing that what appear as regulated patterns in society are not the result of adherence to rules. Rather, these "structures" are imminent in and generated by human dispositions and actions that, in turn, are shaped by social relations and material conditions (Bourdieu 1977). Nonetheless, while certain theories of the state and society have moved away from the implication that form is external to and transcendent of the "matter" that it shapes, the hylomorphic assumption continues to find its way into social science's conception of the economy—tethered as it is to the binary of formality and informality.

What would it mean to see the work vest not as a regulatory mechanism of Comlurb, a labor contract insisted upon by scrap dealers, or an object of resistance for catadores, but rather as what emerges out of the interplay of all these forms? First and foremost, it would require abandoning the notion of the informal once and for all. Every dimension of the social life of work vests involved some kind of form or structure, whether that be the policies implemented by Comlurb, the scrap dealers' methods of allocating vests, or the network and timed coordination of catadores who shared vests. The story of the work vest is a story of improvisation, spontaneity, transience, modification, and flux—all of which are qualities usually associated with informality. But such qualities involve *changing* form, not the lack of form. Over the course of many years, the work vest remained, just not in the way anyone had intended.

The story of the work vest is thus a story of plasticity, the capacity to receive form *and to give form*. It is important to emphasize the latter dimension of plasticity because livelihoods like that of catadores often appear as undoing form, not creating it. For all the efforts on the part of Comlurb to order the dump into a proper "work environment" with policies, uniforms, schedules, and controlled access, the adaptive actions of catadores and scrap dealers made it such that the dump never functioned as planned. However, the actions of everyone involved with the vests did not dissolve form but rather altered it in ways that are not recognized (or desired) as order from the perspective of bourgeois principles of regularity, predictability, and efficiency.[20] In other words, to view the modifications of the work vest as leading to a lack of form is to impose only one form in the world. This precludes the possibility of alternatives to hegemonic order and denies certain actors (in this case, those living and working in conditions of urban poverty) the creative potential to give form to their worlds. It is no accident that wageless workers and favela residents are continually perceived as objects of formalization.

Plasticity, which is fundamentally relational, draws attention to the everyday encounters that make up economic life. In doing so, it allows us to rethink economy not as a "real" structure in the world that can be measured and modeled (even if imperfectly) but as the effects of all this interplay between different forms of living. In her discussion of metaphors used to characterize the brain, Malabou (2008) notes that we continue to perceive the brain as being like a mechanical, programming computer, even though extensive scientific research has shown the brain's supple, adaptive, and improvisational capacities. Analogously, the idea of the economy as a self-contained structure or sphere remains hegemonic in the social sciences and in popular understanding despite all the ethnographic evidence to the contrary. The plasticity of the brain, Malabou argues, "is in fact so familiar to us that we do not even see it" (9). The same could be said for plastic economy.

5 · From Refuse to Revolution

The headquarters of the Association of Catadores (ACAMJG)[1] is located at the end of a long dirt drive. Nothing surrounds it—no other buildings, no houses, just tall grasses and a thicket of overgrown bushes. Sunk low on the left-hand side of the drive is a one-story, cinder-block building. But what immediately draws my gaze is the towering open-air shed in front of me. Its structure is simple: red metal beams support a corrugated roof over a concrete patio. At least, I think it is concrete. It is hard to see the floor of the shed because it is filled with an assortment of stuffed burlap sacks, blocks of baled recyclables lined up in rows, and several raised tables like the kind used in scrapyards to sort different types of plastic containers. All is quiet with the exception of a steady, grinding noise that seems to be coming from the far left side of the patio. As I come a bit closer, I spot its source: a vertical baler. Someone—I cannot quite tell who it is, with their back to me—is stuffing black plastic bags into the baler, continuing to press the bags into place as the heavy metal plate slowly descends. It makes me nervous to see a hand so close to the descending plate. I want to keep watching, but I look away.

"You arrived!"

I turn back toward the cinder-block building to find Gordinho, one of the founding members of ACAMJG, calling out to me, arms wide, ready for an embrace. It has been over a year since I last saw Gordinho. He has put on some weight but little else has changed—he still has a beard, those shoulder-length dreadlocks, and a wide smile that always puts me at ease. I think back to the day during my last visit in January 2007 when Gordinho and several other members of ACAMJG showed me the empty plot of land where we are now standing. They were still working to pressure the city of Duque de Caxias to donate the land so that they could build a recycling center, or what they simply called the *Polo*. They had already acquired funding to construct the building and shed from part of a fine that Brazil's state-run oil company, Petrobras, had to pay toward environmental projects in the area as a result of a 1.3-million-liter oil spill in Guanabara Bay in early 2000. Though at the time ACAMJG's project seemed within reach, I had not imagined the immense structures before me now. How could I? When I first started coming to Jardim Gramacho in 2005, ACAMJG consisted of little more than a group of friends who held weekly meetings at a local bar.

Gordinho grabs my two bags despite my protestations and ushers me into the office—a room with three mismatched desks, a computer, and a few shelves stacked with an assortment of pamphlets, loose papers, and books. As I enter, I am pleased to see Glória and her brother Tião, two other founding members of ACAMJG and the first two catadores to befriend me when I arrived in Jardim Gramacho several years before. Glória is hunched over one of the desks, punching a calculator with one hand and recording its results on some kind of form with the other. A lit cigarette is perched precariously on the edge of her desk. Tião is at the computer, his back to me, typing what looks like an email in a Hotmail account. I wonder where everyone else is. The sole sounds of tapping calculator and computer keys makes the room seem strangely quiet.

I hesitate to interrupt them, but when Glória looks up and sees me, she lets out a shriek and jumps up to give me a hug. We spend the rest of the afternoon catching up, with Glória filling me in on ACAMJG's latest developments.

The Polo, she tells me, was inaugurated nearly four months ago. The building consists of an office, a kitchen, and men's and women's bathrooms complete with showers. The shed is where recyclables are sorted, baled, weighed, and either loaded directly onto buyers' trucks or emptied into large, detachable dump truck containers that buyers pick up whenever they are full. There is a baler—I noticed that when I arrived, I tell Glória. They also bought two trucks. One is for *coleta seletiva*, meaning that it is used for retrieving preseparated recyclables from businesses willing to donate their discarded paper, cardboard, and other material. The other truck picks up recyclables from ACAMJG members who collect on the dump. Bypassing the intermediary scrap dealers in Jardim Gramacho, ACAMJG sells everyone's material jointly to recycling companies for nearly double the normal price. Each person is then paid in accordance with the amount of material (measured in weight) that they contribute to ACAMJG's total sale. Glória is especially proud that ACAMJG is self-sufficient. She deducts 15 percent of each member's earnings to pay a full-time truck driver, a security guard who stays at the Polo overnight (a measure taken after repeated instances of theft), diesel for the trucks, utility bills, and any needed maintenance.

"Impressive!" I reply when Glória finishes her account. The Polo's infrastructure, organization, and built environment seem surreal, the actualization of what only existed as a concept the last time I was here. Glória suggests I take another look around. There are only a handful of remaining payment sheets to calculate, and once she finishes we can go back to her house to rest.

I leave Glória to her work and step outside. I am struck again by how quiet it is. Tião and Gordinho left at some point when I was talking with Glória. Whoever had been operating the baler must have gone as well. I notice a couple of women sweeping up debris surrounding one of the raised tables, but I do not know them. It is now late in the afternoon on a Friday, and Glória mentioned that most people leave the Polo once they receive their weekly payment. But still, I keep searching for a familiar face. Perhaps Zumbi or Funabem? Both of them were founding members of ACAMJG and played central roles in the political mobilization of catadores on the dump. Why haven't I seen them? Where are they?

The sun has sunk low in the sky, and with a light breeze I feel chilled. I go back inside to grab a sweater from my bag, and Glória tells me she is ready to go. As we make our way to her house, I ask about Zumbi and Funabem. They both left ACAMJG, she tells me. Zumbi could not adapt to the Polo's rules. In Funabem's case, there was a dispute over a container of cardboard. I am shocked but do not push the matter further. Her short replies suggest she does not want to talk about it—at least not now.

IN HIS ETHNOGRAPHY of popular politics in Mexico City, Matthew Gutmann (2002: 51) draws attention to several blind spots in social theories of agency and the poor: "Those of us who write books and articles for a living often champion the poor when they stand up to unfair government authorities and win. We are often at a loss when they stand up and lose. Or when they do not even stand up." This chapter tells the story of ACAMJG, a political association and worker cooperative that emerged from almost nothing to become one of the most important organizations in Brazil's National Movement of Catadores (MNCR) and the most economically viable cooperative of catadores in the metropolitan area of Rio de Janeiro. As such, it is the story of the poor who stand up and win. However, in tracing ACAMJG's history, I am primarily concerned with understanding why Zumbi, Funabem, and many other members left the association over time, and furthermore why most catadores on the dump never chose to participate in ACAMJG at all. Such departures or absences are often perceived as a nonstory—a failure, negativity, or lack of something (agency, political consciousness, will). As a result, successful political organizations, projects, or movements like ACAMJG exert a powerful pull on scholars interested in positive social change.[2] Left aside are the poor who seemingly, in Gutmann's framing, stand up and lose or never stand up.

There are risks, argues Elizabeth Povinelli (2011), in celebrating those (rare) alternative social projects that manage to exist and endure. The poor who do not engage in such projects are not only left in the "analytical shadows," but also implicitly blamed for their failure to keep struggling for something more (33). She suggests that by focusing on the success stories and being disinterested in those who lack them, even the most critical social scholarship can end up buttressing late liberal logics that see the difference between those who endure and those who do not as a difference of will. In what follows, I suggest that this difference is itself a question of what constitutes a political project. That is, I argue that what is often interpreted as a nonproject, inaction, or a failure to endure is instead a form of politics that is not recognized as such. Over two thousand catadores collected on the dump, and yet there were at most fifty active members of

ACAMJG, some of whom eventually left—even despite the ability to sell recyclables at higher prices through the cooperative. To disregard the experiences of these catadores is to miss the values, social relations, and modes of inhabiting the world that catadores let go of or took up in their departures from ACAMJG. It is also to miss a variety of other, less visible political projects that emerged through the very labor of catadores on the dump.

I begin with the story of ACAMJG as it evolved from informal gatherings of a small group of catadores into an organized political struggle and worker cooperative. Since its founding in 2005, its members have participated in congresses, meetings, and marches of national and transnational social movements, including the National Movement of Catadores (MNCR) in Brazil, the national Forum on Garbage and Citizenship (Fórum Lixo e Cidadania), and the World Social Forum. Though some of its leaders have continued to be involved in political mobilization, the inauguration of the Polo in 2007 shifted ACAMJG's primary focus to the day-to-day operations of the recycling cooperative. ACAMJG's development over time shows how an increasing concern for viability comes into tension with counter-hegemonic aims and practices. Such tensions complicate both celebratory and pessimistic views of the potential for organizing among wageless workers in what is often described as a crisis of labor movements.[3]

I then turn to stories of departure—to the experiences of catadores who joined ACAMJG and then gradually left the cooperative to go back to collecting on their own. Some of these, like Zumbi and Funabem, were founding members and key leaders in the organization's history. Others were members who joined ACAMJG after the Polo was built. I interpret their withdrawal from ACAMJG not as a negative moment of giving up or giving out, but rather as an affirmative act of returning to the dump. Here again, I conceptualize the return to the dump less as a return to a place than as a return to a particular form of living. With the exception of some of the leaders, most members of ACAMJG continued to collect on the dump, only bringing their material to the Polo to sort and sell. Yet participating in ACAMJG required adapting to certain habits, rules, and institutional structures that many members perceived as antithetical to their valued rhythms of life. To withdraw from ACAMJG was thus to turn back to the modes of being made possible through the conditions of labor on the dump. I also consider how the break with ACAMJG enabled more autonomous forms of cooperative labor to emerge.

"The revolution starts in the bar!" Glória laughed when she said this on the first night we ever went out for drinks together. I hardly knew her at the time, and only later realized that she was chiding me for having spent most of the evening asking questions about politics in Jardim Gramacho—not necessarily the most relaxing topic of conversation for a Friday night. In the case of ACAMJG, however, Glória's statement proved literally true. The first meetings of the association in 2004, when ACAMJG existed only as an idea, took place in an outdoor bar in Jardim Gramacho, called the Botequim do Gringo.

"I wanted nothing to do with it," Glória later told me. "Tião kept begging me to go to their meetings and I finally caved in and went. A group of people gathered, everyone said what they wanted, what they hoped for, what was important. There wasn't any kind of focus at all. No objective. It was like group therapy. One person would say something, another person would swear. Every week, we would go to the bar, drink beer, talk about our dreams. Our meetings were basically weekly group therapy sessions."

When I arrived in Jardim Gramacho in 2005, a group of twelve catadores were still meeting regularly at the Botequim do Gringo. ACAMJG was not yet an officially registered association, and the group still did not have a place that they could use as an office. However, they had begun to publicize ACAMJG to other catadores through a monthly newsletter called *O Mensajeiro da Verdade*, "The Messenger of Truth," named after the Brazilian rap singer and social activist MV Bill (the initials MV in his name stand for "Mensajeiro da Verdade"). The newsletter's first issue focused on the group's primary incentive for mobilization at the time: an announcement by the city of Rio de Janeiro that the dump had reached its capacity and that it would close by the end of the year. The front cover of the newsletter read:

> If you carefully analyze what you are about to read, you will see that, I am here to speak about a matter that interests everyone (Regardless of whether they are Men or Women, old hands or novices). Registered or not, we are catadores, this is a reality, the landfill is about to close, but, if we work together, we can organize, together we will create a center to struggle for our rights as catadores. . . . Therefore I count on the collaboration of everyone in order to unite together in this struggle, more organized. Thank You and Look for the Next Communication.[4]

Subsequent issues of *Mensajeiro da Verdade* included accounts of the experiences and activities of catadores in other cities, information on health and safety issues, general news items excerpted from other media sources, short quotes (*mensagens*) for reflection, and an announcement regarding the time and location of ACAMJG's weekly meetings. Parts of the newsletter were often composed on the dump and only later pieced together in a collage that was photocopied and taken back to the dump to distribute. On several occasions, I saw Zumbi and Funabem huddled together on overturned buckets during a break from collecting, one of them dictating a few sentences of copy while the other wrote them down.

ACAMJG's origins as an informal group of friends—most of whom had collected together since their early adolescence and were now in their late twenties and thirties—distinguished it from the cooperative Coopergramacho. The waste management company Comlurb initiated Coopergramacho as part of its effort to remove catadores from the dump in the late 1990s. A sociologist from the State University of Rio de Janeiro (UERJ) coordinated the formation of the cooperative, and after its founding Coopergramacho continued to be administered by a manager and social worker paid by Comlurb. The lack of a shared history of struggle, coupled with the continuing role that outside managers played in the organization's daily operations, made Coopergramacho seem more like a social assistance project than a worker-run cooperative.

In contrast, ACAMJG charted its own course in its early organizing days, due in part to a lack of resources. When the group eventually found a house in Jardim Gramacho that could serve as an office, they were unable to find a funder that could help pay for the rent. At the time, IBASE (Brazilian Institute for Social and Economic Analysis), a progressive institution that has served as one of the primary organizers of the World Social Forum, was conducting a "social diagnostic" in Jardim Gramacho. "We asked IBASE for funding for the office," Glória recalled, "but they wouldn't give money to ACAMJG. No one ever gave us money." The twelve active members ended up dividing the rent among themselves, each paying a part from their own earnings each month. They did the same with the costs of registering ACAMJG. A pro-bono lawyer helped them complete the necessary paperwork for legalization, but the members wrote their own statutes and each contributed a portion of the registration fee, which totaled several hundred reals.

Nonetheless, despite ACAMJG's relative independence, it emerged in part out of experiences that Tião and Glória had had as a result of their

FIGURE 5.1. ACAMJG headquarters in the early days. *Photo by the author.*

earlier membership in Coopergramacho. Tião, for example, received in-vitations to participate in NGO projects and events when he served as vice president of Coopergramacho in the early 2000s. One of these involved a "Young Black Leaders" group organized by a Dutch-funded NGO called IBISS (Brazilian Institute for Innovations in Social Health), which seeks to reduce violence in Rio's favelas by educating youth to become effective, positive leaders in their communities. As part of this program, Tião took courses on Brazilian history, political organizing, social movements, and civil rights, and met over forty other youths from favelas throughout Rio's metropolitan area. Furthermore, in 2003, the MNCR organized the first meeting of catadores from across Latin America. The MNCR's branch in the state of Rio de Janeiro sent out invitations to the leaders of all coopera-tives of catadores in the state. Tião responded and received MNCR funding to travel to Caxias do Sul in the far south of Brazil to attend the meeting, where he met hundreds of catadores from across Brazil as well as from Chile, Argentina, and Uruguay. Many of Tião's ideas involving *coleta sele-*

tiva, the formation of a network of cooperatives, and the creation of the Polo emerged from conversations he had with other catadores at these meetings.

Though such experiences beyond the dump and beyond Jardim Gramacho were significant, Tião and Glória often pointed to their family as the first and most important influence in their political formation. As a shipyard worker, their father was heavily involved in his trade union, and dinner conversations during their childhood often included lively political debates. When their father lost his job during the debt crisis of the 1980s, their mother began going to the dump in search of food. Those were difficult times, Glória told me, with eight children in the family to feed. But her mother fought hard. She started collecting a variety of recyclable materials: plastic bags, newspaper, cardboard, scrap metal, and hard plastics. On Saturdays and Sundays, when there was no school, Glória accompanied her parents and older brothers to the dump to help sort different types of recyclables that they had collected over the course of the week. She was eleven years old at the time. (Tião, the youngest of the family, was only seven and stayed behind.) During these early years on the dump, Glória witnessed several forms of collective action, often initiated by her mother, that Glória saw as some of the most influential moments of her life. One of these was a three-week "strike" during a sharp reduction in the price of recyclables, when catadores jointly refused to sell their materials. "That strike," Glória told me, "was the moment when I really began to think about how catadores could be more organized. I began to see what is obvious: that when you are together, you have more strength."

As ACAMJG developed, its relationship to outside influences became fraught. Though the organizations that sought to partner with ACAMJG were diverse—ranging from an internationally funded foundation (IBISS), to a local research and activist organization promoting radical democracy (IBASE), to a program in corporate social responsibility (the organization Donate Your Trash in partnership with Institute Coca-Cola Brazil)— members of ACAMJG usually identified them by the broad category of "the NGOs" and critiqued them for similar reasons. I often heard complaints that NGOs were only interested in producing reports on poverty "as if we don't already know what it is to be poor," or that they were only interested in "meetings upon meetings." Most of these meetings were held in downtown Rio, which required at least two bus fares for catadores to attend. The location also placed catadores in social spaces where they felt they did not belong. After returning, along with Tião and Zumbi, from a meeting with the State Forum on Garbage and Citizenship that was held in the Bank of Brazil Cultural Center, Nilson was fuming. "We had to go all the way downtown to sit in a meeting on a Friday afternoon in some chic lounge." It was not only the class disparities but the invisible racial boundaries that Nilson found disturbing. "Do you know what it is like," he asked, "to walk through a part of Rio that is hostile to or at least suspicious of three black men?"

By far, though, most of ACAMJG's critiques of NGOS centered on the question of empowerment. Tensions emerged over unequal access to resources, claims to knowledge and expertise, and the power to define social and political goals. Glória often commented that NGOS[5] did not like ACAMJG, that the association had a reputation for being "unmanageable." The problem, she claimed, was that NGOS sought to involve ACAMJG in projects on *their* terms, not the association's. This became clear on a busy and tiring afternoon, after a representative from the NGO Donate Your Trash stopped by the Polo to solicit the participation of ACAMJG in a Coca-Cola–funded project. The project revolved around a course on environmentalism for catadores. Glória was livid: "They like to use people. They sustain misery. If they really wanted to solve the problem of the catador, they would buy trucks, build sheds, donate a mill to grind plastics. They want ACAMJG's participation. And they aren't going to get it, because I'm going to put my foot down." "Which project is this one?" I asked.

> Empowerment [*capacitação*]. "Ah, we are going to make you environmental agents!" But who the hell wants to be an environmental agent? What's an environmental agent, really? Because I don't know how they define what it means to be an environmental agent. So I said, "Man [*cara*], let me explain something to you. People work with recycling for financial reasons. Because, frankly, if you ask the members of ACAMJG if they want to protect the Pantanal—none of them are ever going to travel there. Fuck the tourist who has money to spend to go to the Pantanal. You want to protect the environment? Great! But here everyone is working for an income."

Glória picked up her glass of coffee as if to take a sip, but then set it back down and continued.

> "Ah, but Glória, [the woman replied] you are saying this without even having seen the course we would offer." And I said, "I've already

seen plenty of courses just like yours. It's not going to work. And there's no use signing up the members, because no one here likes to waste time. They work up on the dump and the day that they are here at the Polo, they aren't going to spend eight hours sitting around listening to you speak. They are going to be here sorting material, so that they can receive their payment on Friday. Because that's what they live off of, they don't live off of the environment. Now, if you really want to help ACAMJG, buy a mill. I sell plastic at R$0.40. If I had a washer and dryer to clean the plastic, I could sell at R$0.50. And if you gave me a mill to grind the plastic, I could sell at R$3.50 a kilo. If you really want us to rise in the chain of production, since you talk so much about the chain of production in your courses, then start supplying us with equipment. ACAMJG's problem, my dear, isn't empowerment. It's equipment."

Glória consistently refused to adopt the subject position of the "needy poor" that would define her life and social world by what they lacked. Implicit in the framing of many NGO projects she encountered was a view of the poor as void of knowledge, expertise, and even social, political, or environmental consciousness. For Glória, the reluctance on the part of NGOs to invest in equipment and infrastructure for ACAMJG stemmed not from a lack of funds but rather from a failure to see catadores as *already* capable—as having a deep history of struggle, multiple forms of knowledge, and the necessary experience to author their own projects.

Over time, I began to see the fraught relationship between ACAMJG and NGOs as inseparable from other tensions in ACAMJG's development that arose from processes of institutionalization. Some of these tensions emerged early on, when ACAMJG was still holding its meetings in the bar. Glória was one of the first to push the group to adopt more systematic and methodical practices, beginning with the practice of taking meeting notes. She initially brought up the issue with Tião:

I told Tião: "Look, our objective is cool [*legal*], our history is cool. But if we don't focus on something, we won't go anywhere with this. It won't turn into anything. You need rules. Even to have a meeting, you need rules." All of the ideas and objectives of ACAMJG—the idea to divide money by percentage, even the idea of the Polo itself—came out of these meetings. But no one was taking notes. No one was writing anything down. So I bought a notebook and said to Tião:

"Hey, I am going to write the meeting minutes, because if we have minutes, we will be able to refer back to them the next day." He said, "Ah, Glória, you are being very bureaucratic," and I said, "I am not bureaucratic. I just think things have to be a certain way to work."

Not long after Glória began recording the meeting minutes, Nilson proposed the idea of creating membership forms that catadores could fill out and sign. Glória developed the form, which included information on place of birth, residence, educational background, racial identity, age, family (both parents and children), marital status, monthly income, number of dependents supported by this income, and length of time on the dump. They made photocopies of the forms, found a tent, borrowed a table and chairs from a friend who owned a bar by the entrance to the dump, and hung a sign by the table reading: "Join the association that is being founded to fight for your rights. Sign up here."

Glória later told me that the membership sign-up was the "first action" taken by ACAMJG. "It caught everyone's attention," she recalled. "No one knew why they were filling out a form, but everyone did it anyway. They thought it was cool to stop at the tent and fill out a form. The guards noticed. Comlurb saw the entire action, because a huge line formed that went far beyond the entrance to the landfill. That's really when the history of ACAMJG began, when ACAMJG finally caught everyone's attention."

I was not expecting ACAMJG's first public act to involve the filling out of forms. It seemed to reduce the emphasis on "dreams" in those early meetings at the bar to a standardized procedure and instrument of regulation. I thought of Robert Michels's (1968) classic thesis on the "iron law of oligarchy" that argued over a century ago that as organizations evolve, they become increasingly bureaucratic in the Weberian sense—emphasizing rules and formal processes, adopting pragmatic goals intended to strengthen the organization, and developing an internal division of labor that eventually leads to a hierarchical structure.[6] For Michels, this process was inevitable regardless of the democratic or counter-hegemonic values of the organization, emerging from the problem of administration, or what he described as the "tactical and technical necessities" of organization (365). Yet what seemed to matter to Glória was not the form itself but the *action* involved in creating a public enrollment in ACAMJG. "It caught everyone's attention," she repeated. By emulating what were seen as "official" or professional practices, the membership forms provided a means to become visible not only to catadores but also to entities like Comlurb on which ACAMJG would later make claims. In other words, to see meeting minutes and membership forms as constituting an inevitable process of bureaucratization is to miss how such practices were primarily about a political struggle for recognition.

"They did not have much faith in us in the beginning," Glória told me. "They didn't think we would last two months." At the time, Glória was talking about ACAMJG's efforts to attract the attention of Comlurb, and I assumed that the "they" referred to Comlurb personnel. I later considered whether the "they" referred to a much broader category of persons—the NGO workers who approached catadores as objects of assistance, the local politicians who initially refused to meet with members of ACAMJG, and perhaps even other catadores who had long grown wary of any organization claiming to work on their behalf. Tião sometimes confessed, late in the evening after a tiring day or disappointing setback, that he felt that no one believed in him, that no one believed that ACAMJG would "work out" (*dar certo*). He knew how easy it was to dismiss the capabilities of a group made up of poor, black youth who had been collecting on a garbage dump since their early adolescence.

Over time, however, ACAMJG's struggle for recognition produced tensions over the type of collectivity that the group would become. Actions like the membership forms, which were intended to emulate the practices of the very institutions from which ACAMJG sought credibility, risked producing a modus operandi that Tião thought was too "bureaucratic." This tension between the form that ACAMJG took at the bar and the form it took as it sought to become a publicly recognized organization was not easily resolved. As we will see in what follows, it foreshadowed conflicts that arose following the establishment of the Polo—conflicts that ultimately led to departures from ACAMJG.[7]

THE SPIRIT OF COOPERATIVISM

By the time I returned to Jardim Gramacho in 2008, the Polo had been built and was fully functioning as a cooperative with a few dozen active members. At first only the twelve catadores who had founded ACAMJG brought their material to the Polo, and there was little differentiation among the roles of the members. The group agreed that once a week each member would volunteer a day of work for the Polo—whether helping load and unload the truck, cleaning the shed, or sorting and baling the recyclables. They called this arrangement the "duty system" (*sistema de plantão*), and years later pointed to this volunteer labor as an example of the unity that defined their early days. Eventually, after multiple meetings with Comlurb's social worker, ACAMJG convinced Comlurb to grant them fifty work vests that they could give to new members, making it easier for catadores who were collecting with a vest from a scrapyard to bring their material to the Polo instead. ACAMJG's numbers grew, and as they did the quantity of material that ACAMJG sold increased, along with its income. ACAMJG was able to pay the salary of a full-time truck driver and security guard. Glória began working full-time at the Polo's office, making arrangements with buyers and overseeing the Polo's day-to-day operations. Tião, ACAMJG's president, was now free enough to spend most of his time outside Jardim Gramacho, building relationships with public officials and NGOs.

ACAMJG's development, however, was not a linear process. In the first year after the Polo was established, numerous conflicts arose. One of the most contentious of these involved the establishment of weekly pay cycles. Because ACAMJG only accumulated enough material to sell a full container once a week, and because it did not have extensive funds in reserve, catadores at the Polo received payments every Friday instead of every day that they worked. "There were all kinds of fights over this," Glória told me. "Some people left. Those who stayed got used to it." Other conflicts arose over behaviors that Glória described as the "culture of catadores, a culture of not having rules." Some of the new rules at the Polo included the requirement to wear ACAMJG uniforms while sorting or baling material, the prohibition on bringing *podrão* (food, clothing, or any other reusable items found on the dump) to the Polo, the requirement to schedule in advance when ACAMJG's truck would pick up collected material on the dump, a policy of discounting material that was deemed "dirty" (soaked or muddied to increase its weight), the prohibition on selling any part of one's material to a scrapyard (*desviar material*), and the prohibition on drug use at the Polo. On this last point, Glória emphasized that members could do what they wanted at home, just not at the Polo. "I wanted it to be a respectable business," she said.

These early conflicts illuminate how the regimentation of labor involves disciplinary practices oriented toward the production of new subjectivities. Work, as Foucault (2008: 223) has argued, is about economic *conduct*. The various rules that Glória sought to implement at the Polo were not only aimed at making the Polo more efficient and productive, but were also oriented toward reshaping the habits of ACAMJG members as a means to becoming a "respectable business." These new habits emphasized the value of rationalized budgeting, orderly appearance, structured time use, professionalization, and the distinction between work and nonwork spheres of life. "Every single change generated a protest," Glória told me, "but they eventually grew accustomed to another kind of deal. Those who are still at ACAMJG have now changed. Others call them"—Glória laughed—"they call them VIP catadores."

It might seem odd that Glória was the one to spearhead efforts to produce new worker subjectivities at the Polo, given her own history and self-identification as a catadora. However, these efforts always stemmed from her goal of making ACAMJG viable and self-sufficient. In a neoliberal context in which social activism has increasingly taken the form of the professional NGO, this meant adopting market-based rationalities of instrumentalism, efficacy, and accountability so as to be visible to the state and to potential funders.[8] Furthermore, recognizing that even as a worker cooperative ACAMJG was forced to operate within competitive markets in the recycling industry, Glória thought ACAMJG's success was only possible by emulating the practices of modern capitalist enterprises—acting like, as she put it, "a respectable business." Her efforts echoed challenges that scholars have described in the vast literature on worker cooperatives that arose in recuperated factories in Argentina following the country's 2001 economic crisis. Over time, many of these worker-run factories struggled to reconcile their social values of cooperative, human-centered production with the constant pressures for profitability (Bryer 2010; Vieta 2010).

I did not realize the extent to which Glória felt similar tensions until a Sunday afternoon visit, late in my fieldwork. I had come over to Glória's house to hand wash laundry with her while sharing a few cold beers and blasting old *pagode* songs on her stereo—a weekly ritual from the days when I had lived with her and her daughter. However, on this particular Sunday afternoon, Glória seemed tired. She had suggested that we leave a pile of clothes soaking in the tank and sit down at the kitchen table to talk. I waited as Glória lit a cigarette, using the spark of an empty green lighter to ignite a burner on her gas stove. As she tapped her lit cigarette absentmindedly on the rim of an empty glass, she told me that she had not slept, that it had been a hard week at the Polo. When I asked what had happened, she began to talk about *vales*, advances that members of ACAMJG sometimes requested when they needed money before they received their weekly payment. She explained:

> Catadores are always asking me for *vales*. And you know, it's not always easy saying no, no, no. Someone comes to me and says, "Glória, can't you give me a *vale* of R$50? My propane just ran out." They were just paid and will be paid again on Friday. I know I can't keep giving out *vales*. ACAMJG can't function like that. And so, I say no.
>
> But then at night, I am trying to sleep and I can't. Others, like Tião—if someone asks him for something, he always tells them to go ask me. I am the one who has to say no. I don't blame him. I know how hard it is. It's hard because the other person's story is your story, too. It is the same story. The story of the poor: Father drank. Mother was beaten. This person was raped. That person was robbed. You know that the person's life hasn't been easy because your life wasn't easy either. You know that everyone is suffering in Jardim Gramacho. We all grew up together. But Tião sends them to me. And I have to say no, no, no. I have to, because otherwise things wouldn't work. It is a business that has to run [*tem que funcionar*]. I am tired of being the one who always has to say no. I am the one who does not sleep at night.

Glória's account of her insomnia points to conflicts, similar to those experienced by catadores when they acquire wage-labor jobs, between the conditions of production in neoliberal capitalism and the precarious conditions of life in Rio's periphery. How does one reconcile the demand for solvency with an empty container of cooking gas? Members' protests about new rules often stemmed from such conflicts. ACAMJG's schedule of weekly payments made it difficult to respond to immediate, unexpected expenses. The prohibition on selling a sack or two to a scrapyard on the side (*desviar material*) precluded another way that members had found to address this issue—when they needed a little cash, they would simply sell a portion of their material to a scrap dealer on the spot. Furthermore, ACAMJG's requirement to schedule pick-ups of material in advance and the prohibition on certain kinds of activities at the Polo prevented more fluid work–life rhythms. For many catadores, to collect as a part of ACAMJG began to feel like any other wage-labor job.

As a result, members of ACAMJG began to leave. "The ones who withdrew from ACAMJG," Glória told me, "withdrew because they were not able to live under rules. They were not able to adapt, and I'm telling you, there are some who will never be able to adapt." I was struck by how her language echoed the way I heard catadores speak of their orientation to the dump as a process of "adapting" to a different life rhythm that prevented them from readapting to the conditions of wage labor. Joining ACAMJG meant becoming a different worker-subject, one made to conform to bourgeois values of industriousness, punctuality, obedience, and propriety. Far from an expression of political apathy, the departures of catadores from ACAMJG could thus be read as a class critique. Moreover, becoming an active member of ACAMJG also meant leaving the dump—not as a place but as a form of living. Though members of ACAMJG continued to collect on the dump, the requirement to adapt to institutional norms involved breaking with modes of being that the dump enabled and signified.

Funabem made this explicit. He did not tell me that he withdrew from ACAMJG, but rather that he returned to the dump: "[ACAMJG] was carrying on, carrying on, and I started to see things I didn't like. I thought to myself, 'the dump still continues on there. Why am I enduring this here?' So, what did I do? I returned to the dump." For Funabem, to return to the dump also meant returning to the work of mobilization. Once the Polo was built and began to occupy ACAMJG's time and energy, the group abandoned many of its wider organizing efforts. ACAMJG stopped producing their newsletter, the *Mensajeiro da Verdade*. Funabem complained that ACAMJG leaders only came to the dump to take back the work vests of members who had stopped bringing their material to the Polo. Zumbi pointed out that the leadership no longer held meetings or gave interviews on top of the dump. "They don't come up here. The focus is on the outside and that's not my style," Zumbi remarked.

Several months after my conversation with Funabem about his departure from ACAMJG, I ran into him on a street corner near the base of the dump. He was speaking intently with a young man whom I did not know and was showing him some kind of document. They both were still wearing their "dump clothes" (*roupa da rampa*)—worn boots, knee-high socks, stained shorts, and the requisite work vest. As I passed by, Funabem waved me over and explained that they were in the process of starting a new cooperative, Cooperjardim, and that they were having a meeting that night to sign the cooperative's statutes. The Community Forum was not available, so they were planning on meeting at a church in Chatuba, an area on the other side of the entrance to the dump. He asked if I could come to the meeting to help record the official minutes of the meeting.

When I arrived at the church that evening, it was dark and no one was there. As I waited for Funabem to arrive, I noticed a group gathering outside a house next door, and when I inquired, they explained that the church had a scheduled *culto* in an hour, and so they decided to move the meeting. It was a one-room house, and though there were only seven people inside when I arrived, it was already crowded. I realized the limited space must have been the reason so many people were still lingering outside. Funabem explained the process: each of the twenty-three founding members had to initial each page and sign their full name on the last page in the same order. This immediately caused confusion, as not everyone had arrived on time, and those who were present had to keep circulating in and out of the one-room house. To further complicate matters, Funabem understood from the lawyer assisting them that they had to do the same process with a second copy of the constitution, that there could not be any mistakes, and that they were not allowed to use liquid paper. Several people present did not know how to write, an issue that was resolved by having someone who was literate take the hand of someone who was not and carefully move the hand through the motions of signing their name on the page. The process went slowly. About half-way through the names, someone made a mistake in the order on six of the pages that were initialized, and so they started over with a new copy. When another mistake was made two hours later, Funabem decided to try again another day—with a different strategy. He planned to seek out each founding member, either at their home or on the dump, one by one, to have them sign the two copies of the statute. Over the next several weeks, I periodically saw Funabem in the staging area on the dump, carrying a pen and folder and asking around for whoever was the next catador who needed to sign the statute.

Funabem's perseverance in creating a new cooperative defied the expectation of disillusionment, or what Elizabeth Povinelli (2011) describes as exhaustion—the slow wearing out of counter-hegemonic projects.[9] What was it that kept Funabem seeking what he often referred to as a "society"? I wondered the same for Zumbi. Long after he withdrew from ACAMJG, he remained active in the MNCR, attending marches and congresses and encouraging other catadores to participate. When I asked Funabem what had

FIGURE 5.2. Signing the statute door-to-door. *Photo by the author.*

led him to mount another cooperative, he replied that it was the garbage: "The garbage is there. And so I got this idea: why don't I call others? I am still here inside [meaning, on the dump]. Why don't I call the people here to walk on our own? And so I got this idea of creating another cooperative. Yes, I left ACAMJG, but I did not lose the spirit of cooperativism."

It was as if, for Funabem, the potentiality of the garbage—of what could be found and transformed—made alternatives possible. Yet it was certainly not the case that everyone who left ACAMJG and returned to the dump initiated a new cooperative or even joined Funabem in his efforts. There was also the vast majority of catadores to consider—those who never sought out ACAMJG. I had long understood their nonparticipation as a politics of detachment from institutional forms of power, but Funabem pushed me further. His emphasis on the way the dump could give life to other projects made me rethink various forms of collective practice that I had come to know on the dump but whose political significance, until that point, I had easily missed.

One of these forms of collective practice that I had long taken for granted was the *truta*. I first learned about this practice through Eva, when she suggested the night we met that we collect jointly on the dump or as she put it, *"de truta."* I did not quite understand what she meant by "truta," thinking only that she wanted us to go together to the dump. The first few times I accompanied her, I continued to collect cardboard on my own while she focused mainly on plastics. Finally, at the end of a day when neither of us had managed to collect much of anything, Eva suggested again that we collect *de truta*. This time I asked her what she meant by the term. To collect with a truta (*catar de truta*), she explained, meant that two or more catadores reclaimed and sold recyclables together, dividing their earnings equally. In some cases, trutas created a division of labor. One catador might pull bags from unloading waste and toss them to another catador, who would then sort through the bag to retrieve any recyclables. Or one catador might focus solely on collecting in the unloading zone, while the other carried the material to the staging area and unloaded it. It was more common, however, for trutas to perform the same tasks, working side-by-side. She suggested that this was what we should do, offering to teach me the necessary skills to collect plastics (how to identify the material through bags and distinguish different types). Such an arrangement, Eva thought, would help motivate us both.

I initially translated the word *truta*, as it was used on the dump, as "partner." Yet over time, I noticed that catadores never used the word *partner* in standard Portuguese (*parceiro*) to refer to this relationship. In its more general usage, the word *truta* is a form of Brazilian slang that originated in prisons to indicate an accomplice or cell mate, and later expanded to refer to a friend or companion, especially someone with a shared ideology or someone who "has your back" (*guarda-costas*). It also commonly appears as a synonym for "black brother" (*mano*) in politically conscious Brazilian rap and hip-hop.[10] In this sense, to collect as a truta meant more than being a work partner. It suggested a relationship of alliance, affinity, collusion, and solidarity. Its meaning on the dump might be better translated as "comrade."

This became clear as I learned to work closely with Eva and as I began to meet other trutas on the dump. Trutas often colluded with each other to hide from scrap dealers who were seeking to take back a work vest. They provided mutual assistance with carrying heavy sacks or loading a truck. And they protected each other from injury—a truta, for example, was another set of eyes to watch out for an oncoming bulldozer. Furthermore, the primary emphasis in collecting with a truta was not greater efficiency or yields. Rarely did catadores earn more money by collecting together than they did individually; in fact, most catadores who worked with a truta told me that they actually made less. Rather, a truta was expected to raise another's spirits—to encourage, uplift, and enliven (*animar*) the other person. Collecting on the dump can be overwhelming and heavy work, I was often told. A truta made the work lighter. When I asked Brenda, who had long worked with her friend Jaqueline, why she preferred this arrangement, she told me that a truta provided motivation. "When you are tired, sitting on your burlap sacks, your truta will say: 'Come on! Let's collect a little more!'" She added that there were also more possibilities for fun. I thought of Eva's penchant for jokes and pranks while collecting, and of the times she had insisted that I join her in singing a song as we made our way to or from the dump.

The kind of collective labor involved in the truta emerged in other social formations on the dump, particularly in camps of catadores that were nicknamed the "unions" (*sindicatos*). Most of these camps were created by long-term moradores, like Vidal and Fabinho, for whom the dump was a place where life with addiction could be lived. But I also encountered camps consisting of catadores who lived far from Jardim Gramacho and preferred to stay on the dump in between their trips home. These catadores tended to be relatively new to the dump—they had not yet found a shack to rent at the base of the dump, and furthermore found the camaraderie of the "unions" helpful in learning to collect as a novice catador. This was the case for Rafael, a young catador from the favela Antares in Santa Cruz, the furthest western neighborhood of Rio de Janeiro. At the time Rafael came to Jardim Gramacho, he was living with his aunt in Santa Cruz (he had lost both his parents to alcoholism during his youth), and she was pressuring him to find a job to help with the household expenses. "I looked at the newspaper every day but there was nothing," Rafael told me. After several months, Rafael ran into an old friend from the orphanage he had lived in during a period of his childhood, who suggested that Rafael accompany him to Jardim Gramacho. When they arrived on the dump, Rafael was surprised to find several acquaintances he knew from Santa Cruz. They invited him to join a union they had formed with other catadores. The group constructed tents out of burlap sacks and stakes they retrieved from the garbage. They also reclaimed rugs to line the ground and blankets for sleeping. Meals and the provisioning of supplies were organized collectively. Rafael explained how the union worked:

> Each person had their own specialty. My specialty was to fetch water down below. I would come back up with twenty two-liter bottles of water for a total of forty liters of water. We always made soup because we needed to eat something heavy. One person would go get those twenty-liter metal cans, cut them, wash them. Another person cut vegetables, another cut meats, another prepared the pasta. When it was time to eat, everyone gathered and ate together. That is, everyone who was part of the group. To participate in the group, you had to do a task. We would say, "Go fetch water. When you finish, wash the dishes." But there wasn't any leader. Everyone gave instructions [*mandava*]. If I thought something wasn't right, I could say so.

When I asked Rafael how the union handled conflicts, he replied that most conflicts involved the failure of a catador to complete his assigned task. In such cases, the person was not allowed to partake in that particular meal but was welcome to join again so long as they resumed contributing to the collective labor of the camp. Inclusion in the group was thus determined not by fixed membership but by one's participation. As a result, unions were ephemeral—any particular one might form, disband, or shift in composition over time. Yet unions were also a constant, always present in some form on the dump. Indeed, it was this nonstructured structure that ensured the continued existence of the union as a collaborative social project, enabling catadores to come and go from a group depending on the often turbulent conditions of their lives.

While collectivities on the dump were often transient, there were also moments in which they spurred large-scale collective action. The oral history of Jardim Gramacho was filled with stories of struggle (*luta*) that veteran catadores often began with phrases like "it was the time of the donkey without a tail [*burrinho sem rabo*]"—a reference to an era when catadores transported their material off the dump, not on trucks, but in large carts that they pulled by hand. I was struck when I first heard these stories by how different the dump seemed from the place I had come to know. In the early years of the dump, fires erupted spontaneously from the untrapped methane gas. Instead of two locations (*rampinha* and *rampão*) where trucks unloaded waste, there were three, and they had different names: the Vulture (*Urubu*), the Scobs (*Serragem*), and the Private (*Particular*). And then there was the "organization of leaders." To collect during the day, a catador had to agree to work three days of the week for one of the "leaders" who controlled access to the dump. These leaders were the first to arrive on the dump in Jardim Gramacho—coming from the dump that Comlurb closed in Caju, a neighborhood in the North Zone of Rio de Janeiro. The organization of leaders, however, did not last. When I asked Glória's mother, Dona Gerusa, if she could take me through the history of the dump, she began with a story of the leaders and of a collective struggle to break their power.

"It was a difficult time," Dona Gerusa told me. The prices of recyclable materials had dropped. What she earned in the four days she worked for herself was no longer enough to cover her household expenses. She began to question the system of leaders, and so did some of the other women who worked alongside her (women worked only for women leaders and men worked only for men). Dona Gerusa thought it was unjust, and everyone agreed: "Yeah, that's right. We are no longer going to collect for anyone. Everyone who wants should be able to work for themselves." They refused to hand over the material to the leader and were subsequently barred from the dump—even at night. They spent three months "going hungry." To cut costs, some of the women moved in with Dona Gerusa, sleeping in a three-room house with eight children. Eventually, one of the women, Dona Marlene (who became Glória's godmother), suggested that they go speak to the bandidos about their situation. She had lived the longest in Jardim Gramacho and knew one of the bandidos well enough to approach him. He sided with the women, telling them that they could return to the dump and "resolve the situation however they liked." When they arrived back on the dump, the leaders left them alone and they began collecting for themselves, every day of the week. Dona Gerusa added that it did not take long for other catadores to notice, and soon no one wanted to collect for anyone else. The history of the leadership came to an end.

Throughout the history of the dump, catadores united for struggles much as Dona Gerusa's group of women had, only to seemingly demobilize once the struggle had passed. There was the "strike" that Glória mentioned as a formative moment in her politicization. Scrap dealers sought to take advantage of the confusion in prices caused by the hyperinflation in Brazil's shortlived currency, the *cruzeiro real*, and the gradual introduction of the new currency, the *real*, in 1994. The prices of recyclables plummeted in Jardim Gramacho. In response, catadores held a meeting on the dump and jointly agreed not to sell any material until the prices improved. The staging area became dense with overflowing burlap sacks. No one went hungry, Glória said, because they all collected podrão, as if the dump as a whole had become one big "union." In contrast, the scrapyards were silent and empty. Without any incoming material from the dump, there was nothing to sort and bale, nothing to sell to the recycled packaging and plastics factories outside Jardim Gramacho. Finally, after three weeks, the scrap dealers acquiesced and began raising their prices.

Catadores also told stories of struggles with the management of the dump. One of these occurred during the period when Comlurb hired the engineering company Queiroz Galvão to coordinate the social and environmental remediation of the dump. One of the engineers redesigned the spatial layout of the dump such that the staging area where catadores placed their sacks was located a full kilometer from the zone where trucks unloaded. After three days of long treks between the garbage and their sacks, a catador fell and was run over by one of the bulldozers. Convinced that their friend had fallen from excessive fatigue, a group of catadores descended to the offices at the base of the dump and demanded a meeting with the engineer. When the engineer continued to insist that the location of the staging area remain the same, the group returned to the top of the dump and organized a blockade of arriving trucks. As catadores gathered, they began shouting that not a single truck would unload on the dump so long as the staging area remained far from the garbage. They insisted that if a truck unloaded, they would set it on fire.

In his work on urban politics, Asef Bayat (2010) describes the collective action of the self-employed and other "marginals" as episodic. These actors mobilize only when a particular gain that they have achieved is threatened—as in the case of a police crackdown on street vendors who have long operated, albeit illegally, in a particular city square. Bayat argues that once the threat has passed, this more contentious form of politics tends to fade away and the participants resume their individual, everyday efforts to survive and improve their lot in a process he calls "the quiet encroachment of the ordinary" (56). While the everyday struggles of the marginalized can gradually achieve gains at the expense of the powerful (for example, tapping electric lines, squatting on public land, or selling pirated goods), Bayat sees their actions as constituting a "social nonmovement."

It is a *non*movement, he explains, because the actors are atomized and lack a shared political ideology, leadership, and organization.

Moments of mobilization on the dump could certainly be described, following Bayat, as episodic. Yet it would be difficult to see the "ordinary" life of the dump—that stretch of time between instances of contentious collective action—as a world of fragmented, atomized, individual actions. Social projects like the trutas and "unions," however tenuous, were part of the fabric of everyday life on the dump, and when needed, they helped produce the relationships and collectivities that sustained more overt struggles. Furthermore, the ephemerality of the overt struggles of catadores did not result from a lack of leadership and organizational power, or to be more precise, from a lack of the *capacity* for political organization. If this were the case, the story of ACAMJG and its achievements would never have been possible. Rather, the collective struggles of catadores did not last— did not become a social structure or institution that endured—because this was never their aim. When catadores returned to the "ordinary" after a moment of mobilized action or when some returned to the dump after departing ACAMJG, they came back to other ways to labor in common. They returned to other forms of living.

Conclusion · The Garbage Never Ends

On June 3, 2012, the Metropolitan Landfill of Jardim Gramacho closed. In a ceremony marking the end of the dump's thirty-four years, the mayor of Rio de Janeiro, Eduardo Paes, climbed atop the bulldozer that dispersed the final pile of garbage ever to be unloaded on the dump. The mayor then returned to the entrance to the dump, pulled a metal chain across the drive, and snapped it shut with a padlock. Behind him, a bright blue sign with white lettering read: THE METROPOLITAN LANDFILL OF GRAMACHO—CLOSED—DUMPING GARBAGE IN THIS LOCALE IS PROHIBITED.

I had anticipated this moment for years, but like most catadores, I found it difficult to believe that it would actually occur. In Comlurb's original projection, it was predicted that the dump would reach capacity and have to close by the year 1998. The date of closure was later revised to 2000 and then 2004. By the time I began conducting research in Jardim Gramacho in 2005, discussions about the dump's imminent closure were common. Yet when year after year passed and nothing happened, many catadores began to doubt the claims. Some catadores told me that there was no way to know when the dump would close, that it would occur without warning from one day to the next. Others dismissed the possibility of closure entirely.

Pointing to the line of semitrailers arriving on the dump to discard their loads of waste, one catador asserted that the dump would not close simply because "the garbage never ends."

But it seemed as if the garbage did end. When I returned to Jardim Gramacho a month after the dump closed, I was struck by the silence. The main street, Monte Castelo, was eerily still. For-rent signs hung on the gates of yards and warehouses that had once been filled with an array of bottles, cans, containers, crushed boxes, loose paper, and plastic bags. I stopped at Deca's bar and was surprised to find that no customers were there. Only two rotisserie chickens were being kept warm in the case at the edge of the bar, and they looked as if they had been there for days. Deca had never been especially talkative, but when I asked him how he was doing, he only replied, "Things got worse," pointing his right thumb down. As we shared a couple beers, Deca told me that he thought of quitting, that it had been too many years and he was tired. Perhaps, he wondered aloud, he could rent out the bar.

The entrance to the dump was just as calm—no semitrailers, no compactor trucks, no flatbed trucks, no catadores with barrels and sacks sitting on the curb waiting for rides or piling onto the back of a truck that had stopped. There were no pigs roaming at the edge of the road, no stands selling gloves and bottles of iced water, no signs for showers for R$1, no music blaring from nearby bodegas. On the left-hand side of the entrance, I noted the new biogas plant that was built to convert the methane produced by the dump's decomposing garbage into energy. Part of this project was inaugurated when I was still in Jardim Gramacho in August 2009, but the plant seemed much larger than I remembered. Protective plastic covered part of the metal piping, as if the plant were a commodity so shiny and new that it had not yet been removed from its packaging.

When I finally arrived at the Polo, I found that it had also expanded, though its new building lay empty. Glória's aunt gave me a tour of the larger headquarters. Our voices echoed as we passed through the building's open lobby, which was bare except for a built-in, L-shaped counter like the kind commonly used for an office reception desk. To the right was a large kitchen with a counter and two tables that occupied hardly half of the space. Along the back side of the building, there were four other rooms. The first contained an assortment of desks and computers, some of which lacked monitors or otherwise looked obsolete. Glória's aunt told me that at one point there had been computer classes but not anymore. There was no one to fill them. The next room was Tião's office, neatly arranged with another L-shaped desk and a table with various trophies and awards that Tião had won for his leadership of ACAMJG. Here the furniture appeared new and maintained, but I learned that Tião had not been there for a month. Glória's aunt did not bother to open the door to the next room. It was supposed to be divided from the fourth and final room and turned into a library, but that never happened. The last room seemed to be functioning as a storage closet stuffed with old furniture. It looked like part of the Polo's original office building. I had found the old kitchen in the original building, for example, to be filled with a mishmash of tires, broken rolling chairs, smashed desks, paint cans. The combination of emptiness and clutter made me feel as though I had arrived too late—that I had come to a site that was now abandoned.

Beneath the shed, a group of five women and three men were sorting plastic containers. Glória told me that there was not enough material at the moment to sustain more catadores. Now that the dump had closed, they depended entirely on donations from businesses that set aside their recyclable material for the cooperative. She was hopeful, though, that their project would grow and that they would eventually be able to acquire a steady source of separated recyclables that would support a network of four cooperatives, all based at the Polo. That was the plan. There was a meeting scheduled for later in the week with Duque de Caxias's secretary of the environment to discuss the necessary license to begin construction of additional sheds. I wondered if there would be enough catadores to fill the four cooperatives, since it seemed that nearly everyone had left ACAMJG when the dump closed. Glória replied that catadores had not left but rather were "waiting" (*aguardando*)—waiting in the sense of being expectant, keeping watch, or holding out for what might come.

I walked around the shed, passing the press and the truck, and then back to the office buildings. These structures stood like frames around a void. At least for the moment, there was nothing to fill them—no garbage, little material, few catadores. Glória told me that one of the odd things about the dump's closure was that the Association of Catadores of the Metropolitan Landfill of Jardim Gramacho was an association of something that no longer exists.

A DUMP WEARING MAKEUP

Later in the evening, while discussing plans for my stay, Glória suggested that I visit a CTR. The acronym for Center for the Treatment of Solid Waste (Central de Tratamento de Resíduos), the CTR is the new model of waste disposal in Rio de Janeiro. In the years leading up to the closure of the dump in Jardim Gramacho, several CTRs were inaugurated throughout the metropolitan area, the largest in the municipality of Seropédica on the northwestern edge of Rio de Janeiro. Glória suggested instead that we go to the CTR in Nova Iguaçu. It was much closer, it predated the CTR in Seropédica, and most importantly, her ex-boyfriend, Paulo, worked as an operator at the CTR in Nova Iguaçu and would be able to give us a tour.

The following Saturday, Glória and I meet Paulo at the entrance to the CTR and the three of us pile into his car. I am surprised to find that our first stop is a greenhouse. Paulo explains that they grow various bushes and trees in the greenhouse and then plant them in finished areas of the landfill. The area closest to the entrance seems to be one of these finished parts—a terraced hillside covered in bright green grass and small plants that are evenly spaced. The hillside could easily be mistaken for a garden, with the exception of white boxes that I notice jutting out of each level. Beneath the white boxes are instruments, Paulo tells us. They measure the pressure between layers to detect any forward or sideways sliding. We stop next at the main office, and I ask to use the bathroom. As I am washing my hands, I notice a bright sign with a reminder to turn off the faucet and not waste water. Outside the office door, there are a series of recycling bins that are colorful and clearly marked with diagrams for glass, plastic, paper, and aluminum. Pointing to the bins, Glória remarks that they have made everything "cute" (*bonitinho*). But in reality, beneath the surface, the place is still a garbage dump. "It's simply a dump wearing makeup" (*um lixão com maquiagem*), she says.

We get back in the car and drive up to the top of the landfill, stopping at a spot where garbage is being unloaded. When I get out of the car, I feel as though I am standing on the edge of a vast mine—the small mountainside in front of me has been cut away. Paulo explains that they first create a valley and then fill it with garbage deposited in five-meter-high layers, each covered with an impermeable liner and dirt. When they reach the top, they finish with two additional layers and then plant grass and the trees that we saw in the greenhouse. We move on to another area where small compactor trucks are unloading garbage, reminding me of the rampinha in Jardim Gramacho. Glória makes the same observation and begins to point out crushed PET bottles that are scattered throughout a layer of waste that the bulldozer has just dispersed. She asks for my camera, telling me she wants to take photos of all the recyclables being dumped on the landfill so that she can send them to the press and prove that the CTR is burying recyclable material that is supposed to be recovered. Paulo warns Glória to keep her distance from the bulldozer, but she keeps walking over the layer of garbage, picking up bottles as she goes. "The only time I knew for certain that material was being recovered," Glória says, "was when I was in Jardim Gramacho and I saw all those sacks full of material, all the traffic of flatbed trucks carrying material out of the dump." Paulo ignores Glória's comments but allows her to take photos for a while before suggesting that we go visit the treatment plant.

On our tour of the treatment plant, we pass three large ponds filled with leachate—the toxic liquid exuded by decomposing waste. At the point where the leachate enters the plant, the smell is more acrid and overpowering than anything I experienced while on top of the dump in Jardim Gramacho. Inside the plant, a young operator shows us a computer that is continually taking readings of each tank in the three-part system. He explains that the first part is biological, with bacteria eating the organic matter contained in the leachate. The second part is chemical, using a process called "ultrafiltration" to control the ammonia levels of the liquid. As far as I can understand, the final stage seems to be mostly about making the liquid clearer through a process called "nanofiltration." I ask the operator what they do with the toxic material that is filtered out of the liquid, and he responds that it becomes a substance resembling a paste that is deposited back onto the landfill.

"But isn't the toxicity concentrated?" Glória asks. "Doesn't [the paste] contaminate the landfill even further?"

The operator responds that the toxins have been neutralized. And furthermore, any leachate that the paste might release on the landfill would make its way back to the plant and be treated. I can tell that Glória is not convinced by the answer. Her eyebrows are furrowed in an expression similar to the one I often witnessed over the years whenever Glória interacted with NGO workers or other officials she found condescending. I thought that Glória was going to drop the subject, but she insists that the explanation does not make any sense, that it seems as though they are simply treating the leachate, putting the leachate (minus the water) back on the landfill, and then treating the leachate again.

"After passing through the system, the leachate is 90 percent less toxic than when it entered," the operator tells us.

"Well, really, how toxic is it?" Glória replied. "If the leachate began very toxic and you remove 90 percent of the toxicity, the remaining 10 percent would be super toxic."

The operator continues to answer our questions with patience, responding that the levels of the remaining 10 percent are within the margins allowed by the INEA (Instituto Estadual do Ambiente, the state of Rio de Janeiro's environmental agency) and can be discharged into the nearby river. He tells us that though the treated liquid is not potable, once it is mixed with the river water and then treated, it is potable. I am unfamiliar with the area and ask the name of the river. At this point, Paulo intervenes and explains that the river is just a little creek (*riozinho*) and that they mostly use the treated water to wash their vehicles and wet the roads to keep down the dust. As we leave the plant, Glória turns to me and says, "I doubt that they wash their cars with that water. It would strip a car's paint."

On the bus ride home, Glória tells me that she does not see how the CTR has improved anything. All the CTR does is hide garbage, make things look beautiful, and use technology so that it seems good for the environment, she argues. It is all about appearance. In her mind, what the CTR does is take away what was "ugly" about Jardim Gramacho: the image of people in the midst of garbage. That is what is disturbing (*incomoda*), Glória insists, and it's the reason catadores are removed when the dumps close and the CTRs open. It's not because others care about the well-being of catadores. It's not because they care about the environment.

As I listen to Glória's reflections, I think back to the greenhouse, the grass-covered terraces, the brightly colored recycling bins. "A dump wearing makeup"—that is how Glória described it. She tells me about a time that catadores held a demonstration outside the new CTR in Seropédica: "When we saw the CTR, everyone cried. It looked so much like Jardim Gramacho but there were no people, there was no movement. The technology took away the human side."

SAUDADES

Eva was working as a street cleaner for the local waste disposal company, Locanty. When I had called her to let her know I was in town, she had told me that she would meet me at the Polo the next day. It was a Thursday. Eva was regularly scheduled to work Monday through Saturday, and when I found this out, I suggested that she should not have missed work for our visit. I could easily have come to her home in Ibarié on Sunday, her day off. But Eva quickly dismissed my concerns. She told me that she had already missed three days of work in the past month and would not care all that much if she were fired. Her boss was arrogant and she felt humiliated at her job. It was difficult to be paid only once a month. She ended up borrowing money between paychecks and amassing too much debt. And she found her job to be dull and tiresome (*aborrecido*).

When Eva arrived at the Polo, she suggested we go for a walk along the route we had always taken to the dump. As we crossed the shed and left from the rear of the Polo, we ran into a catadora who had worked for over thirty years on the dump and was known among catadores as Irmã, meaning "sister." Irmã became famous when she was chosen as a subject of one of the photographs taken by the Brazilian artist Vik Muniz as part of his series *Pictures of Garbage*, a project that was documented in the 2010 Oscar-nominated film *Waste Land*. I was surprised to see Irmã at the Polo. She had never been an active member of ACAMJG, spending most of her time cooking meals that she sold to other catadores on the dump. When I asked how she was doing, she replied that she had been traveling with journalists, that she had given many lectures, that she had flown on a plane several times, all in connection with her role in Muniz's project. "But it ended," she said. At first I was not sure if she was referring to the travel or the dump, but as she continued I realized that she meant both. "After thirty years," she told Eva and me, "from one day to the next, for it to end, ah no. . . ."

Irmã was now sorting material for ACAMJG, but she thought she might do something else next week. She didn't know. Eva suggested that she take a break and join us on our walk to the dump, but Irmã declined. She did not go near the entrance to the dump anymore. It was too hard. She used to like to hang out near the entrance, to watch people coming and going. And then there were all the meals she had made on the dump. Smiling, she told me that she even remembered the first meal she had made for me.

After parting from Irmã, Eva and I made our way along the dirt road that led to a newer part of Jardim Gramacho that was called the *favelinha* (little favela). I suggested that we pay a visit at the house of Dona Heloísa, an older woman who had stopped working on the dump years ago due to various chronic health problems. Eva and I had come to know her well from all the times we had passed by her house on our way to and from the dump. When we arrived, no one was home, but a neighbor informed us that she was taking care of her grandchildren at her daughter's house and showed us the way. When Dona Heloísa came to the door, she expressed surprise at seeing the two of us, apologizing for the mess as she invited us in for coffee. Eva and I took a seat on a bed that was kitty-corner from another bed where her two grandchildren were napping in what was a cramped one-room shack. A soap opera played on a small television set placed precariously on top of a chest of drawers.

Things had been difficult, Dona Heloísa told us. The police presence in Jardim Gramacho had increased. The other day, on her way home with her daughter, around lunchtime, a police car had nearly run them over. And then there was the problem of so many people without work. For now, most ex-catadores were living off of the R$14,000 (roughly US$7,000) that they had received, but she was not sure what they would do when that money was gone.

The R$14,000 referred to the compensation (*indenização*) that catadores received when the dump in Jardim Gramacho closed. This money came from the capitalization of the dump's biogas. In 2006, when Comlurb and the company Novo Gramacho were in the process of negotiating a contract to capture and burn the dump's biogas for energy production, ACAMJG pressured Comlurb to include a clause in the contract that would allocate a portion of the earnings to a fund for catadores. The fund was originally intended to support recycling cooperatives and other initiatives to help catadores transition to finding new employment in the wake of the dump's closure. However, prior to the dump's closure, ACAMJG helped organize an open assembly of over a thousand catadores to decide jointly how best to distribute the funds. The assembly resulted in an agreement that the fund would be divided evenly among all catadores currently collecting on the dump, as well as elderly catadores who were now retired and could show that they had once worked on the dump. This registration process resulted in a total of 1,709 catadores. A new Center for Social Assistance (CRAS) opened in April 2012 in Jardim Gramacho to help both with this registration process and with the acquisition of government documents that were necessary for catadores to open bank accounts to receive the funds.

Eva told Dona Heloísa that the R$14,000 did not last, but that she had spent the money only on household goods: a chest of drawers, a coffee pot, microwave, washing machine, television. She gave the rest to her son, who had not been registered and was not eligible to receive the compensation. Dona Heloísa replied that she knew some people who bought a furnished shack with the money and that spending on the household was the best use of the funds. At least those who had bought their own shack no longer needed to worry about rent—only food.

Dona Heloísa needed to finish washing the lunch dishes before her grandchildren woke up from their naps. We followed her outside and behind the shack, where there was a pipe and a small sink. Next to the sink, on the ground, was a stack of plates, and on top of these, a couple of pots. We offered to help, but Dona Heloísa sent us off, insisting that we come pay another visit the next day.

A few doors down from Dona Heloísa's, Eva and I ran into Leonel, one of the moradores. I almost did not recognize him. His face was swollen. His eyes were bloodshot. Deep wrinkles lined his cheeks, making him look as though he had aged twenty years. I had seen Leonel drunk many times before while on the dump, but there he usually passed out under a tarp in the camp of the moradores. It was strange to see him now alone and on the street—stumbling as he walked. I asked him about the other moradores: Vidal, Fabinho, Mineiro. Where had they gone when the dump closed? Leonel responded, but his speech was garbled. He kept trying to tell me something, but I could not understand a single word that he said.

As we walked away from Leonel, Eva told me that Vidal had died. He had fallen on the street and was run over by a truck. Pointing to her stomach, Eva said, "Everything burst."

I DECIDED TO GO to the new CRAS in Jardim Gramacho because I had heard that Juliana was working there. She had helped CRAS with the registration and documentation of catadores during the closure of the dump, and afterward was hired full-time to do all the cleaning at the center. When I arrived, I asked for Juliana and was directed to the kitchen, where I found her preparing the staff's lunch. Juliana told me that it was the birthday of one of the social workers, that she was preparing a special meal in celebration, and that I should stay and join them. In the meantime, she suggested I wait in the computer room and led me to a back room filled with desks arranged in two neat rows. I took a seat and looked around. Several posters hung on the wall in the front of the room. One announced a "Day of Social Action" that had already passed. Another provided information about daily courses in computing and "digital literacy and citizenship," sponsored by FUNDEC, a local vocational school, and the city of Duque de Caxias. I wondered if these classes were connected to the other job training courses that the city of Duque de Caxias had offered catadores after the garbage dump closed. The program had reserved 350–400 openings for catadores at the vocational schools SENAC-Rio and SENAI in roughly month-long courses to become a cook, baker, pizza maker, maid, waiter, event organizer, travel agent, electrician, and computer technician. Only a couple of catadores I knew told me that they were taking these courses—Nicole was enrolled in the electrician's course and Rodrigo in the one on baking. Neither was convinced that the course would lead to a job, but they were doing them to have something to do while "waiting" (*aguardando*) to see what opportunities might arise. The courses were a way not to feel "idle" (*parado*).

At lunch, I met three of the social workers at CRAS, including Danilo, whose birthday we were celebrating. When I introduced myself, Danilo told me that he took an anthropology course as part of his degree, that he learned to write fieldnotes, and that he continues to use that technique in his day-to-day work. Social work in Brazil differs significantly from the field in the United States, Danilo told me. In contrast to the U.S. focus on the individual case, the Brazilian approach draws from Marxist lines of analysis and tends to emphasize the larger socioeconomic conditions of a person's life. For example, Danilo continued, one of the most important services that CRAS has provided catadores is the enrollment of families in Bolsa Família, Brazil's conditional cash transfer program. Many families in Jardim Gramacho never enrolled in the program because they did not have proper documents, such as birth certificates. Others never enrolled because they did not realize that they were eligible. I asked Danilo if catadores had acquired jobs after the dump closed, wondering if the social workers had also found that most catadores seemed to be waiting or holding out for something else—"aguardando," as they put it.

"Jobs? Absolutely not," Danilo replied. "Work they might get, but it's rare they'll get a job." He added that people always figure out something to get along, always "find a way" (*dar um jeitinho*), using the common Brazilian saying for using one's resources creatively to circumvent laws, rules, conventions, or other obstacles to achieve a desired end. For example, Danilo told me, there was recently an "invasion" in an old, abandoned metallurgical factory a couple of doors down from CRAS. He suggested that we visit it after lunch.

When we arrived at the factory, Danilo knocked several times on a door that formed part of a metal wall that separated the factory from the street. It was impossible to see anything on the other side. We waited. Only silence. Danilo knocked again. Eventually, a girl who looked to be about eight years old opened the door just far enough to poke her head out. Danilo explained who he was and asked for Gabriel. Once Danilo had mentioned Gabriel's name, the girl opened the door all the way and let us inside, slamming the door securely behind us. I found myself standing in front of a two-story building surrounded by a large, open yard. Behind the building, a few men were busy constructing a small house. Next to this house were several others that were in various states of completion. Gabriel came out of the main building to greet us and invited us back to his home—an expansive room on the building's ground floor that was almost empty except for a mattress and a stove. We stood as Gabriel told us a story about how he had come to the factory when he started having trouble paying his rent. He had worked as a nurse's aide, doing home care. His client treated him like a maid, making him do the dishes and all the cleaning and only giving him leftovers to eat. He had to sleep on a tiny mattress that was too small for him to roll over on. When Gabriel could no longer endure the conditions, he quit his job. He heard about the factory from a friend and decided to come and see what it was like.

Gabriel told us that there were now about forty families living in the factory. Newcomers were building houses in the yard, often with old materials that they found on the factory grounds. Everyone divided the electricity bill and shared a well for water. They were careful with security, making sure the front door to the factory remained shut at all times. We went back outside and Gabriel offered to show us the second floor, but that would require climbing a makeshift ladder that one of the residents had built. Uneasy with heights, I declined. As I waited for Danilo and Gabriel to return, I walked across the open yard. Clotheslines were hung and laundry was drying. One of the men who was building a house passed me with a wheelbarrow filled with various pieces of broken lumber. I came back to the ladder, an improvised staircase to the second floor. I was amazed by all the ways this abandoned factory had been transformed. The dump had closed in Jardim Gramacho, but the work of reclaiming the discarded clearly had not.

When I arrived back at CRAS, I found Juliana in the back left-hand corner of the computer room. Her head was down on her right arm, which was stretched out between two computer monitors. I approached her and tapped her lightly on the shoulder. "Just dozing," she said as she looked up at me. She told me that the afternoons were difficult. In the morning, there was a lot to do: sweep the rooms, clean the bathrooms, prepare the lunch for the staff. But there were hardly any tasks to fill the four hours of the afternoon until her workday ended at five o'clock.

Juliana's comments reminded me of Rose. The demand to stay at work with nothing to do was one of the reasons Rose gave for quitting the only job with a signed worker ID that she held in her life. I thought of mentioning Rose to Juliana but decided against it. At that moment, I did not know how to bring up the subject of Rose's death or how to talk about it with Juliana, who had been one of Rose's closest friends. Gordinho had been the one to contact me—almost a year ago. It happened on the morning of Father's Day, he said. The night before, Rose had been fine and everything was normal. She went out with Carlos to a pagode and danced until the early hours of the morning—a sign that she had felt well. When Rose and Carlos arrived home, she told him she would clean the house and start preparing the barbecue for their Father's Day celebration. Carlos told her not to worry, that they had already bought everything they needed for the barbecue, and that they should lie down for a few hours and rest. Carlos awoke to Rose shaking. It was a seizure. She had been diagnosed with epilepsy as a child, but as she aged the seizures had abated and the doctor had informed her that she no longer needed to take medication. Gordinho explained that Rose's seizures had recently returned. By the time they got Rose to the hospital, she had already passed away. The doctors said the cause of death was an "excess of water in the lungs."

Gordinho kept repeating that it was a shock, unexpected, that Rose had been fine the night before. In response, I kept thinking about the intermittent health care that she had received, about the time that it took them to get her to the hospital. Rose's life had involved so many instances of caring response to everyday emergencies that arose from the multiple forms of precariousness in Rio's periphery. Yet as I listened to Gordinho, I found it difficult to accept that Rose's life could end, suddenly, as one of these emergencies for others in her social world.

Juliana suggested that we go outside where she could smoke a cigarette and we could talk. We passed through a crowded front room where about a dozen people were waiting to be attended by one of the social workers. It was quiet outside. We took a seat on a bench in front of the building and Juliana looked out through the blue-painted fence posts toward the empty street. At the moment, no vehicles were passing by. "I miss the dump [*estou com saudades da rampa*], that lively activity [*movimento*]," Juliana said, more to herself than to me. I suggested that her job at CRAS seemed to be a good one. It was, she replied. All the members of the staff were good people and they treated her well. Perhaps, I suggested, it would just take time to adjust to the schedule and other aspects of the job. She told me that she agreed. "You adjust because you have to adjust," she said.

Juliana looked back toward the street. I realized she was looking in the direction of the dump. "But for sure," she added, "if the dump still existed, I would be there. For sure."

INTRODUCTION

1   To protect their identities, I use pseudonyms for most people who appear in this book, with the exception of those who specifically requested that I use their names. These requests often came from catadores who were politically active and publicly known and wished to be credited with their own words, views, and life stories. I also use the real names of public figures.

2   See, for example, Mike Davis's account of the rise of a "surplus humanity" in Third World cities (2004a: 28); Loïc Wacquant's claim that "a significant *fraction of the working class has been made redundant* and constitutes an 'absolute surplus population'" (2008: 266); Achille Mbembe's call to consider "the human itself *as* a waste product at the interface of race and capitalism" (2011: 7; see also Yates 2011); Gavin Smith's arguments regarding how "surplus populations" are generated in capitalism (2011: 14); and Neferti X. M. Tadiar's analysis of what she calls "remaindered lifetimes," the modes of living people engage in "under conditions of their own superfluity or disposability" (2013: 23). For a different, though related, use of *waste* as a metaphor for understanding contemporary labor, see Melissa Wright's (2006) study of Mexican and Chinese female factory workers. In her account, she argues that the disposability of women workers forms part of the ideological framework of factory managers, who see these workers as easily used up, discarded, and replaced, and who therefore literally lay waste to their bodies (through repetitive stress injuries and other illnesses).

3   Marx also described the industrial reserve army (the unemployed or partly employed) as a relative surplus population that can be disposed of by capital in periods of crisis and stagnation (1990: 781–94). However, though Marx's discussion of the industrial reserve army provides much of the language used in accounts of twenty-first-century capitalism, his use of "superfluous" or "surplus" does not signify waste in the same way as found in contemporary accounts for two reasons. First, for Marx, the industrial reserve army is not disposed of indefinitely, but rather is at times expelled and at times reabsorbed within capitalist production cycles. Bauman (2004) makes this distinction explicit: "The destination of the *un*employed, of the 'reserve army of labour,' was to be called back into active service. The destination

of waste is the waste-yard, the rubbish heap" (12). Wacquant (2008: 266) makes a similar point by differentiating between a relative and absolute surplus population, the former constituting the industrial reserve army and the latter referring to those who will likely never find work again and are therefore permanently discarded. Second, in other parts of his work, Marx used waste metaphors to describe how capitalism "squanders" human lives and individual development (1991: 182). In contrast, Achille Mbembe (2011) has argued that capitalism is not just wasteful of human life, but rather turns *the human itself into waste*, adding that race has played a central role in capitalism's production of superfluous people. For a different history of the use of garbage metaphors to describe unproductive populations in the area of mental illness, see Lovell (2007).

4   Literature on the informal economy in the 1970s was dominated by a dual-ist approach that associated the informal with "tradition" and the formal with "modernity" and viewed the former as gradually withering away as developing countries modernized (Emmerij 1974; Sethuraman 1976). This view, however, did not go uncontested. Marxist critiques soon emerged that conceptualized the informal economy as a *consequence* of modernization and underdevelopment (see Castells and Portes 1989; Gerry 1987; Malaguti 2000; Moser 1978). Yet by arguing that the informal sector is a "reflection of the distortions and failures of the development process" (Centeno and Portes 2006: 24), the Marxist literature still implied that the informal sector might disappear if such "failures" were resolved. A third perspective, spear-headed by Hernando de Soto (1989), argued that the informal economy resulted from too much state regulation, which pushed small "entrepre-neurs" to operate outside the law. Again, the implication was that if the problem—here understood as oppressive state regulation—were addressed, the informal would vanish or become merged with the formal.

5   See Davis (2006); Hall and Pfeiffer (2000); UN Habitat (2008). Ulrich Beck (2000: 93) goes so far as to argue that the rise of informality not only in the Global South but also in "late modern" societies has brought about the "Brazilianization of the West."

6   There has also been a revival of the very term *marginality* in notions of a "new marginality" or "advanced marginality" (Caldeira 2009; González de la Rocha et al. 2004).

7   Bureau of International Recycling, www.bir.org/industry/, accessed April 22, 2015. Journalist Adam Minter (2013) has estimated that the global recycling industry turns over $500 billion a year and is likely to reach $1 trillion by 2020.

8   Feminist critiques of what counts as labor in capitalism were part of the extensive domestic labor debates in the 1960s and 1970s. For an overview of this literature that also critiques its underlying assumptions, see Molyneux (1979).

9   As part of an effort to valorize their work as "real" work, catadores in Jardim Gramacho frequently corrected others who described them as *catadores de*

lixo (collectors of garbage) and not *catadores de materiais recicláveis* (collectors of recyclable material). Furthermore, Brazil's National Movement of Catadores (MNCR), in which catadores from Jardim Gramacho have participated, has fought for the recognition and valorization of the work of catadores as a "profession." However, a bill (Projeto de Lei 6.822/2010) that would have regulated the profession of catadores was vetoed by President Dilma Roussef in 2010 because it did not have the support of the MNCR. While the MNCR supported the law's recognition of collecting recyclables as a profession, it expressed concern that the regulations outlined in the proposed legislation (such as having to acquire documents) would become too bureaucratic and onerous for catadores. I discuss the place of catadores within Brazil's moral imaginary of work in more detail in chapter 2.

10 Here I am inspired by Claudia Fonseca's (2006: 28) critique of an "ethnographic refusal" in studies of urban poor, in which she argues that such studies tend to privilege the economic "as if the only concern of the poor ought logically to be survival and financial improvement" (my translation).

11 One area where these separate conversations have come together is in literature describing how the neoliberal erosion of stable jobs has produced pathological subjectivities of loss, anomie, and alienation. Richard Sennett (1998), for example, argues that the increasing demand for flexibility has led to what he calls the "corrosion of character" or an individual's personal incapacity to maintain loyalty to ethical values and social relationships (see also Standing 2011). As Franco Barchiesi (2012a: 239) astutely observes, "By casting precarious employment as a condition that obliterates the wholeness of personality and political agency, [such work] has achieved the result of silencing precarious workers' strategies, autonomy and signifying practices as effectively as the economic liberalization it deprecates." By instead examining forms of living fashioned beyond conditions of wage labor, I am interested in precarious work as a site of existential aspiration and political struggle.

12 For an overview of these debates, see chapter 4.

13 Timothy Mitchell (1998, 2002, 2005, 2008) and J. K. Gibson-Graham (1996, 2006, 2014) have been the most influential thinkers in this project to rethink economy. They have inspired and directly contributed to several edited collections devoted to this theme in recent years (see Lee et al. 2008; Narotzky and Besnier 2014). Carolyn Nordstrom's (2007) work on contraband economies has also problematized the idea of economy.

14 While there is not a general consensus as to which municipalities make up the Baixada Fluminense, the following eight are usually included: Belford Roxo, Duque de Caxias, Japeri, Mesquita, Nilópolis, Nova Iguaçu, Queimados and São João de Meriti. Sometimes the eastern municipalities of Magé

and Guapimirim or the western municipalities of Itaguaí, Seropédica, and Paracambi are also included (Sampaio de Souza and Barbosa 2013).

15 See also Pires Junior and Santos de Souza (1996).

16 Cited by Cantalejo (2008: 22).

17 At the time the contract was negotiated, Duque de Caxias was considered an "Area of National Security" by the military dictatorship, meaning that its mayor was directly appointed by the military (Cantalejo 2008: 96–100).

18 See, for example, Freire-Medeiros (2009).

19 This letter to the editor appeared in *O Globo* on July 21, 2005.

20 For a fuller analysis of the role that the Jardim Gramacho dump played in the intermunicipal politics of metro Rio de Janeiro, see Millar (2012).

21 See also Cavalcanti (2014).

22 Alba Zaluar and Marcos Alvito (2004) describe how the favela has long been perceived as a lack or emptiness to be filled by humanitarian sentiments.

23 For some of the most influential work on drug trafficking and urban violence in Rio, see Arias (2006a); Gay (2005); Larkins (2015); Leeds (1996); Penglase (2014); Zaluar (1994, 2004).

24 ACAMJG stands for Associação dos Catadores do Aterro Metropolitano de Jardim Gramacho.

25 For the Brazilian context, see Domingues Junior (2003); Freitas (2005); Gonçalves (2003); Kemp and Crivellari (2008); Magera (2003).

26 See also Gandolfo (2009: 110–11) for a discussion of how activism that does not conform to traditional workers' unions and movements is often dismissed as apolitical in social scientific research.

27 Garbage has often been associated with hell in the history of Christianity. John Scanlan (2005) notes that the iconography of hell in the Middle Ages included images of rubbish, excrement, and the discarded entrails of butchered animals.

28 The idea that garbage is the product of ordering the world or of "creating and maintaining form" (Reno 2016: 10) has long been a dominant approach to waste in the social sciences (see Scanlan 2005; Thompson 1979). Even studies that emphasize the materiality of waste (see Gille 2007; Hawkins 2006) take as a point of departure Douglas's conceptualization of dirt as a product of social classification (Reno 2014).

29 I follow other recent work in discard studies that has shifted focus to the afterlife of waste (Giles 2014; Reno 2015). However, I prefer to think of the social life of waste rather than its *after*life so as to emphasize that at no point is waste outside the social world.

30 My interest in the generativity and vitality of waste resonates with Jane Bennett's (2010) work on vital materiality, or what she calls "thing-power." Here I am more interested in exploring the phenomenology of waste—how catadores engage with and experience the materiality of garbage—than in demonstrating the agency of waste in itself.

1   In the eighteenth and nineteenth centuries, the area that is now Jardim Gramacho and its environs in the Baixada Fluminense consisted of large plantations (*fazendas*) that cultivated sugarcane, rice, corn, and beans (Ferreira 1959).

2   For an excellent analysis of the complex, confusing, and ambivalent ways environmental toxicity is experienced and interpreted by those impacted by the combined effects of social, economic, and environmental inequality, see Auyero and Swistun (2009).

3   See Mintz (1985); Nash (1979); Roseberry (1983); Wolf (1982).

4   The book was translated into English as *Child of the Dark* in 1962.

5   Research on the number of street children in Rio de Janeiro was carried out by IBASE, a Brazilian NGO that focuses on social and economic change. The IBASE study is cited in Hecht (1998: 101).

6   This figure is based on the number of catadores registered by ACAMJG.

7   The GDP growth rate data was retrieved from World Bank data, http://data .worldbank.org/indicator/NY.GDP.MKTP.KD.ZG, accessed October 10, 2014. Though growth declined in 2009 as a result of the global recession, Brazil's economy expanded by 7.5 percent in 2010. For the impact of the global recession on Brazil's economy, see Salama (2009). Brazil's GDP growth began to slow in 2011 and contracted by 2015.

8   See Morais and Saad-Filho (2011: 36). Classe C is defined as having family income between R$1,064 and R$4,561 per month. For critiques that the notion of a "new middle class" is a market logic that fails to examine and thereby prevents real changes to Brazil's social structure, see Pochmann (2012).

9   This article, which appeared in the print edition of *The Economist* on November 14, 2009, was followed by another, four years later, that questioned Brazil's success in the wake of the 2013 street protests. The image accompanying the article was of the statue Christ the Redeemer crashing toward Earth ("Has Brazil Blown It?," *The Economist*, September 28, 2013).

10 Few catadores were enrolled in Bolsa Família prior to the dump's closure. See the conclusion.

11 Cited in Hunter and Sugiyama (2009: 34).

12 Those with eight to eleven years of education tend to have the highest rate of unemployment. Though the unemployment rate drops for workers with an education level greater than eleven years, the segment with the lowest unemployment rate is workers with no education at all (Ernst 2008). Brazilian economist Marcio Pochmann (2008: 39) has called this phenomenon "the anomaly of intellectual unemployment." It should be noted that Brazil's domestic household survey (PNAD) defines the unemployed person as someone who did not work a single hour in the week prior to the survey and was seeking work during that week. As a result,

this measurement does not include those who have become discouraged or for other reasons are not looking for a job.

13 Anthropologist Livio Sansone (2003) distinguishes between "soft" and "hard" areas or moments of life with respect to race relations in Brazil. Soft spaces are those in which racial distinctions are seen as less relevant than other social differences such as class, age, neighborhood, and gender. Hanging out at a bar in Jardim Gramacho or collecting on the dump were "soft" spaces, in which race was rarely commented upon, as racial difference was not seen as impinging on social interaction. In contrast, when I collected cans in a middle-class neighborhood during carnival alongside catadores from Jardim Gramacho, the topic of race or color arose multiple times. In Sansone's analysis, this would be considered a "hard" moment of race relations. The carnival parades were also the only time during my fieldwork in which my racial difference was called into question while I was collecting. A carnival reveler in a middle-class neighborhood who saw me pick up a can said in surprise, "You are blue-eyed and collecting?!," implicitly associating catadores with blackness. Sansone also emphasizes that one of the most noted hard areas of race relations in Brazil is work, especially the search for employment (52). For another discussion of soft and hard race relations in Rio de Janeiro, see Penglase (2014: 140).

14 For a discussion of the commonly used term *bandido* (bandit) to refer to drug dealers, see Penglase (2014: 31–32).

15 Jardim Gramacho was not at all unusual in the ways that drug dealers sometimes intervened in local disputes. Many of the first studies of drug trafficking in Rio de Janeiro showed how drug dealers create a parallel justice system in the favelas and maintain public order, such as by punishing petty theft (see Goldstein 2003; Leeds 1996). More recently, studies have examined the complex relationships between drug traffickers, police, and favela residents in the production of security and insecurity (see Arias and Rodrigues 2006; Penglase 2009).

16 See DaMatta (1979, 1984).

17 Medical waste was disposed of in a separate area of the dump, though it was common to encounter distinctly colored blue bags filled with used rubber gloves, syringes, and other hospital supplies amid household waste. I learned to avoid these blue bags, but some catadores sought them out because medical supplies were often made out of relatively high-priced plastics.

18 Caju is a neighborhood in the North Zone of Rio where there used to be a dump and where there is now a waste transfer station. Small compactor trucks that collect on the streets in that area unload waste at this transfer station. The waste is then loaded into the containers of semi-trucks, which then make the trip to Jardim Gramacho for final disposal.

19 In his ethnography of a Michigan landfill, Josh Reno (2016) concludes with a policy proposal to help remind us that waste management is a social process and relationship. He suggests that landfills double as cemeteries—that we bury our dead in the same place and with the same ritual that we discard our weekly garbage. While intentionally provocative and wonderfully disruptive of commonsense ways of approaching garbage, this proposal misses how for certain poor, racialized, and marginalized bodies, dumps and landfills already are burial grounds.

20 This is consistent with homicide statistics in Rio de Janeiro, which show that youth who are fifteen to twenty-four years old are more than twice as likely to be killed than the average citizen and are disproportionately black and mixed-race males (Penglase 2014: 14–15).

21 Arthur Kleinman (1995) uses this term in a different context to refer to the generativity that has arisen from his own anthropological work that has developed in the margins—between anthropology and medicine and between social theory and the ethnography of social suffering.

2 · THE PRECARIOUS PRESENT

1 Wages in Brazil are commonly expressed as multiples of the official monthly minimum wage. At the time of my conversation with Rose (2009), the monthly minimum wage in Brazil was set at R$465 or roughly US$233.

2 See also Molé (2010).

3 The literature on the history of neoliberalism is extensive. For an overview, see Harvey (2005).

4 For studies of precarity as a symptom of neoliberalism, see Bourdieu (1998); Johnson (2011); Standing (2011). For views of precarity as a global condition, see Comaroff and Comaroff (2012); Wacquant (2008).

5 For a different use of this term in feminist philosophy and ethics, see MacKenzie and Stoljar (2000).

6 This job security fund is called the Fundo de Garantia por Tempo de Serviço (FGTS). According to Brazilian labor law prior to 2001, the employer had to deposit the equivalent of 8 percent of a worker's monthly salary into a blocked account, opened in the employee's name, in the Caixa Econômica Federal (Federal Savings Bank). A worker could only access these funds if fired without just cause (or in the case of special circumstances such as purchasing a home or becoming seriously ill). The employer also had to pay a penalty, but because this penalty was paid directly to the employee, the two parties could easily make an agreement around a "fake dismissal" (Paes de Barros and Corseuil 2004). In September 2001, an additional half percent of the worker's salary was added to the monthly deposit and an additional fine of 10 percent of the FGTS funds, to be paid directly to the government, was added to the penalty. These changes reduced the

incentives for fake dismissals since they were now more expensive (Gonzaga 2003).

7   This is also the case for street catadores, who must maintain their routes and relationships to businesses and condominium owners who "donate" their recyclables (see Natalino and Eckert 2003).

8   For an analysis of the worker's symbolic value in Argentina, see Perelman (2007).

9   The phrase *carteira assinada* is shorthand for a signed *carteira de trabalho*. It is difficult to translate the name of this document into English. The carteira de trabalho is sometimes translated as "labor card," though this can be misleading as the document consists of a small booklet. A better translation, therefore, might be "labor passbook." However, because the English term *passbook* in a labor context is often associated with apartheid South Africa, I have opted to refer to the carteira de trabalho by a more general descriptor of a "worker ID."

10 See Perlman (2010: 157); Roth-Gordon (2009: 58).

11 For police violence against the poor, including street children, see Caldeira (2000: 138–39); Scheper-Hughes (2006: 154). For arguments concerning elite disregard of Brazil's lower classes, see Skidmore (2010: 191).

12 For example, Ben Penglase (2007) describes an incident in which police systematically stopped and searched black, male youth on their way to beaches in Rio's wealthy South Zone.

13 For a fascinating history of Brazil's vagrancy laws, see Huggins (1985).

14 This language comes from the document *Rio Cidade*, produced by the city of Rio de Janeiro in October 1996 (Oliveira 2008).

15 Cited in Oliveira (2008).

16 Cited in Magalhães (2001).

17 For an account of the ways such efforts to sanitize urban space and protect public patrimony intersect with changing racial politics in Brazil, see Collins (2015).

18 The mayors of Rio de Janeiro who succeeded Cesar Maia have only reinforced his politics of bringing "order" to the city. Luiz Paulo Conde, Maia's secretary of urbanism during his first term, held office between 1997 and 2000 and continued the policies that he had helped Maia initiate. Eduardo Paes, who took office in 2009, further intensified the repression of unlicensed vendors as part of an operation named the "Shock of Order." The city of Rio de Janeiro justified this operation as necessary to create the "sensation" of public security—a goal increasingly pursued by the city in preparation for hosting the 2016 Olympic Games.

19 The guarda municipal was instated in Rio de Janeiro by Municipal Decree Number 12.000, on March 30, 1993. For more on the history of the guarda municipal, see Nacif, da Costa Cardoso, and Baldo Ribeiro (2011); Valverde (2009).

20 The objectives of the guarda municipal are outlined in a section of the 1988 Brazilian constitution that addresses public security (Chapter III, Article 144); it reads: "Municipalities may form guardas municipais with the purpose of protecting their goods, services, and installations according to the law" (my translation; see also Miranda et al. 2003).

21 See Dent (2012).

22 See also Bourdieu (2000).

23 For critiques of the neoliberal conception of autonomy, see Brown (2005); Gershon (2011); Rimke (2000).

24 For an extended discussion of relational labor in the context of volunteerism and care work in post-Fordist Italy, see Muehlebach (2012).

25 See Graeber (2009); Nash (2001); Williams (2008).

26 See Clara Han (2012) for an analysis of an alternative, though similarly oriented, way of living through the present, by way of credit taken up by urban poor families in Santiago, Chile.

3 · LIFE WELL SPENT

1 I hesitated initially when asked for loans, worrying about the ethics of my involvement in these exchanges. However, over time I came to understand that lending and borrowing were constitutive practices in the social worlds of catadores and that to refrain from engaging in this exchange would mean withdrawing from relations of reciprocity and mutual dependence. Philippe Bourgois and Jeff Schonberg (2009: 6) describe a similar "moral economy of sharing" among heroin addicts in San Francisco and their own involvement as researchers in these exchanges.

2 There have long been debates in moral philosophy over whether what is moral and ethical should be based on "the good" or "the right" (see Larmore 1990 for an overview of these debates). Aristotle, along with other ancient Greek philosophers, is usually seen as occupying "the good" camp, as opposed to modern philosophers such as Kant who instead argued for "the right" as the foundation of morality. For Aristotle, living well did not involve following objective rules, obligations, and duties—that is, doing what is right. Rather, he saw something as morally good if it led to human flourishing. This is what Henri Sidgwick (1981) called the "attractive" (versus the imperative) notion of the moral ideal (Larmore 1990: 15–16; see also Robbins 2015: 443). It might therefore seem odd that I emphasize that Aristotle's notion of the good life was about a *right* way of living. While the good is certainly the foundation for Aristotle's conception of the moral, his idea of how the good is pursued implies the right insofar as he advocates for cultivating particular forms of character (the virtues) and believes that there is a single, best life (which, not surprisingly, happens to be the contemplative life). Aristotle's notion of the good life is therefore still normative and

exclusionary. For extended anthropological engagements with Aristotle, see Lambek (2010).

3 For examples of studies that apply Agamben's conception of "bare life" to precarious workers and urban poor, see Arnold (2008); Barchiesi (2011); Lund and Malgarejo (2008); Telles and Hirata (2007). Debates around the notion of a "surplus population" of workers have also invoked the language of bare life (see Smith 2011; Watts 2011).

4 Some of the traits Oscar Lewis (1961: xxvi) outlines in his brief description of the "culture of poverty" relate to the spending patterns of the poor. These include the "absence of savings," "chronic shortage of cash," and "present time orientation with relatively little ability to defer gratification and plan for the future." Though Lewis first proposed the concept of a culture of poverty, its elaboration and applications have often strayed from Lewis's ethnographic work. In a close reading of Oscar Lewis's ethnographies, Matthew Gutmann (2002) cautions against simplistic critiques or outright dismissals of Lewis's work, arguing that Lewis contributes to discussions of structure and agency through his willingness to question how the behaviors and rationales of the poor are mechanisms that at once enable their survival in oppressive conditions and play a part in the reproduction of these conditions.

5 For similar critiques of political-economic approaches to spending and consumption of the poor, see Martínez (2010); Miller (2001).

6 This literature is extensive. For the analysis of barren and baptized money, see Taussig (1980); for dirty money, see Werthmann (2008); for bitter money, see Shipton (1989); for hot money, see Walsh (2003) and Znoj (1998); and for money that burns like oil, see Gamburd (2004). For critiques of the notion that the introduction of money into "traditional" societies destroys existing social relations and culturally embedded forms of exchange, see Mauer (2006) and Parry and Bloch (1989).

7 The reasoning is that the tainted money would harm or ruin essential resources necessary for the long-term reproduction of the family or community. As a result of these prohibitions, tainted money is usually spent on luxury or consumer goods like clothing, alcohol, cigarettes, and marijuana (see Shipton 1989; Taussig 1980; Walsh 2003).

8 The five-year term of registration in the Sistema de Proteção ao Crédito (SPC) is the limit set by Brazilian civil law. For an excellent study of the extension of credit to low-income groups in Brazil, see Yaccoub (2011). In her analysis, Yaccoub points out that Casas Bahia was the first retailer in Brazil to offer credit to those unable to provide proof of income or other documents such as a signed worker ID. For more on the extension of credit to poor in other Latin American contexts, see Han (2012).

9 In her study of debt in a poor neighborhood of Santiago, Chile, Clara Han (2012) shows how the unpredictability of income makes it difficult for residents to make regular credit card payments. In certain ways, the challenge

of paying debts for catadores is the reverse. Precisely because their income is predictable—in that they know they will be paid each day they work and that this work is always available—debt payments are difficult to evade. The immediate demands placed on this income furthermore make it more likely that at some point they will be in need of a loan.

10   Benoît de L'Estoile (2014) similarly observes a tendency to spend money immediately among rural workers in the northeast of Brazil. Here I want to emphasize how immediate spending is a means to hold on to one's earnings in some form.

11   Crack cocaine arrived in Brazil in the early 1990s. However, unlike in other Brazilian cities, such as São Paulo, crack did not play a major role in Rio's drug trade nor was it widely distributed in Rio de Janeiro until the mid-2000s.

12   This comparison was noted in an article by Juan Forero in the *Washington Post* on December 26, 2012.

13   Jason Pine (2007) has noted a similar connection between hard labor (such as truck driving, meat packing, and construction) and the use of methamphetamines in the rural Midwest. The use of narcotics *in order to work* challenges popular associations between drug use and the homeless, unemployed, unproductive, or nonworking poor.

14   Most of this food was usually still in good condition, having been discarded by grocers only because it was near or at the expiration date.

15   The words *nega* and *nego* refer to a black woman or man and have traditionally been understood in Brazil as extremely derogatory racial terms. However, they were commonly reappropriated and used among catadores (nearly all of whom were nonwhite) as terms of endearment. Vidal, who was black, had a habit of calling those he addressed in his speech "Nega" or "Nego." The fact that he also referred to me in this way suggests that his use of the term was more about creating a sense of affinity or affection than it was a reference to race. For a distinction between the use of Brazilian racial terms in pragmatic versus referential speech, see Sheriff (2001).

16   For an analysis of the breque as a temporality that disrupts work/life divisions, see Millar (2015).

17   Beginning in September 2008, prices of recyclable materials began to drop in Jardim Gramacho. This was part of a worldwide slump in the recycling industry, as reported in a *New York Times* article by Matt Richtel and Kate Galbraith on December 7, 2008. A few materials, such as cardboard, declined in value to such an extent that scrap dealers in Jardim Gramacho would no longer buy them. Most catadores offset the decline in prices of materials by working longer hours or more frequently. In other words, their incomes stayed roughly the same. What changed was how much they collected on the dump.

18   Anthropologists studying capitalist development in subsistence or peasant societies have described similar reactions to wage incentives, wherein new

wage laborers would work less when wages or prices of cash crops increased (see Sahlins 1972; Taussig 1980).

19 For a collection of anthropological essays on present-time orientation among a range of marginalized groups, see Day et al. (1999). It should also be noted that Oscar Lewis (1961) identified a focus on the present as one of the defining characteristics of a "culture of poverty."

20 The specific discourse expressing a distinction between the deserving and undeserving poor shifts across different cultural contexts (Corboz 2013). In Brazil, it has often taken the form of oppositions between the hustler (*malandro*) and the worker or, more recently, between the bandido and the worker. For more on these distinctions, see chapter 2.

4 · PLASTIC ECONOMY

1 The decline of the U.S. stock market in September 2008 resulted from the collapse of major financial institutions including Lehman Brothers and the American International Group (AIG). For more on the financial crisis of 2008, see Helleiner (2011).

2 See Baxi (2008).

3 See Hamilton (2009).

4 Oil prices fell significantly in mid-September 2008 in the wake of the collapse of U.S. financial institutions (as Catherine Clifford noted in a CNN story on September 16, 2008). However, the average for oil prices in the full month of September was over $100 a barrel. Oil prices reached a low in December of just over $40 a barrel, which coincided with a temporary drop in the price of recycled PET. For more on the correlation between oil prices and prices of recycled PET, see Plastic Zero (2013).

5 This conference paper was published two years later in Hart (1973).

6 For an overview of various methodologies used in measuring the informal economy, see Portes (1994).

7 See Mazumdar (1976); Weeks (1975). Sethuraman (1976) proposed yet another rationale for distinguishing the two sectors that examined specific characteristics of informal enterprises, such as their size and ease of entry. For an overview of dualist approaches, see Moser (1994).

8 See also Gerry and Birkbeck (1981); Portes (1989).

9 A 1979 decree (Portaria No. 53/79) by Brazil's National Council on the Environment (Conselho Nacional do Meio Ambiente or CONAMA) stipulates that waste cannot be deposited in waterways. The mangrove swamp in Jardim Gramacho would fall under this decree. Article 225 of Brazil's 1988 federal constitution designates the Atlantic forest and coastal areas as national patrimony, and article 268 of Rio de Janeiro's state constitution specifies that Guanabara Bay and its mangrove swamps are areas of permanent conservation. These constitutional articles reinforce Brazil's federal

law 4.711, passed on September 16, 1965, which made mangrove swamps protected areas (Área de Preservação Permanente).

10 For studies that critique the concept of informality while arguing for its retention, see Goldstein (2016); Guha-Khasnobis et al. (2006); Lazar (2012).

11 Refer to chapter 2 for a fuller discussion of the signed worker ID.

12 Larissa Adler Lomnitz's (1988) study of personalistic favors and illicit exchanges within political systems could be considered a precursor to more recent work on the ways informality is produced by the state.

13 More specifically, Daniella Gandolfo (2013) theorizes the force often associated with the "informal" as "formless." Drawing on Georges Bataille's (1985) idea of "formless," she describes this quality as the excess of governing structures and systems. This understanding of formless is groundbreaking in the ways it draws attention to a particular mode or force, while challenging the powerful assumption that informal workers desire inclusion in formal state apparatuses. As such, Gandolfo's approach has been inspirational for my own conceptual work on plasticity. However, I do not adopt the concept of formless here in an attempt to move away from terms that have a negative construction (form*less*).

14 The company in charge of implementing the remediation of the dump was the civil engineering firm Queiroz Galvão, which was subcontracted by Comlurb. Other companies, including S.A. Paulista and Novo Gramacho, managed the dump in later years. Because Comlurb oversaw the management of catadores and because social work on the dump maintained continuity despite changes in the subcontracted firms, I refer to Comlurb when discussing the administration's dealings with catadores.

15 When work vests were first instituted in 2001, those distributed through scrapyards were yellow. By the time of my fieldwork in 2008, the color of scrapyard vests had changed to fluorescent green. Because ACAMJG was not a scrapyard but a cooperative of catadores, Comlurb made their vests orange, the same color as the vests of catadores who were registered by Comlurb in 1996.

16 Scrap dealers also paid bribes to police and local bandidos for protection and support. In the former case, these payments helped ensure that police would overlook the scrapyard's unlicensed operations, including the use of trucks that lacked a current registration or were driven by motorists without a proper license. Payments to bandidos enabled scrap dealers to appeal to their power in case of conflicts. For example, when ACAMJG first began organizing and was perceived as a threat to the scrapyards, its founders received numerous threats from local bandidos. For other accounts of bribery to police and drug dealers for protection, as well as bribes *between* drug dealers and police, see Arias (2006b); Larkins (2013); Zaluar (2004).

17 For similar arguments that garbage pickers are disguised proletarians, see also Birkbeck (1979); Gerry and Birkbeck (1981); Wilson (2005). For

critiques of this argument, see Blincow (1986); Medina (2007); Sicular (1991, 1992).

18   See Levi Bryant, "Hylomorphism: The Myth of Formlessness," *Larval Subjects*, April 13, 2012, http://larvalsubjects.wordpress.com/2012/04/13 /hylomorphism-the-myth-of-formlessness/. The italicized and bolded text appears in the original.

19   Claude Lévi-Strauss was the primary anthropologist to develop this school of thought in the 1960s in a four-volume work called *Mythologiques* (published in English in 1969, 1973, 1978, and 1981). See Ortner (1984) for an excellent overview of structuralism and its critiques in anthropology.

20   To say that form is altered and not dissolved does not mean that plasticity cannot at times be disruptive. Catherine Malabou (2008, 2010) draws on a third meaning of plasticity as explosive (*plastique*) to argue that plasticity is also the power to blow up forms. However, this explosion does not result in no form, the informal, the formless, or chaos. Rather, it "allows for the possibility of change and transformation"—that is, for fundamentally new forms to emerge (Crockett 2010: xiii). Furthermore, the explosive power of plasticity is inherent to form itself. It does not come from an external or transcendent force nor from what we might see as the antithesis of form in messiness or chaos. In other words, there must be form for there to be explosive power.

5 · FROM REFUSE TO REVOLUTION

1   The full name of ACAMJG is Associação dos Catadores do Aterro Metropolitano de Jardim Gramacho (Association of Catadores of the Metropolitan Landfill of Jardim Gramacho). Catadores tend to use the word *landfill* (*aterro*) rather than *dump* (*lixão*) when referring to the official name of the site.

2   Most studies of catadores in Brazil, for example, have focused on associations and cooperatives of catadores (see Domingues Junior 2003; Freitas 2005; Gonçalves 2003; Kemp and Crivellari 2008; Magera 2003).

3   See Burawoy (2010); Gallin (2001); Moody (1997); Silver (2003).

4   I have retained the punctuation and capitalization as written in the original text.

5   As much literature on nongovernmental organizations (NGOs) has noted, the NGO is not a homogeneous category. NGOs vary with respect to scale, types of funding sources, organizational structure, relationship to social movements, relationship to the state, and types of services, projects, and aims of the organization (Mercer 2002; Srinivas 2009; Vakil 1997). Glória's statement here refers to characteristics of NGOs that proliferated in the 1980s in Brazil. These NGOs were largely created by middle-class activists who began working in poor neighborhoods or favelas and who professionalized many of Brazil's social movements (Baiocchi 2005: 29). I draw

on Sonia Alvarez's observation that NGOs in Latin America are commonly defined as "intermediary organizations" that "are typically composed of middle-class, educated and professional people who have opted for political or humanitarian reasons to work with (or on behalf of) the poor and the marginalized" (Pearce 1997: 259, cited by Alvarez 1999: 186).

6 Michels's work was heavily influenced by Weber's conceptualization of bureaucracy as a form of power involving rational, calculative logic and action. Characteristics of bureaucracy, for Weber, included hierarchy, the general application of rules and regulations, the use of standard operating procedures, an emphasis on written records (the "files"), and the separation of the personal from official business (Weber 1978: 956–1005).

7 João Biehl (2007) describes a similar process in which the institutionalization of an AIDS clinic in the northeast of Brazil, called Caasah, led to the departures of some residents who were unable or unwilling to adapt to new rules and norms of behavior.

8 For an excellent discussion of neoliberal logics in NGOs in the Brazilian context, see Biehl (2007). While the professionalization of NGOs began in the 1980s and 1990s in Latin America, Sujatha Fernandes (2010) has argued that even in the post-neoliberal order in Venezuela in the late 1990s and 2000s, market-based rationalities continued to shape state and private funders' approaches to social movements.

9 See also Povinelli (2012).

10 For a discussion of *truta* as part of slang in Brazilian prisons, see Resende (2013). For a discussion of its usage in Brazilian hip-hop, see da Silva (2016).

Agamben, Giorgio. 1998. *Homo Sacer: Sovereign Power and Bare Life.* Translated by Daniel Heller-Roazen. Stanford, CA: Stanford University Press.

Ahmed, Sara. 2010. *The Promise of Happiness.* Durham, NC: Duke University Press.

Allison, Anne. 2012. "Ordinary Refugees: Social Precarity and Soul in 21st-Century Japan." *Anthropological Quarterly* 85, no. 2: 345–70.

———. 2013. *Precarious Japan.* Durham, NC: Duke University Press.

Alvarez, Sonia E. 1999. "Advocating Feminism: The Latin American Feminist NGO 'Boom.'" *International Feminist Journal of Politics* 1, no. 2: 181–209.

Anjaria, Jonathan Shapiro. 2011. "Ordinary States: Everyday Corruption and the Politics of Space in Mumbai." *American Ethnologist* 38, no. 1: 58–72.

Arias, Enrique Desmond. 2006a. *Drugs and Democracy in Rio de Janeiro: Trafficking, Social Networks, and Public Security.* Chapel Hill: University of North Carolina Press.

———. 2006b. "The Dynamics of Criminal Governance: Networks and Social Order in Rio de Janeiro." *Journal of Latin American Studies* 38, no. 2: 293–325.

Arias, Enrique Desmond, and Corinne Davis Rodrigues. 2006. "The Myth of Personal Security: Criminal Gangs, Dispute Resolution, and Identity in Rio de Janeiro's Favelas." *Latin American Politics and Society* 48, no. 4: 53–81.

Aristotle. 1985. *Nicomachean Ethics.* Translated by Terence Irwin. Indianapolis: Hackett Publishing Company.

Arnold, Kathleen R. 2008. *America's New Working Class: Race, Gender, and Ethnicity in a Biopolitical Age.* University Park: Pennsylvania State University Press.

Aronowitz, Stanley, and William DiFazio. 1994. *The Jobless Future.* Minneapolis: University of Minnesota Press.

Auyero, Javier, and Débora Alejandra Swistun. 2009. *Flammable: Environmental Suffering in an Argentine Shantytown.* Oxford: Oxford University Press.

Baiocchi, Gianpaolo. 2005. *Militants and Citizens: The Politics of Participatory Democracy in Porto Alegre.* Stanford, CA: Stanford University Press.

Barchiesi, Franco. 2011. *Precarious Liberation: Workers, the State, and Contested Citizenship in Postapartheid South Africa.* Albany: State University of New York Press.

———. 2012a. "Liberation of, through, or from Work? Postcolonial Africa and the Problem with 'Job Creation' in the Global Crisis." *Interface: A Journal for and about Social Movements* 4, no. 2: 230–53.

———. 2012b. "Precarity as Capture: A Conceptual Reconstruction and Critique of the Worker-Slave Analogy." *UniNomade*, October 10. Accessed January 23, 2017. http://www.uninomade.org/precarity-as-capture/.

Bastos, Valéria Pereira. 2008. "Catador: Profissão: Um Estudo do Processo de Construção Identitária, do Catador de Lixo ao Profissional Catador. Jardim Gramacho, de 1996 aos Dias Atuais." PhD diss., Pontifícia Universidade Católica do Rio de Janeiro.

Bataille, Georges. 1985. "Formless." In *Visions of Excess: Selected Writings, 1927–1939*, ed. Allan Stoekl. Translated by Allan Stoekl, Carl R. Lovitt, and Donald M. Leslie Jr., 31. Minneapolis: University of Minnesota Press.

Bauman, Zygmunt. 2004. *Wasted Lives: Modernity and Its Outcasts*. Cambridge: Polity Press.

Baxi, Ranjit. 2008. "Paper Division." In *Bureau of International Recycling Annual Report 2008*, 14–15. Brussels: Bureau of International Recycling.

Bayat, Asef. 2010. *Life as Politics: How Ordinary People Change the Middle East*. Amsterdam: Amsterdam University Press.

Beck, Ulrich. 2000. *The Brave New World of Work*. Translated by Patrick Camiller. Cambridge: Polity Press.

Beloch, Israel. 1986. *Capa Preta e Lurdinha: Tenório Cavalcanti e o Povo da Baixada*. Rio de Janeiro: Record.

Bennett, Jane. 2010. *Vibrant Matter: A Political Ecology of Things*. Durham, NC: Duke University Press.

Bergson, Henri. 1998 [1911]. *Creative Evolution*. Translated by Arthur Mitchell. Mineola, NY: Dover Publications.

Berlant, Lauren. 2011. *Cruel Optimism*. Durham, NC: Duke University Press.

Biehl, João. 2005. *Vita: Life in a Zone of Social Abandonment*. Berkeley: University of California Press.

———. 2007. *Will to Live: AIDS Therapies and the Politics of Survival*. Princeton, NJ: Princeton University Press.

Birkbeck, Chris. 1978. "Self-Employed Proletarians in an Informal Factory: The Case of Cali's Garbage Dump." *World Development* 6, nos. 9–10: 1173–85.

———. 1979. "Garbage, Industry, and the 'Vultures' of Cali, Colombia." In *Casual Work and Poverty in Third World Cities*, ed. Ray Bromley and Chris Gerry, 161–83. New York: John Wiley.

Blincow, Malcolm. 1986. "Scavengers and Recycling: A Neglected Domain of Production." *Labour, Capital and Society* 19, no. 1: 94–115.

Bourdieu, Pierre. 1977. *Outline of a Theory of Practice*. Translated by Richard Nice. Cambridge: Cambridge University Press.

———. 1998. *Acts of Resistance: Against the Tyranny of the Market*. Translated by Richard Nice. New York: The New Press.

———. 2000. *Pascalian Meditations*. Translated by Richard Nice. Stanford, CA: Stanford University Press.

Bourgois, Philippe. 1995. *In Search of Respect: Selling Crack in El Barrio*. Cambridge: Cambridge University Press.

Bourgois, Philippe, and Jeff Schonberg. 2009. *Righteous Dopefiend*. Berkeley: University of California Press.

Brown, Wendy. 2005. *Edgework: Critical Essays on Knowledge and Politics*. Princeton, NJ: Princeton University Press.

Bryant, Levi R. 2012. "Hylomorphism: The Myth of Formlessness." *Larval Subjects Blog*. April 13. Accessed May 9, 2016. http://larvalsubjects.wordpress.com/2012/04/13/hylomorphism-the-myth-of-formlessness.

Bryer, Alice. 2010. "Beyond Bureaucracies? The Struggle for Social Responsibility in the Argentine Workers' Cooperatives." *Critique of Anthropology* 30, no. 1: 41–61.

Burawoy, Michael. 2010. "From Polanyi to Pollyanna: The False Optimism of Global Labor Studies." *Global Labour Journal* 1, no. 2: 301–13.

Caldeira, Teresa P. R. 2000. *City of Walls: Crime, Segregation, and Citizenship in São Paulo*. Berkeley: University of California Press.

———. 2009. "Marginality, Again?!" *International Journal of Urban and Regional Research* 33, no. 3: 848–53.

Cantalejo, Manoel Henrique de Sousa. 2008. "O Município de Duque de Caxias e a Ditadura Militar, 1964–1985." MA diss., Universidade Federal do Rio de Janeiro.

Castells, Manuel, and Alejandro Portes. 1989. "World Underneath: The Origins, Dynamics, and Effects of the Informal Economy." In *The Informal Economy: Studies in Advanced and Less Developed Countries*, ed. Alejandro Portes, Manuel Castells, and Lauren A. Benton, 11–37. Baltimore: Johns Hopkins University Press.

Cavalcanti, Mariana. 2014. "Threshold Markets: The Production of Real-Estate Value between the 'Favela' and the 'Pavement.'" In *Cities from Scratch: Poverty and Informality in Urban Latin America*, ed. Brodwyn Fischer, Bryan McCann, and Javier Auyero, 208–37. Durham, NC: Duke University Press.

Centeno, Miguel Angel, and Alejandro Portes. 2006. "The Informal Economy in the Shadow of the State." In *Out of the Shadows: Political Action and Informal Economy in Latin America*, ed. Patricia Fernández-Kelly and Jon Shefner, 23–48. University Park: Pennsylvania State University Press.

Collins, Jane L. 1990. "Unwaged Labor in Comparative Perspective: Recent Theories and Unanswered Questions." In *Work without Wages: Comparative Studies of Domestic Labor and Self-Employment*, ed. Jane L. Collins and Martha Gimenez, 3–24. Albany: State University of New York.

Collins, John F. 2015. *Revolt of the Saints: Memory and Redemption in the Twilight of Brazilian Racial Democracy*. Durham, NC: Duke University Press.

Comaroff, Jean, and John L. Comaroff. 2012. *Theory from the South: Or, How Euro-America Is Evolving toward Africa*. Boulder, CO: Paradigm Publishers.

Corboz, Julienne. 2013. "Asentamientos and Cantegriles: New Poverty and the Moral Dangers of Proximity in Uruguayan Squatter Settlements." *Latin American Research Review* 48, no. 3: 44–62.

Crockett, Clayton. 2010. "Foreword." In *Plasticity at the Dusk of Writing: Dialectic, Destruction, Deconstruction*, by Catherine Malabou, xi–xxv. New York: Columbia University Press.

DaMatta, Roberto. 1979. *Carnavais, Malandros e Heróis: Para uma Sociologia do Dilema Brasileiro*. Rio de Janeiro: Zahar.

———. 1984. "On Carnaval, Informality and Magic: A Point of View from Brazil." In *Text, Play and Story: The Construction and Reconstruction of Self and Society*, ed. Edward M. Bruner, 230–46. Washington, DC: American Ethnological Society.

da Silva, José Carlos Gomes. 2016. "Juventude, Cultura e Política: Repensando os Estudos Culturais, Revisitando o Hip-Hop." *Projeto História: Revista do Programa de Estudos Pós-Graduados de História* 56:39–68.

Davis, Mike. 2004a. "Planet of Slums: Urban Involution and the Informal Proletariat." *New Left Review* 26(March/April): 5–34.

———. 2004b. "The Urbanization of Empire: Megacities and the Laws of Chaos." *Social Text* 22, no. 4: 9–15.

———. 2006. *Planet of Slums*. London: Verso.

Day, Sophie, Evthymios Papataxiarchis, and Michael Stewart. 1999. "Consider the Lilies of the Field." In *Lilies of the Field: Marginal People Who Live for the Moment*, ed. Sophie Day, Evthymios Papataxiarchis, and Michael Stewart, 1–24. Boulder, CO: Westview Press.

de Jesus, Carolina Maria. 1995 [1960]. *Quarto de Despejo: Diário de uma Favelada*. São Paulo: Editora Ática.

de L'Estoile, Benoît. 2014. " 'Money Is Good, but a Friend Is Better': Uncertainty, Orientation to the Future, and 'the Economy.' " *Current Anthropology* 55, no. S9: S62–73.

Denning, Michael. 2010. "Wageless Life." *New Left Review* 66(November/December): 79–97.

Dent, Alexander S. 2012. "Piracy, Circulatory Legitimacy, and Neoliberal Subjectivity in Brazil." *Cultural Anthropology* 27, no. 1: 28–49.

Desjarlais, Robert. 1994. "Struggling Along: The Possibilities for Experience among the Homeless Mentally Ill." *American Anthropologist* 96, no. 4: 886–901.

Desjarlais, Robert, and C. Jason Throop. 2011. "Phenomenological Approaches in Anthropology." *Annual Review of Anthropology* 40:87–102.

de Soto, Hernando. 1989. *The Other Path: The Invisible Revolution in the Third World*. Translated by June Abbott. New York: Harper and Row.

Domingues Junior, Paulo Lourenço. 2003. *Cooperativa e a Construção da Cidadania da População de Rua*. São Paulo: Edições Loyola.

Douglas, Mary. 1996 [1966]. *Purity and Danger: An Analysis of the Concepts of Pollution and Taboo*. London: Routledge.

Edelman, Marc. 2012. "E. P. Thompson and Moral Economies." In *A Companion to Moral Anthropology*, ed. Didier Fassin, 49–66. Malden, MA: Wiley-Blackwell.

Edmonds, Alexander. 2010. *Pretty Modern: Beauty, Sex, and Plastic Surgery in Brazil*. Durham, NC: Duke University Press.

Emmerij, Louis. 1974. "A New Look at Some Strategies for Increasing Productive Employment in Africa." *International Labour Review* 110, no. 3: 199–218.

Ernst, Christoph. 2008. *Recent Dynamics in Brazil's Labour Market*. Geneva: International Labour Office.

Fernandes, Sujatha. 2010. *Who Can Stop the Drums? Urban Social Movements in Chávez's Venezuela*. Durham, NC: Duke University Press.

Fernández-Kelly, Patricia. 2006. "Introduction." In *Out of the Shadows: Political Action and Informal Economy in Latin America*, ed. Patricia Fernández-Kelly and Jon Shefner, 1–22. University Park: Pennsylvania State University Press.

Ferreira, Jurandyr Pires. 1959. *Enciclopédia dos Municípios Brasileiros*, vol. 22. Rio de Janeiro: IBGE.

Fischer, Brodwyn. 2014. "A Century in the Present Tense: Crisis, Politics, and the Intellectual History of Brazil's Informal Cities." In *Cities from Scratch: Poverty and Informality in Urban Latin America*, ed. Brodwyn Fischer, Bryan McCann, and Javier Auyero, 9–67. Durham, NC: Duke University Press.

Fonseca, Claudia. 2006. "Classe e a Recusa Etnográfica." In *Etnografias da Participação*, ed. Claudia Fonseca and Jurema Brites, 13–34. Santa Cruz do Sul: EDUNISC.

Foucault, Michel. 2008. *The Birth of Biopolitics: Lectures at the Collège de France, 1978–1979*. Edited by Michel Senellart. Translated by Graham Burchell. New York: Palgrave Macmillan.

Freire-Medeiros, Bianca. 2009. "The Favela and Its Touristic Transits." *Geoforum* 40, no. 4: 580–88.

Freitas, Maria Vany de Oliveira. 2005. *Entre Ruas, Lembranças e Palavras: A Trajetória dos Catadores de Papel em Belo Horizonte*. Belo Horizonte: Editora PUCMinas.

Frow, John. 2003. "Invidious Distinction: Waste, Difference, and Classy Stuff." In *Culture and Waste: The Creation and Destruction of Value*, ed. Gay Hawkins and Stephen Muecke, 25–38. Lanham, MD: Rowman and Littlefield.

Gallin, Dan. 2001. "Propositions on Trade Unions and Informal Employment in Times of Globalisation." *Antipode* 33, no. 3: 531–49.

Gamburd, Michele Ruth. 2004. "Money That Burns Like Oil: A Sri Lankan Cultural Logic of Morality and Agency." *Ethnology* 43, no. 2: 167–84.

Gandolfo, Daniella. 2009. *The City at Its Limits: Taboo, Transgression, and Urban Renewal in Lima*. Chicago: University of Chicago Press.

———. 2013. "Formless: A Day at Lima's Office of Formalization." *Cultural Anthropology* 28, no. 2: 278–98.

Gay, Robert. 2005. *Lucia: Testimonies of a Brazilian Drug Dealer's Woman*. Philadelphia: Temple University Press.

Gerry, Chris. 1987. "Developing Economies and the Informal Sector in Historical Perspective." *Annals of the American Academy of Political and Social Science* 493:100–119.

Gerry, Chris, and Chris Birkbeck. 1981. "The Petty Commodity Producer in Third World Cities: Petit-Bourgeois or 'Disguised' Proletarian?" In *The Petite Bourgeoisie: Comparative Studies of the Uneasy Stratum*, ed. Frank Bechhofer and Brian Elliott, 121–54. New York: Palgrave.

Gershon, Ilana. 2011. "Neoliberal Agency." *Current Anthropology* 52, no. 4: 537–55.

Gibson-Graham, J. K. 1996. *The End of Capitalism (As We Knew It): A Feminist Critique of Political Economy*. Minneapolis: University of Minnesota Press.

———. 2006. *A Postcapitalist Politics.* Minneapolis: University of Minnesota Press.

———. 2014. "Rethinking the Economy with Thick Description and Weak Theory." *Current Anthropology* 55, no. S9: S147–53.

Giles, David Boarder. 2014. "The Anatomy of a Dumpster: Abject Capital and the Looking Glass of Value." *Social Text* 32, no. 1: 93–113.

Gille, Zsuzsa. 2007. *From the Cult of Waste to the Trash Heap of History: The Politics of Waste in Socialist and Postsocialist Hungary.* Bloomington: Indiana University Press.

Goldstein, Daniel M. 2016. *Owners of the Sidewalk: Security and Survival in the Informal City.* Durham, NC: Duke University Press.

Goldstein, Donna M. 2003. *Laughter Out of Place: Race, Class, Violence, and Sexuality in a Rio Shantytown.* Berkeley: University of California Press.

Gonçalves, Pólita. 2003. *A Reciclagem Integradora dos Aspectos Ambientais, Sociais e Econômicos.* Rio de Janeiro: DP&A Editora.

Gonzaga, Gustavo. 2003. "Labor Turnover and Labor Legislation in Brazil." *Economia* 4, no. 1: 165–222.

González de la Rocha, Mercedes, Janice Perlman, Helen Safa, Elizabeth Jelin, Bryan R. Roberts, and Peter M. Ward. 2004. "From the Marginality of the 1960s to the 'New Poverty' of Today: A LARR Research Forum." *Latin American Research Review* 39, no. 1: 183–203.

Gordillo, Gastón R. 2014. *Rubble: The Afterlife of Destruction.* Durham, NC: Duke University Press.

Gorz, André. 1982. *Farewell to the Working Class: An Essay on Post-Industrial Socialism.* Translated by Michael Sonenscher. London: Pluto Press.

Graeber, David. 2001. *Toward an Anthropological Theory of Value: The False Coin of Our Own Dreams.* New York: Palgrave.

———. 2009. *Direct Action: An Ethnography.* Oakland, CA: AK Press.

Gregory, Steven. 2007. *The Devil behind the Mirror: Globalization and Politics in the Dominican Republic.* Berkeley: University of California Press.

Guha-Khasnobis, Basudeb, Ravi Kanbur, and Elinor Ostrom. 2006. "Beyond Formality and Informality." In *Linking the Formal and Informal Economy: Concepts and Policies*, ed. Basudeb Guha-Khasnobis, Ravi Kanbur, and Elinor Ostrom, 1–18. Oxford: Oxford University Press.

Gutmann, Matthew C. 2002. *The Romance of Democracy: Compliant Defiance in Contemporary Mexico.* Berkeley: University of California Press.

Hall, Peter, and Ulrich Pfeiffer. 2000. *Urban Future 21: A Global Agenda for Twenty-First Century Cities.* New York: Taylor and Francis.

Hamilton, James D. 2009. "Causes and Consequences of the Oil Shock of 2007–08." *Brookings Papers on Economic Activity* 40, no. 1: 215–83.

Han, Clara. 2012. *Life in Debt: Times of Care and Violence in Neoliberal Chile.* Berkeley: University of California Press.

Hart, Keith. 1973. "Informal Income Opportunities and Urban Employment in Ghana." *Journal of Modern African Studies* 11, no. 1: 61–89.

———. 2006. "Bureaucratic Form and the Informal Economy." In *Linking the Formal and Informal Economy: Concepts and Policies*, ed. Basudeb Guha-Khasnobis, Ravi Kanbur, and Elinor Ostrom, 21–35. Oxford: Oxford University Press.

Harvey, David. 2005. *A Brief History of Neoliberalism*. Oxford: Oxford University Press.

Hawkins, Gay. 2006. *The Ethics of Waste: How We Relate to Rubbish*. Lanham, MD: Rowman and Littlefield.

Hecht, Tobias. 1998. *At Home in the Street: Street Children of Northeast Brazil*. Cambridge: Cambridge University Press.

Helleiner, Eric. 2011. "Understanding the 2007–2008 Global Financial Crisis: Lessons for Scholars of International Political Economy." *Annual Review of Political Science* 14:67–87.

Hobbes, Thomas. 1994. *Leviathan: With Selected Variants from the Latin Edition of 1668*. Edited by Edwin Curley. Indianapolis: Hackett Publishing Company.

Höjdestrand, Tova. 2009. *Needed by Nobody: Homelessness and Humanness in Post-Socialist Russia*. Ithaca, NY: Cornell University Press.

Holston, James. 2008. *Insurgent Citizenship: Disjunctions of Democracy and Modernity in Brazil*. Princeton, NJ: Princeton University Press.

Huggins, Martha Knisely. 1985. *From Slavery to Vagrancy in Brazil: Crime and Social Control in the Third World*. New Brunswick, NJ: Rutgers University Press.

Hunter, Wendy, and Natasha Borges Sugiyama. 2009. "Democracy and Social Policy in Brazil: Advancing Basic Needs, Preserving Privileged Interests." *Latin American Politics and Society* 51, no. 2: 29–58.

Jackson, Michael. 2013. *Lifeworlds: Essays in Existential Anthropology*. Chicago: University of Chicago Press.

Jeannerod, Marc. 2008. "Foreword." In *What Should We Do with Our Brain?*, by Catherine Malabou, xi–xiv. New York: Fordham University Press.

Johnson, Cedric G. 2011. "The Urban Precariat, Neoliberalization, and the Soft Power of Humanitarian Design." *Journal of Developing Societies* 27, nos. 3–4: 445–75.

Kemp, Valéria Heloisa, and Helena Maria Tarchi Crivellari, eds. 2008. *Catadores na Cena Urbana: Construção de Políticas Socioambientais*. Belo Horizonte: Autêntica Editora.

Kleinman, Arthur. 1995. *Writing at the Margin: Discourse between Anthropology and Medicine*. Berkeley: University of California Press.

Kristeva, Julia. 1982. *Powers of Horror: An Essay on Abjection*. Translated by Leon S. Roudiez. New York: Columbia University Press.

Lambek, Michael, ed. 2010. *Ordinary Ethics: Anthropology, Language, and Action*. New York: Fordham University Press.

Larkins, Erika Robb. 2013. "Performances of Police Legitimacy in Rio's Hyper Favela." *Law and Social Inquiry* 38, no. 3: 553–75.

———. 2015. *The Spectacular Favela: Violence in Modern Brazil*. Berkeley: University of California Press.

Larmore, Charles. 1990. "The Right and the Good." *Philosophia* 20, nos. 1–2: 15–32.

Lazar, Sian. 2012. "A Desire to Formalize Work? Comparing Trade Union Strategies in Bolivia and Argentina." *Anthropology of Work Review* 33, no. 1: 15–24.

Lee, Roger, Andrew Leyshon, and Adrian Smith. 2008. "Rethinking Economies/ Economic Geographies." *Geoforum* 39, no. 3: 1111–15.

Leeds, Elizabeth. 1996. "Cocaine and Parallel Polities in the Brazilian Urban Periphery: Constraints on Local-Level Democratization." *Latin American Research Review* 31, no. 3: 47–83.

Lefebvre, Henri. 2008 [1947]. *Critique of Everyday Life*, vol. 1. Translated by John Moore. London: Verso.

Leone, Eugenia Troncoso. 2010. *O Perfil dos Trabalhadores e Trabalhadoras na Economia Informal*. Brasília: Escritório da OIT no Brasil.

Lévi-Strauss, Claude. 1969. *Mythologiques*, vol. I. Translated by John Weightman and Doreen Weightman, *The Raw and the Cooked: Introduction to a Science of Mythology*. New York: Harper and Row.

———. 1973. *Mythologiques*, vol. II. Translated by John Weightman and Doreen Weightman, *From Honey to Ashes: Introduction to a Science of Mythology 2*. New York: Harper and Row.

———. 1978. *Mythologiques*, vol. III. Translated by John Weightman and Doreen Weightman, *The Origin of Table Manners: Introduction to a Science of Mythology 3*. New York: Harper and Row.

———. 1981. *Mythologiques*, vol. IV. Translated by John Weightman and Doreen Weightman, *The Naked Man: Introduction to a Science of Mythology 4*. New York: Harper and Row.

Lewis, Oscar. 1961. *The Children of Sánchez: Autobiography of a Mexican Family*. New York: Random House.

Lomnitz, Larissa Adler de. 1975. *Cómo Sobreviven los Marginados*. Mexico City: Siglo Veintiuno Editores.

———. 1988. "Informal Exchange Networks in Formal Systems: A Theoretical Model." *American Anthropologist* 90, no. 1: 42–55.

Lovell, Anne M. 2007. "Hoarders and Scrappers: Madness and the Social Person in the Interstices of the City." In *Subjectivity: Ethnographic Investigations*, ed. João Biehl, Byron Good, and Arthur Kleinman, 315–40. Berkeley: University of California Press.

Luce, Mathias Seibel. 2013. "Brasil: Nova Classe Média ou Novas Formas de Superexploração da Classe Trabalhadora?" *Trabalho, Educação e Saúde* 11, no. 1: 169–90.

Lund, Joshua, and María del Pilar Melgarejo. 2008. "Walking in the Slum: Urban Cultural Production Today." *Hispanic Issues on Line* (fall): 179–88.

Lustig, Nora, Luis F. Lopez-Calva, and Eduardo Ortiz-Juarez. 2013. "Declining Inequality in Latin America in the 2000s: The Cases of Argentina, Brazil, and Mexico." *World Development* 44:129–41.

MacKenzie, Catriona, and Natalie Stoljar, eds. 2000. *Relational Autonomy: Feminist Perspectives on Autonomy, Agency, and the Social Self*. Oxford: Oxford University Press.

Magalhães, Roberto Anderson M. 2001. "O Centro do Rio na Década de 1990: Requalificação e Reafirmação da Centralidade Principal." *Anais: Encontros Nacionais da ANPUR* 9:741–52.

Magera, Márcio. 2003. *Os Empresários do Lixo: Um Paradoxo da Modernidade.* Campinas, Brazil: Editora Átomo.

Malabou, Catherine. 2008. *What Should We Do with Our Brain?* Translated by Sebastian Rand. New York: Fordham University Press.

———. 2010. *Plasticity at the Dusk of Writing: Dialectic, Destruction, Deconstruction.* Translated by Carolyn Shread. New York: Columbia University Press.

Malabou, Catherine, and Noëlle Vahanian. 2008. "A Conversation with Catherine Malabou." *Journal for Culture and Religious Theory* 9, no. 1: 1–13.

Malaguti, Manoel Luiz. 2000. *Crítica à Razão Informal: A Imaterialidade do Salariado.* São Paulo: Boitempo.

Malinowski, Bronislaw. 1984 [1922]. *Argonauts of the Western Pacific.* Prospect Heights, IL: Waveland Press.

Marques, Rosa Maria, and Àquilas Mendes. 2008. "Sobre a Política de Combate à Pobreza no Governo Lula." *Revista de Economia* 34, no. 3: 91–112.

Martin, Emily. 1994. *Flexible Bodies: Tracking Immunity in American Culture from the Days of Polio to the Age of AIDS.* Boston: Beacon Press.

Martínez, Samuel. 2010. "Excess: The Struggle for Expenditure on a Caribbean Sugar Plantation." *Current Anthropology* 51, no. 5: 609–28.

Marx, Karl. 1963 [1852]. *The Eighteenth Brumaire of Louis Bonaparte.* New York: International Publishers.

———. 1964 [1895]. *Class Struggles in France (1848–1850).* New York: International Publishers.

———. 1990 [1867]. *Capital: A Critique of Political Economy*, vol. I. London: Penguin Group.

———. 1991 [1894]. *Capital: A Critique of Political Economy*, vol. III. London: Penguin Group.

Mauer, Bill. 2006. "The Anthropology of Money." *Annual Review of Anthropology* 35:15–36.

Mazumdar, Dipak. 1976. "The Urban Informal Sector." *World Development* 4, no. 8: 655–79.

Mbembe, Achille. 2011. "Democracy as a Community of Life." *The Johannesburg Salon* 4:5–10.

Medina, Martin. 2007. *The World's Scavengers: Salvaging for Sustainable Consumption and Production.* Lanham, MD: AltaMira Press.

Mercer, Claire. 2002. "NGOs, Civil Society and Democratization: A Critical Review of the Literature." *Progress in Development Studies* 2, no. 1: 5–22.

Michels, Robert. 1968 [1911]. *Political Parties: A Sociological Study of the Oligarchical Tendencies of Modern Democracy.* Translated by Eden Paul and Cedar Paul. New York: Free Press.

Millar, Kathleen M. 2012. "Trash Ties: Urban Politics, Economic Crisis and Rio de Janeiro's Garbage Dump." In *Economies of Recycling: The Global Transformation of*

Materials, Values and Social Relations, ed. Catherine Alexander and Joshua Reno, 164–84. London: Zed Books.

———. 2015. "The Tempo of Wageless Work: E. P. Thompson's Time-Sense at the Edges of Rio de Janeiro." *Focaal: Journal of Global and Historical Anthropology* 73:28–40.

Miller, Daniel. 2001. "The Poverty of Morality." *Journal of Consumer Culture* 1, no. 2: 225–43.

Minter, Adam. 2013. *Junkyard Planet: Travels in the Billion-Dollar Trash Trade*. New York: Bloomsbury Press.

Mintz, Sidney W. 1985. *Sweetness and Power: The Place of Sugar in Modern History*. New York: Viking.

Miranda, Ana Paula Mendes de, Glaucia Maria Pontes Mouzinho, and Kátia Sento Sé Mello. 2003. "Os Conflitos de Rua entre a Guarda Municipal e os 'Camelôs.'" *Comum* 8, no. 21: 39–65.

Mitchell, Sean T. 2015. "American Dreams and Brazilian Racial Democracy: The Making of Race and Class in Brazil and the United States." *Focaal: Journal of Global and Historical Anthropology* 73:41–54.

Mitchell, Timothy. 1998. "Fixing the Economy." *Cultural Studies* 12, no. 1: 82–101.

———. 2002. *Rule of Experts: Egypt, Techno-Politics, Modernity*. Berkeley: University of California Press.

———. 2005. "Economists and the Economy in the Twentieth Century." In *The Politics of Method in the Human Sciences: Positivism and Its Epistemological Others*, ed. George Steinmetz, 126–41. Durham, NC: Duke University Press.

———. 2008. "Rethinking Economy." *Geoforum* 39, no. 3: 1116–21.

Molé, Noelle J. 2010. "Precarious Subjects: Anticipating Neoliberalism in Northern Italy's Workplace." *American Anthropologist* 112, no. 1: 38–53.

Molyneux, Maxine. 1979. "Beyond the Domestic Labour Debate." *New Left Review* I/116 (July/August): 3–27.

Moody, Kim. 1997. *Workers in a Lean World: Unions in the International Economy*. London: Verso.

Morais, Lecio, and Alfredo Saad-Filho. 2011. "Brazil beyond Lula: Forging Ahead or Pausing for Breath?" *Latin American Perspectives* 38, no. 2: 31–44.

Morton, Gregory Duff. 2015. "Managing Transience: Bolsa Família and Its Subjects in an MST Landless Settlement." *Journal of Peasant Studies* 42, no. 6: 1283–1305.

Moser, Caroline O. N. 1978. "Informal Sector or Petty Commodity Production: Dualism or Dependence in Urban Development?" *World Development* 6, nos. 9–10: 1041–64.

———. 1994. "The Informal Sector Debate, Part 1: 1970–1983." In *Contrapunto: The Informal Sector Debate in Latin America*, ed. Cathy A. Rakowski, 11–29. Albany: State University of New York Press.

Muehlebach, Andrea. 2011. "On Affective Labor in Post-Fordist Italy." *Cultural Anthropology* 26, no. 1: 59–82.

———. 2012. *The Moral Neoliberal: Welfare and Citizenship in Italy*. Chicago: University of Chicago Press.

Muehlebach, Andrea, and Nitzan Shoshan. 2012. "Post-Fordist Affect: An Introduction." *Anthropological Quarterly* 85, no. 2: 317–43.

Muniz, Vik. 2008. *Pictures of Garbage*. Digital C Prints, 129.5 × 101.6 cm. Accessed May 2, 2017. http://vikmuniz.net/gallery/garbage.

Munn, Nancy D. 1992. "The Cultural Anthropology of Time: A Critical Essay." *Annual Review of Anthropology* 21:93–123.

Nacif, Cristina Lontra, Diego da Costa Cardoso, and Maria Baldo Ribeiro. 2011. "Estado de Choque: Legislação e Conflitos no Espaço Público da Cidade do Rio de Janeiro-Brasil (1993–2010)." Paper presented at the national meeting of the Associação Nacional de Pós-Graduação e Pesquisa em Planejamento Urbano e Regional (ANPUR), Rio de Janeiro, May 23–27.

Narotzky, Susana, and Niko Besnier. 2014. "Crisis, Value, and Hope: Rethinking the Economy: An Introduction to Supplement 9." *Current Anthropology* 55 (S9): S4–16.

Nash, June C. 1979. *We Eat the Mines and the Mines Eat Us: Dependency and Exploitation in Bolivian Tin Mines*. New York: Columbia University Press.

———. 2001. *Mayan Visions: The Quest for Autonomy in an Age of Globalization*. New York: Routledge.

Natalino, Marco Antonio Carvalho, and Cornelia Eckert. 2003. "Carrinheiros: Cotidiano e Itinerários Urbanos de Catadores de Lixo da Vila Cruzeiro em Porto Alegre." *Iluminuras* 4, no. 7: 1–20.

Neilson, Brett, and Ned Rossiter. 2005. "From Precarity to Precariousness and Back Again: Labour, Life and Unstable Networks." *Fibreculture Journal*. Accessed January 23, 2017. http://five.fibreculturejournal.org/fcj-022-from-precarity-to-precariousness-and-back-again-labour-life-and-unstable-networks/.

———. 2008. "Precarity as a Political Concept, or, Fordism as Exception." *Theory, Culture, and Society* 25, nos. 7–8: 51–72.

Nordstrom, Carolyn. 1997. *A Different Kind of War Story*. Philadelphia: University of Pennsylvania Press.

———. 2007. *Global Outlaws: Crime, Money, and Power in the Contemporary World*. Berkeley: University of California Press.

Oliveira, Márcio Piñon de. 2008. "Projeto Rio Cidade: Intervenção Urbanística, Planejamento Urbano e Restrição à Cidadania na Cidade do Rio de Janeiro." *Scripta Nova: Revista Electrónica de Geografía e Ciencias Sociales* 12, no. 270. Accessed January 23, 2017. http://www.ub.edu/geocrit/sn/sn-270/sn-270-117.htm.

Oliven, Ruben George. 1984a. "A Malandragem na Música Popular Brasileira." *Latin American Music Review/Revista de Música Latinoamericana* 5, no. 1: 66–96.

———. 1984b. "The Production and Consumption of Culture in Brazil." *Latin American Perspectives* 11, no. 1: 103–15.

Ortner, Sherry B. 1984. "Theory in Anthropology since the Sixties." *Comparative Studies in Society and History* 26, no. 1: 126–66.

Oxfeld, Ellen, and Lynellyn D. Long. 2004. "Introduction: An Ethnography of Return." In *Coming Home? Refugees, Migrants, and Those Who Stayed Behind*, ed. Lynellyn D. Long and Ellen Oxfeld, 1–15. Philadelphia: University of Pennsylvania Press.

Paes de Barros, Ricardo, and Carlos Henrique Corseuil. 2004. "The Impact of Regulations on Brazilian Labor Market Performance." In *Law and Employment: Lessons from Latin America and the Caribbean*, ed. James J. Heckman and Carmen Pagés, 273–350. Chicago: University of Chicago Press.

Paes de Barros, Ricardo, and Miguel Nathan Foguel. 2000. "Focalização dos Gastos Públicos Sociais e Erradicação da Pobreza no Brasil." In *Desigualdade e Pobreza no Brasil*, ed. Ricardo Henriques, 719–39. Rio de Janeiro: IPEA.

Parry, Jonathan, and Maurice Bloch. 1989. "Introduction: Money and the Morality of Exchange." In *Money and the Morality of Exchange*, ed. Jonathan Parry and Maurice Bloch, 1–32. Cambridge: Cambridge University Press.

Pearce, Jenny. 1997. "Between Co-Option and Irrelevance? Latin American NGOs in the 1990s." In *NGOs, States and Donors: Too Close for Comfort?* ed. David Hulme and Michael Edwards, 257–74. New York: St. Martin's.

Penglase, Ben. 2007. "Barbarians on the Beach: Media Narratives of Violence in Rio de Janeiro, Brazil." *Crime, Media, Culture* 3, no. 3: 305–25.

———. 2009. "States of Insecurity: Everyday Emergencies, Public Secrets, and Drug Trafficker Power in a Brazilian Favela." *PoLAR: Political and Legal Anthropology Review* 32, no. 1: 47–63.

———. 2014. *Living with Insecurity in a Brazilian Favela: Urban Violence and Daily Life.* New Brunswick, NJ: Rutgers University Press.

Perelman, Mariano D. 2007. "Theorizing Unemployment: Toward an Argentine Anthropology of Work." *Anthropology of Work Review* 28, no. 1: 8–13.

Perlman, Janice E. 1976. *The Myth of Marginality: Urban Poverty and Politics in Rio de Janeiro.* Berkeley: University of California Press.

Perlman, Janice. 2010. *Favela: Four Decades of Living on the Edge in Rio de Janeiro.* Oxford: Oxford University Press.

Pine, Jason. 2007. "Economy of Speed: The New Narco-Capitalism." *Public Culture* 19, no. 2: 357–66.

Pires Junior, Roberto, and Marlucia Santos de Souza. 1996. "Terras de Muitas Aguas." In *Socializando a Produção Escrita.* Duque de Caxias, Brazil: Papelaria Itatiaia.

Plastic Zero. 2013. "Action 4.1: Market Conditions for Plastic Recycling." Accessed August 5, 2015. http://www.plastic-zero.com.

Pochmann, Marcio. 2008. *O Emprego no Desenvolvimento da Nação.* São Paulo: Boitempo Editorial.

———. 2010. "Estrutura Social no Brasil: Mudanças Recentes." *Serviço Social e Sociedade* 104: 637–49.

———. 2012. *Nova Classe Média? O Trabalho na Base da Pirâmide Social Brasileira.* São Paulo: Boitempo Editorial.

Portes, Alejandro. 1989. "La Informalidade Como Parte Integral de la Economía Moderna y no Como Indicador de Atraso: Respuesta a Klein y Tokman." *Estudios Sociológicos* 7, no. 20: 369–74.

———. 1994. "The Informal Economy and Its Paradoxes." In *The Handbook of Economic Sociology*, ed. Neil J. Smelser and Richard Swedberg, 426–49. Princeton, NJ: Princeton University Press.

Povinelli, Elizabeth A. 2011. *Economies of Abandonment: Social Belonging and Endurance in Late Liberalism.* Durham, NC: Duke University Press.

———. 2012. "The Will to Be Otherwise/The Effort of Endurance." *South Atlantic Quarterly* 111, no. 3: 453–75.

Prado, Marcos, dir. 2004. DVD. *Estamira.* Rio de Janeiro: Riofilme and Zazen Produções Audiovisuais.

Reno, Joshua. 2015. "Waste and Waste Management." *Annual Review of Anthropology* 44:557–72.

Reno, Joshua O. 2016. *Waste Away: Working and Living with a North American Landfill.* Berkeley: University of California Press.

Reno, Joshua Ozias. 2014. "Toward a New Theory of Waste: From 'Matter Out of Place' to Signs of Life." *Theory, Culture and Society* 31, no. 6: 3–27.

Resende, Selmo Haroldo de. 2013. "Narrativas de Presos Condenados: Um Vocabulário da Prisão." *Revista Eletrônica de Educação* 7, no. 1: 361–68.

Rifkin, Jeremy. 1995. *The End of Work: The Decline of the Global Labor Force and the Dawn of the Post-Market Era.* New York: G. P. Putnam's Sons.

Rimke, Heidi Marie. 2000. "Governing Citizens through Self-Help Literature." *Cultural Studies* 14, no. 1: 61–78.

Robbins, Joel. 2015. "Ways of Finding the Good in Ethnography." In "There Is No Such Thing as the Good: The 2013 Meeting of the Group for Debates in Anthropological Theory," ed. Soumhya Venkatesan. *Critique of Anthropology* 35, no. 4: 440–45.

Rocha, Geisa Maria. 2007. "Celso Furtado and the Resumption of Construction in Brazil: Structuralism as an Alternative to Neoliberalism." *Latin American Perspectives* 34, no. 5: 132–59.

Roitman, Janet L. 2003. "Unsanctioned Wealth; Or, the Productivity of Debt in Northern Cameroon." *Public Culture* 15, no. 2: 211–37.

Rose, Nikolas. 1999. *Powers of Freedom: Reframing Political Thought.* Cambridge: Cambridge University Press.

Roseberry, William. 1983. *Coffee and Capitalism in the Venezuelan Andes.* Austin: University of Texas Press.

Roth-Gordon, Jennifer. 2009. "The Language That Came Down the Hill: Slang, Crime, and Citizenship in Rio De Janeiro." *American Anthropologist* 111, no. 1: 57–68.

Roy, Ananya. 2005. "Urban Informality: Toward an Epistemology of Planning." *Journal of the American Planning Association* 71, no. 2: 147–58.

———. 2009. "Why India Cannot Plan Its Cities: Informality, Insurgence and the Idiom of Urbanization." *Planning Theory* 8, no. 1: 76–87.

———. 2011. "Slumdog Cities: Rethinking Subaltern Urbanism." *International Journal of Urban and Regional Research* 35, no. 2: 223–38.

Sahlins, Marshall. 1972. *Stone Age Economics.* Chicago: Aldine-Atherton.

Salama, Pierre. 2009. "Argentina, Brasil e México diante da Crise Internacional." *Estudos Avançados* 23, no. 65: 27–48.

Sampaio de Souza, Rodrigo, and Ana Carolina Santos Barbosa. 2013. "Representações da Região da Baixada Fluminense: Refletindo sobre o Papel do Poder Político Familiar no Município de Nilópolis/RJ." *Revista Geonorte* 4, no. 12: 831–48.

Sansone, Livio. 2003. *Blackness without Ethnicity: Constructing Race in Brazil.* New York: Palgrave MacMillan.

Scanlan, John. 2005. *On Garbage.* London: Reaktion Books.

Scheper-Hughes, Nancy. 1992. *Death without Weeping: The Violence of Everyday Life in Brazil.* Berkeley: University of California Press.

———. 2006. "Death Squads and Democracy in Northeast Brazil." In *Law and Disorder in the Postcolony,* ed. Jean Comaroff and John L. Comaroff, 150–87. Chicago: Chicago University Press.

Sennett, Richard. 1998. *The Corrosion of Character: The Personal Consequences of Work in the New Capitalism.* New York: W. W. Norton.

Sethuraman, S. V. 1976. "The Urban Informal Sector: Concept, Measurement and Policy." *International Labour Review* 114, no. 1: 69–81.

Sheriff, Robin E. 2001. *Dreaming Equality: Color, Race, and Racism in Urban Brazil.* New Brunswick, NJ: Rutgers University Press.

Shipton, Parker MacDonald. 1989. *Bitter Money: Cultural Economy and Some African Meanings of Forbidden Commodities.* Washington, DC: American Anthropological Association.

Sicular, Daniel T. 1991. "Pockets of Peasants in Indonesian Cities: The Case of Scavengers." *World Development* 19, nos. 2–3: 137–61.

———. 1992. *Scavengers, Recyclers, and Solutions for Solid Waste Management in Indonesia.* Berkeley: Center for Southeast Asia Studies, University of California at Berkeley.

Sidgwick, Henri. 1981 [1907]. *The Methods of Ethics.* 7th ed. Indianapolis: Hackett Publishing Company.

Silver, Beverly J. 2003. *Forces of Labor: Workers' Movements and Globalization since 1870.* Cambridge: Cambridge University Press.

Skidmore, Thomas E. 2010. *Brazil: Five Centuries of Change.* New York: Oxford University Press.

Smith, Adam. 1976 [1776]. *An Inquiry into the Nature and Causes of the Wealth of Nations.* Edited by Edwin Cannan. Chicago: University of Chicago Press.

Smith, Gavin A. 2011. "Selective Hegemony and Beyond-Populations with 'No Productive Function': A Framework for Enquiry." *Identities: Global Studies in Culture and Power* 18, no. 1: 2–38.

Srinivas, Nidhi. 2009. "Against NGOs? A Critical Perspective on Nongovernmental Action." *Nonprofit and Voluntary Sector Quarterly* 38, no. 4: 614–26.

Stam, Robert. 1997. *Tropical Multiculturalism: A Comparative History of Race in Brazilian Cinema and Culture.* Durham, NC: Duke University Press.

Standing, Guy. 2011. *The Precariat: The New Dangerous Class.* London: Bloomsbury Academic.

Starn, Orin. 1999. *Nightwatch: The Politics of Protest in the Andes*. Durham, NC: Duke University Press.

Tadiar, Neferti X. M. 2013. "Life-Times of Disposability within Global Neoliberalism." *Social Text* 31, no. 2: 19–48.

Taussig, Michael T. 1980. *The Devil and Commodity Fetishism in South America*. Chapel Hill: University of North Carolina Press.

Telles, Vera da Silva, and Daniel Veloso Hirata. 2007. "Cidade e Práticas Urbanas: Nas Fronteiras Incertas entre o Ilegal, o Informal e o Ilícito." *Estudos Avançados* 21, no. 61: 173–91.

Thomas, Keith. 1964. "Work and Leisure." *Past and Present* 29:50–66.

Thompson, E. P. 1963. *The Making of the English Working Class*. New York: Random House.

———. 1967. "Time, Work-Discipline, and Industrial Capitalism." *Past and Present* 38:56–97.

———. 1971. "The Moral Economy of the English Crowd in the Eighteenth Century." *Past and Present* 50:76–136.

Thompson, Michael. 1979. *Rubbish Theory: The Creation and Destruction of Value*. Oxford: Oxford University Press.

Tsing, Anna Lowenhaupt. 2015. *The Mushroom at the End of the World: On the Possibility of Life in Capitalist Ruins*. Princeton, NJ: Princeton University Press.

UN Habitat. 2008. *State of the World's Cities 2010/2011: Bridging the Urban Divide*. London: Earthscan.

United Nations Conference on Trade and Development (UNCTAD). 2006. *Trade and Development Report*. New York: United Nations.

Vakil, Anna C. 1997. "Confronting the Classification Problem: Toward a Taxonomy of NGOs." *World Development* 25, no. 12: 2057–70.

Vallim, Danielle de Carvalho. 2012. "As Políticas Públicas Municipais Voltadas ao Enfrentamento de Crack na Cidade do Rio de Janeiro." Paper presented at the sixth meeting of the Asociación Latinoamericano de Ciencia Política, Quito, June 13–15.

Valverde, Rodrigo Ramos Hospodar Felippe. 2009. "Largo da Carioca como um Cenário: Da Representação da Publicidade à Projeção Espacial da Informalidade." *GEOUSP—Espaço e Tempo* 25:22–40.

Veloso, Leticia. 2010. "Negotiating Marginality and Rethinking Labor through the Eyes of Marginalized Youth." Paper presented at the annual meeting of the American Anthropological Association, New Orleans, November 18.

———. 2012. "Child Street Labor in Brazil: Licit and Illicit Economies in the Eyes of Marginalized Youth." *South Atlantic Quarterly* 111, no. 4: 663–79.

Vieta, Marcelo. 2010. "The Social Innovations of Autogestión in Argentina's Worker-Recuperated Enterprises: Cooperatively Reorganizing Productive Life in Hard Times." *Labor Studies Journal* 35, no. 3: 295–321.

Wacquant, Loïc. 2008. *Urban Outcasts: A Comparative Sociology of Advanced Marginality*. Cambridge: Polity Press.

Walker, Lucy, Karen Harley, and João Jardim, dirs. DVD. 2010. *Waste Land*. London and Rio de Janeiro: Almega Projects and O2 Filmes.

Walley, Christine J. 2013. *Exit Zero: Family and Class in Postindustrial Chicago.* Chicago: University of Chicago Press.

Walsh, Andrew. 2003. "'Hot Money' and Daring Consumption in a Northern Malagasy Sapphire-Mining Town." *American Ethnologist* 30, no. 2: 290–305.

Watts, Michael J. 2011. "Planet of the Wageless." *Identities: Global Studies in Culture and Power* 18, no. 1:69–80.

Weber, Max. 1958 [1905]. *The Protestant Ethic and the Spirit of Capitalism.* Translated by Talcott Parsons. New York: Charles Scribner's Sons.

———. 1978 [1922]. *Economy and Society: An Outline of Interpretive Sociology,* vol. 2. Edited by Guenther Roth and Claus Wittich. Berkeley: University of California Press.

———. 2003 [1927]. *General Economic History.* Translated by Frank H. Knight. Mineola, NY: Dover Publications.

Weeks, John. 1975. "Policies for Expanding Employment in the Informal Urban Sector of Developing Countries." *International Labour Review* 111, no. 1: 1–13.

Weeks, Kathi. 2011. *The Problem with Work: Feminism, Marxism, Antiwork Politics, and Postwork Imaginaries.* Durham, NC: Duke University Press.

Werthmann, Katja. 2008. "'Frivolous Squandering': Consumption and Redistribution in Mining Camps." In *Dilemmas of Development: Conflicts of Interest and Their Resolutions in Modernizing Africa,* ed. Jon Abbink and André van Dokkum, 60–76. Leiden: African Studies Centre.

Williams, Gwyn. 2008. "Cultivating Autonomy: Power, Resistance and the French Alterglobalization Movement." *Critique of Anthropology* 28, no. 1: 63–86.

Williams, Raymond. 1983. *Keywords: A Vocabulary of Culture and Society.* New York: Oxford University Press.

Wilson, Tamar Diana. 2005. *Subsidizing Capitalism: Brickmakers on the U.S.-Mexican Border.* Albany: State University of New York Press.

Wolf, Eric R. 1982. *Europe and the People without History.* Berkeley: University of California Press.

Wright, Melissa W. 2006. *Disposable Women and Other Myths of Global Capitalism.* New York: Routledge.

Yaccoub, Hilaine. 2011. "A Chamada 'Nova Classe Média': Cultura Material, Inclusão e Distinção Social." *Horizontes Antropológicos* 17, no. 36: 197–231.

Yates, Michelle. 2011. "The Human-As-Waste, the Labor Theory of Value and Disposability in Contemporary Capitalism." *Antipode* 43, no. 5: 1679–95.

Zaluar, Alba. 1994. *Condomínio do Diabo.* Rio de Janeiro: Editora Revan/UFRJ Editora.

———. 2004. *Integração Perversa: Pobreza e Tráfico de Drogas.* Rio de Janeiro: Editora FGV.

Zaluar, Alba, and Marcos Alvito. 2004. "Introdução." In *Um Século de Favela,* ed. Alba Zaluar and Marcos Alvito, 7–24. Rio de Janeiro: Editora FGV.

Znoj, Heinzpeter. 1998. "Hot Money and War Debts: Transactional Regimes in Southwestern Sumatra." *Comparative Studies in Society and History* 40, no. 2: 193–222.

Note: Page numbers followed by *f* indicate an illustration.

Baixada Fluminense (continued)
as a region of plantations in the eighteenth
and nineteenth centuries, 195n1; as a site
for Rio's heavy industries, 17
bandidos (criminals): bribery and, 130, 203n16;
conflict resolution and, 47–48, 96, 172–73,
196n15, 203n16; favelas as associated with,
21, 75, 202n20; use of term, 196n14; workers
distinguished from, 75–76, 202n20
Barchiesi, Franco, 9, 193n11, 200n3
barrels. *See* collecting
Bayat, Asef, 174–75
biogas and biogas plants, 178, 184
Birkbeck, Chris, 143, 203n17
Bolsa Família, 42–44, 186, 195n10
borrowing and lending: as a by-product of
unexpected emergencies, 87, 96–97, 99;
friends and family as part of the network
of, 96, 104, 107; as fundamental to the relationships among catadores, 96, 101, 107–8,
199n1, 200–201n9; inflexibility of wage payment as a cause of borrowing, 120, 183.
See also debt; everyday emergencies; money
Brazil: attitudes regarding manual labor
in, 74–75; Bolsa Família cash transfer
program in, 42–44, 186, 195n10; carnival
traditions in, 60; employment and social
values in, 70, 74; environmental laws of,
13, 130, 202–3n9; Fordism and post-
Fordist nostalgia in, 70, 76; GDP statistics
for, 195n7; the Gini coefficient for (1998;
2009), 43; *guarda municipal* system created by the constitution of, 79, 199n20;
INCRA, 18; industrialization of, 40–41,
74–76; inequality in, 40, 43–45, 74–75,
131, 159–60, 196n13, 198n11; labor laws in,
74–76, 197n1, 197–98n6; the middle class
in, 43, 44, 70, 195n8; migration of Europe-
ans to, 74–75; MNCR in, 22, 133, 136, 154–55,
158, 169, 192–93n9; the "new middle class"
("Classe C") in, 43, 44, 195n8; NGOs in, 157,
159, 195n5, 204–5n5, 205nn7–8; 1980s debt
crisis in, 41, 159; payment of foreign debt
obligations as a priority for, 42, 69–70;
Petrobras, 17, 124, 152; political economy
of, 39–44; President Fernando Henrique
Cardoso, 42; President Getúlio Vargas, 9,
74–75; President Luiz Inácio Lula da Silva,
42–43; 2014 World Cup hosted by, 19, 43;
2016 Olympic Games hosted by, 19, 43,

198n18; unemployment and unemployment statistics in, 41, 43, 44, 195–96n12;
vagrancy and vagrancy laws in, 21, 56,
75–76, 198n13; wage labor employment
benefits in, 43–44; the worker-citizen in,
74–75
bribery, 103, 130, 143, 203n16
bulldozers: catador accidents from, 2, 142, 174;
catador alertness to, 63–64, 171; constant
movement of on the dump, 14, 59, 62; movements of in the wake of garbage trucks, 49,
58, 62, 124. *See also* dump; trucks
burlap sacks. *See* collecting

capitalism: bureaucratization and, 165;
"disposable" populations created by, 4, 5,
7, 191–92nn2–3; Keynesian-Fordist, 6, 92,
98–99; the legitimation of only certain kinds
of labor by, 8, 9, 13, 15, 103, 192n8; neoliberal, 5, 10, 98, 127, 166; precarity's relation
to, 6, 166; secure employment eroded by
neoliberal, 6, 70, 86, 92, 98; structuralist
understandings of economy and, 129–30;
waste as perceived in, 33; Weber's study of,
119; the work-citizenship nexus in, 9; worker
incentives in, 119; the work-life dichotomy
posited by, 10–11; work redefined by, 119.
See also neoliberalism; precarity; wage labor
carnival, 26, 60, 196n13
carteira assinada (signed worker ID): dismissal from employment for holders of the,
72; as a document of regular employment,
68, 70, 72, 76, 88–89, 91, 131, 198n9, 200n8;
possession of as a personal restraint, 71,
83–85, 89, 92, 188; as a symbol of status
and respectability, 69, 71, 74, 76; as a tool
for labor regulation in Brazil, 74–75, 131,
198n9. *See also* wage labor
cash: Bolsa Família for Brazilian families
below the poverty line, 42, 43, 186; earnings made daily in, 28, 107–8, 114–15, 166;
social science theories regarding the personal financial management of the poor,
200n4, 201–2n18. *See also* money
catadores: accidents experienced by, 2–3, 50,
64–65, 73–74; "arrival" concept among, 27,
39–40, 45, 52, 59; barrels and burlap sacks
used by, 145, 171–72; borrowing, lending,
and sharing among, 96–97, 101, 107–8, 111–
13, 115, 199n1, 200–201n9; Carolina Maria

collecting (continued)
of the dump, 27, 59, 63–65; weather and temperature as influences on, 1, 3, 48–52, 68, 111–12, 117, 118; weight of materials as a consideration in, 25, 30, 50, 59, 123, 153; work patterns among catadores, 24, 25, 48, 50, 87–88, 97, 101–2. *See also* catadores; dump; material; materiality; recyclables; recycling; returns to the dump; vests

collective action: ACAMJG, 25, 156–57, 163; activism, 25, 70, 90, 156, 159, 165, 194n26, 204–5n5; collaboration among catadores, 60–61, 65, 110, 113, 115, 159, 172–73; noninstitutionalized, 29, 149, 174–75; organizing among catadores outside ACAMJG, 29, 167–69; *sindicatos*, 171–72; *trutas*, 170–71. *See also* ACAMJG; labor; MNCR

Comlurb: ACAMJG and, 162–64, 184, 203n15; benefit to of the catadores' reclamation activities, 142; management of catadores by, 28, 47, 130, 133–34, 137, 138, 142, 145, 147–50, 203n14; number of catadores at Jardim Gramacho registered by, 42, 134–35, 142; remediation efforts by at Jardim Gramacho, 134, 174; as Rio's semi-public waste management company, 47, 130, 132; scrap dealers and, 130, 140, 143, 149; work vest requirement of, 28, 138–39, 142–47, 149–50, 164. *See also* recycling

cooperatives: the ACAMJG Polo, 24–25, 29, 154–57, 163, 165, 179, 203n15; cooperativism, 167–68, 184; Coopergramacho, 133–35, 157–58; Cooperjardim, 167–69; the MNCR network of, 158–59, 204n2

credit. *See* debt

crisis of work, 5, 6, 8, 10

CTRs (Centers for the Treatment of Solid Waste; *Central de Tratamento de Resíduos*), 179–82

death: "carnivalesque aesthetic" and, 60; dump as a border between life and, 27, 56, 61, 63–65

debt: cash pay predictability as a tool for collection of, 107–8, 200–201n9; as cause of vanishing or cursed money, 28, 100–101, 103–4; credit card, 48, 101–2, 104, 106–7, 200–201n9; debt payments as everyday emergencies, 27, 69, 88, 106–7; extension of credit to the poor in, 42, 200n8; as an

influence on the timing and frequency of catadores' returns to the dump, 28, 48, 89, 120; intertwining of credit and debt for catadores, 107, 183; personal debts owed to other individuals, 104–5, 107, 116; as a product of social relations, 96–97, 108. *See also* borrowing and lending; money

de Jesús, Carolina Maria, 40–41

dirt: dirty money, 103, 200n6; dirty recyclables, 164; dirty substances as elements of carnival ritual, 60; dried dirt of the dump, 1, 95; hidden dangers contained in, 20, 51; Mary Douglas on, 30, 56; as matter out of place, 30; social classification and, 194n28; as a threat to order, 30, 56; as a tool for hiding waste, 62, 134, 180. *See also* dust

discrimination. *See* inequality

disposability, 5–8, 99, 191n2

Douglas, Mary, 30, 56–57, 194n28

drugs: addiction to in Jardim Gramacho, 88; adulterated, 115; armed violence and, 19–21, 63, 115, 194n23; assumed association of favela residents with drug trafficking, 75, 76; *boca de fumo* (mouth of smoke) selling site in Jardim Gramacho, 20, 47; bribery and, 203n16; catadores and, 109–10, 117, 164; Comando Vermelho gang operations in Jardim Gramacho, 20, 47; crack cocaine, 47, 109–10, 111, 114, 201n11; cursed money and, 109; drug dealers and police, 196n15, 203n16; drug dealing, 13, 19–20, 47, 88, 196n14; labor and, 110, 201n13; marijuana, 47, 110; powder cocaine, 47, 110; power exercised by drug traffickers over neighborhoods and at the dump, 20, 47, 196n15, 203n16; rivalries among drug trafficking gangs, 20, 81; "soldiers" at the bottom of the gang hierarchy, 63; trafficking organizations, 21, 47; vanished earnings and expenditures on, 109–12. *See also* addiction

dump: as a border between life and death, 27, 59–64; bulldozers at, 2, 14, 58–59, 62–64, 142, 171, 174; charred remains of stolen vehicles abandoned at the, 56, 63; closure of in Jardim Gramacho, 2, 29, 156, 177, 180; daily volume of garbage transported from Rio to Jardim Gramacho, 17, 23; dust of the, 23, 37, 59, 96; environmental dangers at, 31–32, 37–38, 59, 73–74, 84, 134–35, 172, 178; fires at, 31, 134, 172; illegality of in Jardim

Gramacho, 130, 202–3n9; leachate at the, 31–32, 37–38, 59, 135, 181–82; *lixão*, 32, 180, 204n1; methane gas at the, 31–32, 38, 84, 134, 135, 172, 178; Metropolitan Landfill of Jardim Gramacho, 23, 32, 82, 156, 162, 177, 204n1; mud and muck of the, 48–51, 59, 68; as ontological experience of labor, 27, 53, 59, 62, 64, 66; pathways and trails inside the, 13–14, 24, 112–13; physical environment of the, 1, 23, 31–32, 37–38, 58–59, 63, 65, 102; physical maintenance procedures of a, 62, 113; rain and mud as dangers at the, 50–51; the *rampão* (big slope), 50, 59, 83, 111–12, 138, 172–73; the *rampinha* (little slope), 50, 59, 112, 172–73, 180; remediation of in Jardim Gramacho, 38, 42, 134, 174, 203n14; rhythms of the, 14, 49, 59, 83; size and scale of the in Jardim Gramacho, 1, 2, 17, 18, 23, 32, 50; traces of violence, death, and of life at the, 41, 58, 61, 63–65, 102, 113, 159; traffic and vehicular dangers at the, 1, 2–3, 14, 49, 64, 73; unloading zones, 13–14, 48–50, 110, 112, 170. *See also* bulldozers; catadores; collecting; garbage; trucks

Duque de Caxias: Jardim Gramacho as a sub-bairro of Gramacho in, 20; job training courses offered by, 185–86; the municipality of, 16–20. *See also* Baixada Fluminense

dust: the catadores' endurance of, 2, 37, 96; garbage trucks and, 38–39, 96; omnipresence at the dump, 2, 23, 37, 59; omnipresence in homes and businesses near the dump, 24, 38–39. *See also* dirt

economy: anthropological typologies of, 16; challenges to social science theories of, 14–15, 128–33, 193n13; exclusion of certain income-generating activities from economic analyses, 128–29; formal-informal dichotomy, 127–31, 149, 150, 192n4; GDP measurements for Brazil, 195n7; inequality, 43–45, 131; influence of neoliberal economic policies on Brazil's development, 42, 44, 69–70; J. K. Gibson-Graham on the modern concept of, 16, 193n13; Keith Hart's concept of formal and informal economies, 14–15, 128; Max Weber's concept of a rationalization of economic activity, 14–15; measurements of an, 128–29, 202n6; as a principle of frugality, 128; realities and plasticity of income-generating activities, 28, 127–33, 150; social science notions of economy as a distinct material domain of human life, 15–16, 150; structuralist interpretations of informal activities, 129–30; sugar industry in Brazil, 17, 40, 75–76; theoretical conceptualizations of as a totalizing, self-contained, measurable sphere, 128, 150; theoretical separations of different kinds of income-generating activities, 11, 127–29; theoretical separations of income-generating activities from other elements of life, 15–16; Timothy Mitchell on the shift in the meaning of, 128, 193n13; wage labor and definitions of work in social science analyses, 10, 29; the work-life binary, 11. *See also* informal economy; political economy

empowerment, 89, 160–61

ethnography: metaphors of waste used in, 6–7; political economy and, 11, 40; studies of power and inequality in Latin America and, 39–40. *See also* anthropology

everyday emergencies: collecting recyclables as a way of managing, 86–87, 89, 91, 92, 107–8; damaged household goods as significant sources of, 86–87; debt payments as, 27, 69, 88, 106–7, 183; disruptive impact of on financial planning, 97; as normal to life in Rio's favelas and periphery, 69, 92, 107, 188; origins, nature, and relationships behind, 27, 71, 87–88, 97, 188; physical environment of the favela as causes of, 19, 21, 27, 43, 45–46, 62, 86–87; politics of security and violence as causes of, 87–88; rent and housing as, 87, 105–6, 171; wage employment as impediment to coping with, 27, 71, 90–92; weather and environment as causes of catadores', 17, 20, 46, 86–87, 105. *See also* borrowing and lending; precarity; returns to the dump

favelas: association of with the absence of work, 20–21, 63; bairro versus, 19–20; biases regarding residents of, 19–21, 75, 150; construals of as a place of lack, 21–22, 99, 194n22; drug-trafficking organizations in, 20, 47, 62–63, 196n15; employment and, 21, 62–63; the everyday emergency as constituting normality in, 69, 92, 107, 188; hillside favelas of Rio de Janeiro, 16, 19–20, 22, 47, 62,

favelas (continued)
81, 171; inequality in Rio de Janeiro and, 19, 39–40; infrastructure and service improvements in Rio's favelas, 17, 19; Jardim Gramacho as a favela-bairro, 20; makeshift housing and inadequate infrastructure and services in, 19, 27, 36, 69, 87, 106; NGO programs for Rio's youth from, 158, 204–5n5; police targeting of favelas and their residents, 75, 88; proximity of favelas to upper- and middle-class neighborhoods in Rio de Janeiro, 19, 62; rural-to-urban migration and, 35–37, 40–41; working residents of, 21, 75. *See also* bairro; inequality; poor

fires: catadores' homes and lives destroyed or damaged by, 86, 87; as contributors to precariousness, 87; methane gas as a source of dump, 31, 134, 135, 172

Fordism: existence of as a dream and aspiration in the Global South, 70; expectations of and their continuing influence, 6, 70, 76, 92; full-time, lifelong employment as a standard of, 6, 70; post-Fordist labor, 69, 71, 74; post-Fordist precarity, 69–70. *See also* precarity

friends: borrowing and lending among catadores and their, 87, 96, 100, 107; friendships and collective activities among catadores on the dump, 60–61, 83, 85, 102, 110–15, 138, 144–45, 146–47, 174; friendships and socializing among catadores outside the dump, 86, 104, 115–16, 140, 144, 152, 188; friendships that fostered ACAMJG, 42, 152, 157, 162; as important elements of the relational autonomy of the catadores, 87–90, 100, 114–15; as mentors to novice catadores, 54, 57–58, 80, 82, 84, 171–72; of catadores scattered throughout Rio, 22, 115; as sources of assistance during emergencies, 87–88, 100; trust, loyalty, and the safety of collected materials among catadores, 48, 50, 145–46, 170–71; *trutas*, 170–71

Gandolfo, Daniella, 14–15, 80, 132, 194n26, 203n13
gangs. See *bandidos* (criminals)
garbage: as the abject product of order creation, 15, 30, 194nn27–28; as the basis for commercial activities, 2, 23, 38–39, 123–24, 178; bulldozers and tractors that moved the, 2–3, 52–53, 58–59, 62–65, 73, 84, 113, 142, 174; catadores' experiences of, 49–59, 82–86; corpses in the, 61–65, 102; dangers of working in, 2–3, 8, 32, 37, 49–51, 59, 64–65, 174; "following the garbage," 2, 41, 173; "the garbage never ends," 29, 73, 178; *lixo*, 31, 124, 193–94n9; materiality of, 30–32, 49, 194n30; materials reclaimed from, 2, 14, 40–41, 48–49, 123–25; perception of as formless, 30, 31, 32, 33, 58; polluting aspects of in Jardim Gramacho, 31–32, 37–38, 58–59, 84, 135; the predictable, identifiable qualities of for catadores, 14, 30, 31, 49, 124–25; recyclables versus, 31–32, 192–93n9; smell of, 30, 38, 52, 58–59, 84, 125; the social generativity of, 30, 33, 71–73, 87–93, 110–16, 168–72, 194n29; tonnage of unloaded in Jardim Gramacho, 1, 17–18, 23; traces of violence present in, 56, 61–65, 102; trucks that transported the, 13, 14, 37–39, 48–50, 62, 73. *See also* dump; material; materiality; reclaiming; waste

garbage pickers, trash pickers, and scavengers, 5, 32, 40, 136, 143, 203–4n17
Goldstein, Daniel, 129, 131–32, 203n10
Goldstein, Donna, 39–40, 60, 74, 196n15
Guanabara Bay, 1, 36, 134, 152, 202–3n9

Han, Clara, 71, 199n26, 200–201nn8–9
Hart, Keith, 3–4, 14–15, 128–29, 132
Hobbes, Thomas, 148–49
housing: makeshift camps and, 10, 135, 171–72; materials from the dump fashioned into, 20; rented in Jardim Gramacho, 2, 4, 20, 112; self-construction of in Jardim Gramacho and other favelas, 7–8, 27, 69, 106, 187. *See also* shacks
hylomorphism, 148–49, 204n18

IBASE (Brazilian Institute for Social and Economic Analysis), 157, 159, 195n5
IBISS (Brazilian Institute for Innovations in Social Health), 158, 159
inequality: in Brazil, 6–8, 19, 20–21, 40, 42–44, 70; the *carteira assinada* as a tool that produces, 75–76, 131; in employment opportunities among Brazilians, 43–45, 70, 185–86, 195–96n12; the Gini coefficient measure of, 43; label of "informal" as a source of, 131; NGOs and, 160–61, 163, 204–5n5, 205n8;

leachate, 31–32, 37–38, 59, 135, 181–82. *See also* methane gas

Lula da Silva, Luiz Inácio, President, 42–43

Malabou, Catherine, 127–28, 137, 148, 150, 204n20

mangrove swamps: at and near Jardim Gramacho, 2, 4, 67, 86; environmental remediation of Jardim Gramacho by Comlurb, 38, 42, 134, 174, 203n14; garbage dumping in, 2, 4, 17–18, 23, 130, 134; as housing sites, 20; as protected areas, 17–18, 130, 202–3n9

marginality, 7–8, 21, 120–21, 174–75, 192n6, 202n19, 204–5n6. *See also* inequality; poor

Marx, Karl: industrial reserve army of workers as conceived by, 4, 191–92n3; influence of on the formal-informal theory of labor, 130, 192n4; the lumpenproletariat concept of, 5; the socioeconomic theories of, 186

material: aluminum, 38, 113, 140; cardboard, 13, 22–24, 49, 123–24, 127, 153, 159, 170, 201n17; catadores' engagement with, 32, 33, 192–93n9; "dirty," 164; garbage versus, 31–32, 124, 192–93n9; identification of through garbage bags as a skill, 24, 52, 58, 71, 84, 125, 170; metal, 2, 23, 32, 50, 124, 159; paper, 14, 23, 31–32, 40, 124, 153, 159; PET, 24, 124–27, 130, 138–39, 202n4; physical requirements dictated by for collecting, 49; *plástico fino*, 125; prices and values of, 113, 123–24, 173; prices as the basis for collecting specific, 113, 123–24, 201n17; proper ways for a catador to carry as a skill, 47, 50, 52, 68, 71, 123, 138; removal of from the dump as a means of prolonging its life, 142; rubber, 23, 196n17; sale of collected material by catadores, 25, 28–29, 73, 138–40, 143–44, 155, 166, 173–74; the sorting and bundling of at scrapyards, 23; specific materials targeted by catadores for collection, 31, 32, 159; toxic materials present at the dump, 32, 38, 58–59, 61, 105, 135, 195n2; transport of within the dump, 1, 13, 22–23, 50–51; use of scrap in Jardim Gramacho housing, 20; weight of, 25, 51, 153. *See also* collecting; garbage; PET; plastics; recyclables; recycling

materiality: abjection as an initial refusal to engage the materiality of garbage, 54–57, 58; catadores' engagement with the materiality of garbage as crucial, 30, 32, 33; the corpse

as a materiality of the body and of death, 56; disruptive and transformative powers of garbage, 32–33, 58, 194n30; failure to engage the materiality of garbage as a failure of understanding, 30, 31; of garbage, 30–33; 194n28. *See also* collecting; garbage

methane gas, 31–32, 38, 84, 134, 135, 172, 178. *See also* leachate

middle class: "Classe C" as the "new middle class" in Brazil, 43, 195n8; dominance of middle class outlook and thinking among NGO activists, 204–5n5; Fordist expectations and aspirations of the, 6, 70, 100; "good life" and the, 98–99; influence of Brazil's economic growth and recession on its, 43, 44

migrants: among the catadores, 40; early to Rio de Janeiro, 35–37, 40, 70, 74–75; the income-generating activities of, 3–4, 6, 15, 103, 128; return to place by, 26; social marginalization of, 7, 8

Mitchell, Timothy, 15–16, 128, 193n13

MNCR (National Movement of Catadores of Recyclable Materials), 22, 133, 136, 154–55, 158, 169, 192–93n9. *See also* collective action

money: anthropology of, 103, 200n6; concept of cursed among catadores, 81, 101–4, 116–17; emergencies as destabilizing influences on financial planning, 97, 108, 120; expenditures to finance addictions, 109–11, 114; expenditures of cursed on luxury items, consumer goods, and drugs, 109, 110, 111, 114, 116, 200n7; expenditures on household goods, 87, 117, 120, 184–85; expenditures on rent payments, 87; the manner of earning as an influence on its expenditure, 103–4, 165–66, 183, 200nn6–7, 201n10; personal expenditures on behalf of others as a source of vanished, 106–7; *pessoa ignorante* as one who earns and spends only for personal consumption, 106; predictability of cash payments as a prompt for debt collection, 107, 200–201n9; predictability of cash payments as a prompt for immediate spending, 107, 108, 200–201n9; social science assumptions regarding financial management among the poor, 100–101, 200n4; spending money and spending life as inseparable acts, 97, 99–100, 117–18; spending to save as a strategic use of one's, 107–9, 184–85; wage earnings and periodic

pay as restrictions on the use of, 120, 165–66, 183; Weber's study on workers' attitudes toward, 119. *See also* borrowing and lending; cash; debt; vanished money
moral economy, 11–12, 16, 199n1
Muniz, Vik, 31, 183

neoliberalism: activism against, 90; autonomy as conceived by, 89, 199n23; economic policies of, 42–44; flexibility in the context of, 89, 127; free market economics and, 69; history of, 197n3; influence of on NGO logics and activities, 165, 205n7; job insecurity as a by-product of neoliberal theory and practices, 69–70, 193n11, 197n4; neoliberal capitalism, 5, 10, 98, 127, 166; structural adjustment in, 70. *See also* capitalism
NGOs (nongovernmental organizations), 157–65, 195n5, 204–5n5, 205n8
Nordstrom, Carolyn, 132, 149, 193n13

odor. *See* smell
ontology: of garbage and the dump 27, 53, 62, 64, 66; precarity as an ontological experience, 69

Penglase, Ben, 69, 194n23, 196nn13–15, 197n20, 198n12
PET (polyethylene terephthalate) plastics: Arteplas corporation, 126, 130; baling and trucking of, 125–26; collection of, 24, 124, 125; compared to other plastics, 125; conversion of into new recyclable items, 126–27; markets and prices for, 83, 124, 138, 139, 202n4; material and tactile properties of, 124–25. *See also* material; plastics
plantations, 17, 18, 38, 40, 75, 195n1
plasticity: case of the work vests and, 142–47, 149–50; Catherine Malabou on, 127–28, 137, 148, 150, 204n20; of Comlurb, 133, 137, 147; the concept of, 15, 127–28, 132, 137, 148, 204n20; as a disruption of the formal-informal binary, 15, 132–33; economic life and, 15, 150; flexibility versus, 127; form and, 15, 127, 148, 149; of the human brain, 127, 150; hylomorphism and, 148–49, 204n18; physical plasticity of PET, 126–27; of the work of catadores, 135, 137, 145–47
plastics: baling of, 125; collecting and sale of by catadores, 13–14, 23–24, 32, 49–51, 58,

63, 68, 111; "crystal" (*cristal*), 125; distinctions among types of, 14; milling of, 160, 161; plastic bags, 102, 151, 159, 178; PVC (polyvinyl chloride; *carina*), 125; skills and physical demands required for collecting, 49, 124–25, 132, 170; skin absorption of smells, 125; thin (low-density polyethylene; *plástico fino*), 125. *See also* material; PET
police: bribery of, 130, 203n16; death squads, 41; *guarda municipal* of Rio, 78, 79, 198–99nn19–20; harassment and abuse of street vendors by, 45, 78–81, 175; targeting and abuse of black and brown youths by, 75, 198n12; violence against the poor, 198n11; violence against street children, 41, 75, 79, 198n11
political economy: of Brazil, 27, 39–40, 45; ethnography and, 11, 40; gender analyses of, 10, 192n8; studies of debt and spending among the poor and, 101, 200n5; the work-life binary and, 11–12, 40, 101. *See also* economy; politics
politics: *bandidos* and local politics, 20, 47–48, 96, 130, 173, 203n16; of inequality, 40, 44–45, 74–75, 159–61, 198n12; intermunicipal in the Rio metropolitan area, 18–19, 194n17, 194n20; of labor and of "labor melancholia," 4–5, 8–9, 25, 74, 136–37, 192–93n9; noninstitutionalized collective actions as, 29, 154–55, 167–70, 174–75, 194n26; political mobilization of catadores in Brazil, 22, 25, 42, 154–63; of precarity, 6, 7, 69–70, 92, 193n11, 197n4; of security, policing, and violence practiced against Rio's favela residents, 75, 87–88; of social exclusion, 8–9, 62–63, 74–75; of urban space, 78–80, 198n17, 198n18. *See also* political economy
politics of detachment, 27–28, 91–93
Polo. *See* ACAMJG (Association of Catadores of the Metropolitan Landfill of Jardim Gramacho)
poor: Brazil's Bolsa Família program for, 42–44, 186, 195n10; concept of deserving versus undeserving poor, 75, 121, 202n20; concept of the needy poor, 161; credit availability for Brazil's, 42, 200n8; laboring, 12, 25, 70; mass migrations of the rural into urban areas, 7, 75–76; NGOs and, 159–61, 204–5n5; perceptions of, 7, 75, 76, 131, 201n13; police violence against, 41, 75,

poor (continued)
78, 79, 198n11; precarious work and laboring, 6, 45, 70, 92; reforms by President Luiz Inácio Lula da Silva designed to help Brazil's, 42–43; social nonmovements by, 174–75; theories regarding agency of, 150, 154–55, 159; theories regarding decisions by to quit regular jobs, 72, 89, 91–92; theories regarding financial management among, 100–101, 114, 200nn4–5, 201–2n18; theories regarding social exclusion of, 8, 75; theories regarding wageless economic activities of the urban, 4, 6, 71–72, 89; theories that associate lack and waste with, 7, 8, 99, 200n3; theories that see economic need as the impetus for all actions by, 12, 91–92, 193n10; unplanned settlements of the urban, 6, 19; wageless, income-generating activities of, 3–4, 7–8, 71, 128, 131–32, 137. *See also* favela; inequality; marginality
poverty: concept of cycles of poverty, 26; inequality and, 8, 19, 43–45; Oscar Lewis's concept of the culture of poverty, 100–101, 121, 200n4, 202n19; reforms by President Luiz Inácio Lula da Silva to reduce poverty in Brazil, 42–44. *See also* inequality
Povinelli, Elizabeth, 7, 154, 168
pragmatism, 11, 101, 103–4, 162
precarity: of Brazil's nonwhite population, 44–45, 70, 87, 92; as a characteristic of advanced capitalism, 6, 41, 69–70, 86; as a characteristic of catadores' lives, 86–87, 89, 91–93, 101, 121, 137, 188; as a characteristic of Rio's periphery, 12–13, 70, 86–87, 92, 166; destabilization of daily life by, 69–70, 74; Franco Barchiesi on, 9, 193n11; geopolitical location and social position as influences on, 70, 99, 200n3; global nature of, 5–7, 69–70, 197n4; Guy Standing on the precariat, 92, 193n11; hallmarks of, 5–6, 69–70, 74, 86, 193n11, 197n4; inequality as both cause and effect of, 44–45, 99, 193n11, 200n3; labor precarity versus precarity as an ontological experience, 69, 166; neoliberal capitalism and free market economics as causes of, 44–45, 69–70, 98–99, 197n4; the precariat, 5–6, 92; regular employment and, 87, 89, 92–93, 137, 166; relational autonomy as a means of living through, 91–93, 101, 188.

See also capitalism; everyday emergencies; Fordism; inequality
prices: aluminum, 113; as a basis for sales of materials by catadores to scrap dealers, 73, 138–39, 140, 153, 159, 174; the catadores' knowledge and discussions of market, 123–24, 138; commodity and recyclable price links, 124, 202n4; declines in for recyclables, 113–14, 201n17; the influence of on the collection of recyclable materials, 124, 196n17; longer work hours as a means of counteracting price drops, 201n17; market for recyclables, 113–14; oil and petroleum, 124, 202n4; paid by recycling companies for materials sold through ACAMJG, 153, 154–55; paper, 124; PET, 124; plastics, 124, 196n17; scrap metal, 124; selling strikes by catadores over the exploitative prices offered for recyclables, 159, 173–74; stock, 124; 2008 drop in cardboard, 24, 123, 124; 2008 global economic crisis as an influence on, 113–14, 124, 202n4; vest rental, 139

Queiroz Galvão, 38, 174, 203n14

race and racial inequality: associations of catadores with blackness, 196n13; Brazil's race relations, 159–60, 196n13; capitalism and, 191–92n3; employment and, 44–45; homicide rate and, 63, 197n20; in Jardim Gramacho, 45; 196n13; legacies of Brazil's history of slavery, 74–76; police racialized targeting, 75; 198n12; politics of, 198n17
rampão (big slope), 50, 59, 83, 111–12, 138, 172–73
rampinha (little slope), 50, 59, 112, 172–73, 180
reclaiming: as an act of making visible, 65; the catadores' acts of, 32–33, 39, 50, 53, 65–66, 73; discarded items returned to use, 2, 4, 23, 60–61, 110, 113, 171–72; the life-giving nature of, 23, 32, 33, 70–71, 113, 187. *See also* garbage
recyclables: aluminum as a highly valued recyclable, 113; cardboard, 13, 22–24, 49, 123–24, 127, 153, 159, 170, 201n17; *carina* (flexible plastic; polyvinyl chloride or PVC), 31, 125; *coleta seletiva* (preseparated, donated), 153, 158–59; collection of as basis for a form of living, 9–10, 71, 87–88, 91–92, 113; collection of as dangerous, demanding labor, 2, 24, 48–51, 58–59, 63–65, 134, 142, 170, 174; col-

scrap dealers (continued)

allocation of work vests to for issuance to catadores, 28, 48, 138–39, 142, 145, 203n15; Comlurb's attempts to manage, 28, 130, 136, 147–48, 150; as intermediaries between the dump and recycling companies, 25, 127, 130, 153; new dealers, 140; the payments of for materials by the kilo, 123; point-of-sale cash payments of to catadores, 73, 107; prices and markets as influences on, 123–24, 139, 173–74, 201n17; racial backgrounds of Jardim Gramacho's, 45; registration of by Comlurb, 140; repossession of vests by, 139; sales of Comlurb registration numbers and work vests among, 140; trucks owned by, 24, 39, 48, 140, 145; unregistered, 28, 54, 130, 139–41, 144, 203n16

scrapyards: ACAMJG's bypassing of intermediate, 164, 166; clustering of in Rio's favela-like areas, 20; *depósitos*, 54–55, 57; as intermediate points between the dump and recycling companies, 25, 127, 130, 153; of Jardim Gramacho, 2, 4, 20, 54, 125, 130, 139, 141f, 151; opening a scrapyard, 140; registration numbers of on work vests, 139; sorting and bundling of recyclables at, 23, 141f; trucks, 24, 39, 48, 125, 136, 140; unlicensed in Jardim Gramacho, 130, 139, 203n16

self-employment, 45, 78, 84, 87, 130, 143, 174, 183

shacks: below-sea-level locations of in Jardim Gramacho, 17, 20, 46, 87; built from scrap materials from the dump, 20, 53; fires in, 86; flooding of, 17, 46, 87; located along "the inside" in Jardim Gramacho, 20; occupancy and crowding of in Jardim Gramacho, 20, 86, 88, 173, 184, 185; purchases of furnished, 184–85; rentals of, 2, 4, 20, 72–73, 112, 171; self-constructed, 17, 19, 20, 86. *See also* housing

smell: abjection, social stigma and, 55–57, 73, 125; acclimation to among catadores, 3, 55, 58–59, 84; distinguishing smells as a safety concern for catadores, 30, 52, 58–59; of leachate, 31, 38, 59, 135, 181; of methane gas, 31, 58–59, 84, 135; raw sewage and damp foliage as elements of in Jardim Gramacho, 46; skin absorption of *plástico fino*, 125; toxic substances, materials, and gases, 30, 52, 58–59, 84, 181

social workers: Bolsa Família enrollment of families by, 186; in Jardim Gramacho, 109, 133–37, 142, 157, 164, 203n14, 185–88

spending: as a form of saving for catadores, 28, 107–9, 120–21, 184–85, 201n10; the link between spending money and spending life, 97, 100–101, 104–6, 108, 119–20; *pessoa ignorante*, 106; social by the Brazilian government, 44, 69; social science interpretations of by the poor, 101, 200nn4–5

storytelling, 55–56, 59–65

street vendors: catadores who worked previously as, 45, 70, 78–81; maintenance of claims to space required of, 73, 174; migrants to Rio self-employed as, 70; police harassment of, 45, 78–81, 174; selling locations of, 16–17

structuralism, 30, 56–57, 129, 143–44, 149, 204n19

swamps. *See* mangrove swamps

Thompson, E. P., 11–12, 85, 91

time: boredom and restlessness in employment and, 68, 85, 187–88; present-time orientation, 120–21, 200n4, 202n19; rhythm of life, 15, 17, 34, 38–39, 85, 91–92, 107, 127, 137, 179, 233, 248; temporality of work, 84, 135, 179, 120–21, 201n16; wage labor and, 17, 85, 89, 91, 136

traffic. *See* bulldozers; dump; trucks

transformation: plasticity and, 127–33, 204n20; the politics of, 32–33, 136–37, 169; of waste and recyclables, 32–33, 116, 125–27, 132, 169 187; worker subjectivity and, 12, 57–59, 71, 84–85, 116. *See also* abjection; arrivals at the dump; returns to the dump

trucks: the ACAMJG, 1–2, 24, 50–51, 59, 95, 97, 104, 153, 163–64, 179; accidents involving, 65, 142; bulldozer movements in the wakes of, 49, 62; catador proximity to unloading, 14, 49, 50, 61, 63, 68, 83, 123; compactor, 50, 196n18; constant movement of at the dump, 14, 24, 49, 59, 84; distinguishing characteristics of materials falling from, 49, 123; eighteen-wheelers that transported garbage into the dump, 1, 13, 22–23; flatbed transport of bales of paper to recycling plants, 23; flatbed transport of bales of plastic to recycling plants, 14, 23, 125–27; identification of with garbage types, 31; leachate, dust, and toxic materials in and on, 37, 39, 61, 63, 65; potholes, dirt, dust, mud,

wage labor: as a basis for citizenship, 9, 74–75; E. P. Thompson on the impact of on workers, 11–12, 85, 91; as a hindrance to coping with everyday emergencies, 88, 120, 183; the influence of on an individual's perception and use of time, 10–11, 71, 85, 91; negative human responses to, 119, 201–2n18; perception of as the only form of "real" work, 10, 13, 15, 129; relational autonomy and, 27, 68, 71–72, 90–92, 100, 108, 199n24; as a tool for creating predictable, governable subjects of the state, 9, 72, 75, 127, 136–37, 192–93n10; as a tool for establishing employer ownership of an employee's time, 11, 12, 68, 85, 91, 127, 187–88; worker incentives, 119; work-life binary and, 10–11, 85, 165. See also capitalism; *carteira assinada*; time; work

wageless work: hegemonic interpretations of the nature of and motivations underlying, 4, 5, 26, 29–30, 150; as a means of facilitating desirable forms of living, 4, 27–28; relational autonomy and, 72, 84–85, 87, 183; street vending as a form of, 80–81; unacknowledged, unofficial status of, 13, 44–45, 128–30, 186

waiting, 29, 179, 186

waste: as the abject product of order creation, 30, 194nn28–29; Aristotle on wastefulness and, 98–99; catadores' presence at waste disposal sites, 13, 57–58; Comlurb, 28, 42, 47, 130, 132, 134–35, 157; CTR illegal burial of recyclables, 180–81; CTR management of leachate, 181–82; CTRs as replacements for dumps, 179–80; daily dumping of Rio's at the Jardim Gramacho mangrove swamp, 17–19, 130, 178, 202–3n9; disposal of as an act of forgetting, 62, 197n19; hospital and medical, 61, 196n17; inequality and, 33, 45, 191n2; the life-generating powers of, 30, 32–33, 38–39, 194nn29–30; materiality and dynamic properties of, 32–33, 38, 58–59, 134, 194n30; metaphors for, 6–8, 191–92n3; negative connotations of, 30, 33; the poor, marginalized, and unemployed conceived of as disposable human, 5–8, 10, 99, 191–92nn2–3, 197n19; reclamation and, 65, 71, 113, 116; sensationalization or aestheticization of, 30–31; transfer stations, 50, 83, 196n18; waste disposal sites and transfer stations, 13, 30, 32, 49–50, 58–59, 62, 68. See also garbage

Weber, Max, 14–15, 119–20, 129, 162, 205n6

work: activities beyond the purely economic as kinds of, 10; biases against those not engaged in paid, 7–8, 10, 72–73, 192–93n9; Brazilian attitudes toward, 9–10, 74; Brazil's labor market and economy, 43–44, 45, 69–70, 74–75, 195–96n12; capitalist notion of life as being separate from, 10–11, 85, 136; capitalist notions of as paid employment, 9–10; catadores', 5, 8, 10, 13, 22, 52–57, 72–73, 85, 136–37; catadores' continuous return to the dump, 4, 12–13, 26–30, 67–74, 82–91, 120–21; centrality of among Rio's poor, 2, 22, 44–45, 70, 78–80, 84–85, 121, 201n17; concept of a crisis of, 5–6, 8, 10; concept of work flexibility, 127; conceptions of what does and does not constitute, 13, 29, 136–37; definitions and understandings of the term, 10; as an end in itself, 28, 119; E. P. Thompson's study of workers and, 11–12, 85, 91; favela as symbol of the absence of, 20–21; Fordism, post-Fordism, and the significance of, 69–71, 98; as a form of living, 9, 10–13, 26–29, 71, 85–89, 113, 120–21, 137; inequality and, 44–45, 186, 196n13; informal and the informal economy, 4, 6, 13–15, 127–31, 149, 150, 192n4; interpretations of certain kinds of as survivalism, 3, 4, 11, 26, 29–30; life and, 4, 8, 9, 71, 91–92, 119, 201n16, 201–2n18; Max Weber's study of workers and, 119–20, 205n6; moral interrelationship of with living well, 12–13, 71, 99–100, 119–20; phenomenology of, 12, 24, 26–27; plasticity of the catadores', 127–28, 137; precarity, 5–6, 69–70, 74, 91–92, 97, 197n4, 200–201n9; professionalization of *catação* (collecting recyclables), 136–37, 192–93n9; Protestant ethic as a complement to wage labor, 119, 205n6; self-employment, 45, 78–80, 84, 130, 143, 174; as a source of post-Fordist insecurity, 69–70, 98; as a site of the everyday struggle to construct the good, 12–13; unemployment and, 5–6; wage labor as a constraint on coping with instabilities in life, 71, 85, 88–92; wage labor as a relatively new form of, 10, 85–86, 91, 119; wageless, 4, 5, 26–30, 73, 80–81, 91–92, 150; wages in Brazil, 44; wage versus wageless labor, 13; waste, human disposability, and the absence of, 5–8, 10, 191–92n3; the work-citizenship nexus theorized by Barchiesi, 9, 193n11. See also labor